The Front Page

THE FRONT PAGE

FROM THEATER TO REALITY

By Ben Hecht
and Charles MacArthur

Introduction by Jed Harris

Edited, with an Introduction,
by George W. Hilton

THE ART OF THEATER SERIES

A Smith and Kraus Book

Published by
Smith and Kraus, Inc.
177 Lyme Road, Hanover, NH 03755
www.SmithKraus.com

First edition: September 2002
Printed in the United States of America
9 8 7 6 5 4 3 2 1

Cover and Text Design by Freedom Hill Design, Reading, Vermont
Front cover photo courtesy of The New York Public Library.

Library of Congress Cataloging In Publication Information

Hecht, Ben, 1893–1964.
The front page : from theater to reality / by Ben Hecht and Charles MacArthur ;
introduction by Jed Harris ; edited, with an introduction by George W. Hilton.
p. ; cm. — (The art of theater series)
Includes bibliographical references and index.
ISBN 1-57525-310-0(paper) ISBN 1-57525-
1. Journalists—Drama. 2. Chicago (Ill.)—Drama. 3. Newspaper publishing—
Drama. 4. Hecht, Ben, 1893–1964. Front page. I. MacArthur, Charles,
1895–1956. II. Hilton, George W. III. Title. IV. Series.

PS3515.E18 F7 2002
812'.52—dc21
2002276803

AUTHORS' DEDICATION

To Madison and Clark Streets

Madison and Clark Streets in 1914, looking north along Clark Street past the Planters Hotel. Madison and Clark was the intersection at which Hecht was wont to sit on the curb when too drunk to return to work at the *Journal*. It remained his favorite corner after he moved to New York and Los Angeles; he endeavored to visit it on stopovers in Chicago (see his *A Child of the Century*, p. 148). On the basis of locations of restaurants, hotels, and people mentioned in the play, it is evident how central this intersection was to the lives of the authors in Chicago, (Chicago Historical Society).

PREFACE

My acquaintance with *The Front Page* dates from February 1947, when, during my first year of postgraduate work at the University of Chicago, I saw a performance of the 1946 Broadway revival of the play at the Civic Theatre in Chicago. In one sense, I would like to say that I immediately evaluated the play as a masterwork, but I did not. I did think it extremely funny and exceptionally articulate. In particular, I appreciated the vividness of the delineation of Chicago around the time of my birth. The Civic Theatre could not have been a better place for my introduction, for it is only about a block from the site of the offices of the *Herald and Examiner*, the newspaper about which the plot revolves. More important, as part of the Civic Opera House complex of 1929, it was under construction when the play appeared, and thus represented precisely the architectural tastes of the time.

In another sense, it was good that I did not immediately recognize the play's quality, for my evaluation of it could parallel that of society. As I have endeavored to document in the introduction, it was not until the 1980s that critical opinion fairly universally evaluated the work as a classic. At least I can say in my defense that I had come to this conclusion some twenty years earlier. When the revival of 1969 was mounted on Broadway, I was on leave from UCLA, serving as acting curator of rail transportation at the Smithsonian Institution. I went up to New York for the performance and had no doubt as to the merit of what I was seeing. When that revival played Los Angeles, I had returned to UCLA, and I took Robert Lucas, a British colleague, and Mahrukh Tarapor to see it. Happily, they agreed that I had not exaggerated the play's excellence.

After 1970 I was engaged in an effort to identify the actual persons in Ring W. Lardner's baseball fiction of the 1914-to-1919 period. I had concluded that the quality of the stories could be only imperfectly appreciated without a recognition of their empirical content. By the time my edition of the stories was published in 1995, I had long since concluded that a similar treatment was suitable for *The Front Page*. In the best of the Lardner stories, the hero and the others on whom the plot hangs are fictional, but the teammates and other secondary characters are actual. In *The Front Page*, all the characters with few exceptions are actual and identifiable. Appreciation of the play, even more than of the Lardner stories, depends on recognizing the actual people represented. In particular, the political relationship between the Republican mayor of Chicago, William Hale Thompson, and the Democratic assistant attorney general of Illinois, Samuel E. Pincus, is extremely important to the playing out of the plot.

It will be noted, however, that my efforts were not entirely successful: a large number of identifications eluded me. Where I have referred to a person as "not identifiable," I mean only that I have been unable to identify him or her, not that I believe the person can never be identified. Eventually, the death certificates of the nation will be computerized, greatly facilitating searches of this sort. I suspect that the prototypes of Sidney Matsburg, Max, Eddie, Frank, and Tony, whom I could not identify, may prove as interesting as Mrs. Petras and the Reverend Godolphin, whom I considered unidentifiable until almost the end of my labors. Characters called only by a first name, or by a surname with a nickname, are difficult or impossible to identify with assurance. A century hence, I should like to have it said that this edition initiated the effort to identify all the characters systematically, not that it definitively did so.

My first obligation in this project is to Richard Philbrick, retired religion editor of the *Chicago Tribune*. After expressing surprise that no one had attempted these identifications previously, he encouraged me to continue with them. He also proved a fount of information on the *Tribune*'s practices. He put me in touch with various of his fellow members of the Chicago Press Veterans, of whom Vern E. Whaley, Marilyn Cafferata Lien, George Murray, Ed Baumann, and Dan Friedlander were particularly helpful. Joseph Reilly, chief of the City News Bureau, allowed me to search the bureau's personnel files for early records of many of the journalists in the play. I am especially indebted to Mrs. Geraldine Adelman of Terre Haute, Indiana, and Mrs. Elka Kovitz of River Forest, Illinois, for assistance in finding biographical information on their father, Samuel E. Pincus. Professor of English Howard W. Webb of Southern Illinois University, who had greatly encouraged and assisted me with the Lardner project, also lent his support to this one. William Hyder read the manuscript both early and late, giving me the benefit of his long years of experience with the *Baltimore Sun* and, even more, the remarkable fund of general knowledge he had gathered in the course of a career in journalism. He provides the German translations in the epilogue. Professor Leonard H. Frey of San Diego State University provided his usual counsel and professional wisdom. Professor

John J. Binder of the University of Illinois–Chicago, Richard C. Lindberg, and fellow members of The Merry Gangsters Literary Society were very helpful, especially in the discussion following a talk I gave on the play to the group on May 9, 1995. Eric C. Gabler assisted me with getting the text onto my computer and programming it for indexing. My wife Connie engaged in many discussions of the play and prevented me from putting an axe to my scanner.

—GWH

CONTENTS

EDITOR'S
INTRODUCTION

The time is long past for an editor to attempt to demonstrate that *The Front Page* is a great work. Vincent Starrett in his autobiography of 1965 called the play "an indubitable masterpiece,"[1] and Irving Wardle in his review of the first London professional performance by the National Theatre at the Old Vic in 1972 wrote, with respect to American drama, that the work is "surely as fine a comedy as that country has ever produced."[2] The late Kenneth Tynan, who was serving as literary consultant to the National Theatre, was quoted as saying, "*The Front Page* is the best American comedy ever written."[3] Tynan later quoted Sir Tom Stoppard—as he now is—as saying in 1977, "But my favourite American play is *The Front Page*—even though I might have to admit, if extremely pressed, that it wasn't quite as fine as *Long Day's Journey into Night*."[4]

Kenneth Tynan wrote that Tom Stoppard made the statement just quoted at a press interview in Los Angeles on July 13, 1977, but being unable to find an account of the interview in the *Los Angeles Times*, I wrote Stoppard for confirmation. He responded:

> I probably said this—it sounds like me making an overcorrective overstatement possibly to some underestimation of F. P.—which I have loved since I first read it at the age of 20 or so. I don't know any play which sustains its verve so well[;] it's the "only" American comedy of the 1920's in the way that "Importance" is the "only" English comedy of the 1890's.[5]

The play has, indeed, established itself as the counterpart in American letters of Oscar Wilde's *The Importance of Being Earnest* in British. The plays are not similar in dialogue, but both are works in which great actors or actresses take pride in performing.[6] The leading actresses of the London stage—Dame Maggie Smith as recently as 1993—have considered their careers incomplete without doing Lady Bracknell. Helen Hayes undertook the role of Mrs. Grant in the 1969 revival of *The Front Page* so that she could have acted the role based on her mother in the classic work of which her husband, Charles MacArthur, was coauthor.[7] Robert Ryan, who was terminally ill, wanted to fill out his life's record as Walter Burns in the same revival. James MacArthur, son of Charles MacArthur and Helen Hayes, waited until age forty-three to appear as Hildy Johnson in a performance of *The Front Page* by the Stanford Community Theater in California in 1981, believing that earlier he lacked the maturity necessary for the role.[8] Both plays have had musical versions, *Ernest in Love* and *Windy City*, respectively.[9] The analogy between the two plays cannot be pressed excessively, however. *The Importance of Being Earnest* is an attack on the social standards of the British upper class, as embodied in Lady Bracknell's criteria for marriage. *The Front Page* is a comprehensive affront to all values: friendship, truth, intellectual honesty, the brotherhood of man, sanctity of human life, the law, and much else. The affection of Hildy for his fiancée stands out among all this as a normal, laudable emotional response.

Ben Hecht was active in Chicago journalism from 1910 and Charles MacArthur from 1915. They considered themselves friends, but their relationship was not close enough for them to undertake the play while in Chicago. MacArthur worked for morning papers, the *Herald and Examiner* and the *Tribune*, and Hecht for evening papers, the *Journal* and the *Daily News*. By the time MacArthur became a police reporter, Hecht had moved on to writing features. After they moved to New York, MacArthur in 1924 and Hecht in 1925, they became close friends, united by their common background in Chicago and by great mutual respect.[10] Hecht was explicitly of the opinion that they should never have left Chicago. To celebrate the Chicago journalistic world that had nurtured them, they hit upon a play as the vehicle to express, in a literal way, what they had known. The set would reproduce the pressroom of the old Criminal Court Building; the characters would all be actual. They would base the plot on two events: a practical joke played by Walter Howey, editor of the *Herald and Examiner*, on MacArthur in the summer of 1920, when MacArthur took Carol Frink of the newspaper's staff off to New York to marry her, and the escape of a convict, Tommy O'Connor, from the Cook County jail four days before he was to be hanged in December 1921.

Howey's practical joke, having MacArthur arrested as his train reached Gary, Indiana, was not publicized, but the escape of Tommy O'Connor was reported nationwide. Both Hecht and MacArthur had covered it for their newspapers and were thoroughly familiar with it. The episode, in which O'Connor made use of a smuggled pistol to break out of jail, made the police, both in Chicago and in surrounding Cook County, little short of laughingstocks. They followed a variety of false leads within the city and in the northwest suburbs. None of the leads was productive; O'Connor was never seen again and was rumored in the Chicago Irish community to have made his way back to Ireland unimpeded.

Meanwhile, Prohibition in 1920 gave rise to a proliferation of organized crime on a scale never before observed. The efforts of the Capone mob and its various rivals to control the liquor trade produced murders, hijackings, and miscellaneous crime against which the police appeared impotent. Indeed, the Capone mob apparently corrupted the police in Chicago and especially in suburban Cicero. For most of the time since 1915, William Hale Thompson had occupied the mayor's office; a politician who participated so gleefully in the corruption of the time that, by the end of his tenure, the *Chicago Tribune* had characterized him as a tool of the Capone mob. Thompson's venality had split the Republican party into two factions, one loyal to him and the other allied with the *Tribune*. All this had given the city a reputation worldwide for crime and corruption. This situation provided Hecht and MacArthur with an ideal opportunity for a satirical treatment of a universally recognized local situation. Slightly veiled versions of Thompson, his sheriff, a former police chief, and a representative Chicago hoodlum could take the stage as principal characters.

The play's supporting characters are drawn most conspicuously from the fellow reporters of Hecht and MacArthur at the Criminal Courts, but also from people the authors had met in Chicago. As police reporters, they had necessarily come into contact with a great variety of public officials, criminals, victims, and, in particular, drinking companions in Loop bars. Hecht and MacArthur used the names of these acquaintances, typically altering them slightly to avoid lawsuits. The names of people who had died, such as William Fenton, are regularly used without alteration. MacArthur's relations with Walter Howey are accurately delineated in the play but attributed to MacArthur's colleague, John Hilding Johnson, whose name is lightly altered to Hildebrand Johnson. Hildy Johnson, as he was invariably called, was the most conspicuous reporter in the Criminal Courts pressroom, a figure so dominant that the authors had little choice but to select him as their hero. Walter Howey appears as Walter Burns, a contraction of Walter Noble Burns, author of *The Saga of Billy the Kid*. Hecht and MacArthur adapted two prosecutors, Samuel E. Pincus, by changing his first name to Irving, and John Prystalski, by reversing the *r* and *y* in his name. Restaurateur Charles Appel appears as Charlie

Apfel. Diana Frutkin Margolies, to whom is addressed the second most famous line in the play, is concealed to the extent of reversing her first two initials. The authors habitually dropped or added *e* to names ending in *y* and
altered suffixes.

By recognizing how Hecht and MacArthur altered names, it is possible
to identify in Chicago city directories some of the minor figures mentioned,
notably Herman Schlosser, Bert Neeley, Abe Lefkowitz, William Gilhooly, and
Mittelbaum. It hardly need be said that identifications of this sort are open
to error. The process is much like what Sherlock Holmes described in *The
Hound of the Baskervilles*.

> "We are coming now rather into the region of guesswork," said
> Dr. Mortimer.
> "Say, rather, into the region where we balance probabilities and
> choose the most likely. . . ." [said Holmes]

There is a further problem that those people typically appeared in city directories for only a year or two, and then disappeared with no surviving evidence
for tracing them. Identifications of speakeasies and brothels in the text are necessarily worse than tentative; being illegal, their historical documentation is
inevitably based on hearsay or oral tradition.

Charles MacArthur, while directing a revival of the play on Broadway in
1946, decided to retain—with a single exception—the actual names of newspapers, characters, and persons who are merely mentioned, even though the
Journal and *Post* had gone out of business, the Hearst papers had merged, and
many of the prototypes of the characters had died. He said, "I can't see that
it makes any difference. We could just as well have used fictitious names in
the first place."[11] He was wrong. The newspapers had individual identities,
such that the *Tribune* could be treated as patrician—as in Walter's line, "Save
that for the *Tribune*"—and the *Herald and Examiner* could be represented as
the sleazy sheet it was. The names of individuals give the play an immediate
feel for the multiethnic society of Chicago that a set of fictional names could
never have provided. The weakness, relative to the other names, of Peggy Grant,
the name of the hero's love interest, is conspicuous. Worse, this character, who
is demonstrably fictional, tends to be flat because her lines do not emanate
from a personality that the authors knew. As a consequence, the play has the
unusual organization that the prostitute, Mollie Malloy, not Peggy, is the female lead. From the outset, casting and advertising have given primacy to Mollie Malloy.[12] Mollie, who is the social antithesis of Peggy, is also a weak
character, but in a different sense, being the stock theatrical figure of the noble

prostitute. Mark Amory in his review of *Windy City* in *The Spectator* (London) in 1982 called Mollie "the golden-hearted prostitute[,] surprisingly the whole cliche [played] absolutely straight."[13]

In part, the weakness of the two leading female characters stems from the play being essentially about the interactions of two men, Hildy and Walter, rather than the relations between a man and a woman. Indeed, what is true of the journalists is equally true of the politicians, for the second most important relationship is the interplay between the Mayor, the Sheriff, and Mr. Pincus. The writer who reviewed the first Philadelphia performance for the *Evening Bulletin* noted the primacy of the relationship between Hildy and Walter, saying that "the ladies in the play give the impression of being 'stop-gaps,'" causing the actresses to play the roles "without much enthusiasm in their several parts."[14]

Necessarily, the question arises how the prototypes of the characters viewed the use of their names by Hecht and MacArthur. Hilding Johnson was delighted. When Harold Ricklefs, a Chicago press veteran, met Johnson shortly after the play appeared, Ricklefs asked if Johnson intended to sue the authors. Johnson replied, "Hell no. They've made me famous. I'm a bigger hero than I've ever been. Sue? Have you been in a pressroom? They're all going around swearing louder and worst [sic] than ever. And did you notice [how] many of them are trying to write a play better than Charlie or Ben?"[15] Ricklefs, however, observed that Albert Baenziger, prototype of the neurotic Bensinger, and Sheriff Peter Hoffman, whom none could fail to identify as the Sheriff Hartman of the play, were reported at that time to be considering suit. There is no evidence that either followed through, but Richard Philbrick reported in conversation that when he knew Baenziger in the late 1940s, Baenziger was still irate at the delineation of him as Bensinger. Alone of the reporters, Jimmy Murphy published his reactions in a letter to his paper. In a letter to Art Sheekman, conductor of the *Journal's* literary column, "Little about Everything," Murphy defended himself against the character's use of profanity but concluded that he was not angry, just hurt that the authors made Hilding Johnson the hero, rather than himself.[16] Buddy McHugh revelled in his appearance in the play as McCue, taking pride in it until the end of his life.[17] "Duffy" Cornell, the most important of the characters who do not appear on stage, reportedly disliked the celebrity the mention gave him and, once the play reached Chicago, asked the authors to change the identification. The *Tribune* reported that the actors in the Chicago company began calling him by another name, but he remained "Duffy" in the text.[18] Indeed, in the acting edition of the play of

1950, the last published in the authors' lifetimes, he is explicitly designated—three times, no less—as "Duffy Cornell."[19]

The use of actual names has the incidental benefit of providing chronological detail. No specific date can be assigned to the play; rather, identifiable events range from before 1915 up to the middle of 1927, the year the play was written. Buddy McHugh is placed on the City News Bureau although he left it for the *American* in 1915.[20] John Prystalski served as assistant state's attorney from 1912 to 1920. Two events from 1919 are treated as in the past: establishment of the Chicago Crime Commission in January 1919 and the confession of Thomas Fitzgerald on July 27, 1919 for the murder of a child, Janet Wilkinson. The action occurs during William Hale Thompson's consecutive terms as mayor of Chicago, from April 26, 1915 to April 17, 1923. The preoccupation with Polack Mike's speakeasy and with clandestine transactions for gin places the action after the imposition of Prohibition on July 1, 1920. Although the practical joke that ends the play occurred at an undetermined date in the summer of 1920, the text contains three specific references to events of 1920: the murder-suicide of Ruth Randall occurred on March 8, 1920; assignment of Ernie Kruger to the *Journal of Commerce* requires the action to be after the newspaper's founding on October 14, 1920; and the reference to the Clara Hamon murder puts the play after November 21, 1920.[21]

Mention of the Wrigley Building places the action after the structure began receiving tenants in April 1921. The escape of Tommy O'Connor occurred on December 11, 1921, but the Sheriff is the barely veiled Peter M. Hoffman, who was elected to office on November 7, 1922. Samuel E. Pincus, a Democratic lawyer, was made assistant attorney general of Illinois, the appointment vital to the plot, in 1915; but if the reprieve he delivers is assigned to 1921 along with the O'Connor execution, his appearance is during the tenure of the anti-Thompson Republican attorney general, Edward J. Brundage, who served from 1917 to 1925.[22] Pincus apparently left office when he became city prosecutor of Chicago on April 17, 1923. The action occurs when Hildy Johnson has been a newspaperman for fifteen years, which is to say in 1923.[23] The Tivoli Theatre, to which Walter attempts to direct Pincus for a Greta Garbo film, was opened on February 16, 1921, but no picture of Garbo played there until a silent version of Vincente Blasco Ibanez's *The Temptress* in the week beginning on January 3, 1927.[24] The Durkin case mentioned was the murder of a federal agent on October 11, 1925. Charles Callahan of the Chicago Police Department served as lieutenant, the rank assigned him in the play, from January 4, 1924 to July 1, 1926. The Chinese earthquake that Walter dismisses so unequivocally is probably that of May 23, 1927, in Kansu Province. The reporters' discussion of the imminent hanging is most consistent with the period shortly before the State of Illinois's conversion to electrocution by a statute of July 6, 1927.

The stagebill issued for the opening in Chicago on November 25, 1928, placed the play in "[a]n era which ended about 1912," but that is clearly incorrect.[25] The authors and producer while planning the first Chicago production received formal objections to the treatment of Thompson and sought to blur the delineation of him, partly by instructing actor Willard Dashiell to shift from Thompson's trademark broad-brimmed soft hat, which had been used by George Barbier in New York, to a derby and partly by assigning the action to a period several years before Thompson became mayor.[26] Frederick Donaghey in his review in the *Chicago Tribune* on November 26, 1928, noted the impossibility of the dating in the program: "If the era the authors have footlighted ended in 1912, then Herbert Hoover wasn't elected President in the current month."[27] At the opposite extreme from the Chicago program, the notes for *Windy City*, the musical based on *The Front Page*, done in 1980 for production on the London stage two years later, assign the action to the spring of 1929, several months after *The Front Page* itself appeared.[28] The range of possible dates is narrower than that. One is probably most justified to assign the action to the period from Tommy O'Connor's escape in December 1921 to Samuel E. Pincus's becoming city prosecutor of Chicago in April 1923, with anachronisms both earlier and later.

According to Helen Hayes, Hecht and MacArthur rented the Rockland Female Institute, a girls' school in South Nyack, New York, and wrote the play there in the summer of 1927.[29] Hecht in his biography of MacArthur describes how they collaborated. Hecht sat in a chair with a clipboard and pad. MacArthur, he said, walked about the room, lay on a couch, drew moustaches on cover girls, or prowled about in a fourth dimension, dictating dialogue and turns of plot. They showed great faith in each other's judgment, rejecting what either of them disliked. Hecht reported that they continued in this method through twenty years of collaboration on stage works and screenplays. Upon finishing the play, they went out to lunch at the Algonquin Hotel. When MacArthur asked which author's name should appear first, Hecht replied that he did not know. MacArthur suggested they flip a coin. Hecht flipped a nickel, MacArthur called heads, and the coin came up tails.[30] It does appear to have been a collaboration of equals. Helen Hayes reported that Hecht wrote most of the dialogue and did the turns in the plot, but MacArthur created the characters from people he had known in Chicago.[31] Hecht was more favorable to MacArthur, crediting him for the plot turns and for the sharp characterization in the dialogue: "It was always a character who spoke, not a line born of another line."[32]

The play was to be one of four hits brought to Broadway between 1926 and 1928 by Jed Harris, who thereby established a mercurial reputation as an impresario from the age of twenty-six to twenty-eight. Harris took an option to produce the play late in 1927 and accepted it during the weekend of December 10.[33] Believing the script to be in need of substantial cutting and rewriting, he brought in George S. Kaufman to write a "better, tighter and funnier script," and subsequently hired him as director. Harris stated that Kaufman gave the play its name.[34]

It should be noted that the writing of the play coincided precisely with the apogee of the New York theater. The number of productions rose from 157 in the 1920-to-1921 season to 280 in the 1927-to-1928 season, the highest figure in history. As early as 1939 it was down to 80.[35] In recent years the number of new productions has done well to break 20.

Hecht and MacArthur laid the manuscript on Harris's desk with a note stating that the play should be treated as "a work of art, something like *Hamlet*."[36] No doubt this was intended as a facetious observation, but it probably represents the authors' recognition, even if on a subconscious level, of the quality of what they had done. It is, alas, unlikely that society will ever treat the intellectual heirs of Aristophanes as seriously as the sons of Sophocles. Hecht's and MacArthur's note might have been taken seriously had they tried to relate the play instead to the classic comedies, of which Ben Jonson's *The Alchemist* is probably the closest analog in moral tone. It is notable that *The Alchemist*, also, employs a prostitute as its female lead. Alternatively, if *The Beggar's Opera* is accepted as an attack on Prime Minister Sir Robert Walpole, one may observe the parallel in the treatment of William Hale Thompson in *The Front Page*. An even closer parallel is to a less familiar comedy of the eighteenth century, Samuel Foote's *The Mayor of Garratt* of 1763. The plot concerns an eccentric election in a town in what is now London south suburbia. The characters are mainly identifiable local political figures, but one of the male leads is an obsequious politician easily identifiable by audiences as the recent First Lord of the Treasury, the Duke of Newcastle.[37]

Such analogies could not have been lost on Harris, for in his introduction to the Covici-Friede edition of 1928, reprinted in this edition (see page 33), he noted the parallel between Constable Dogberry of Shakespeare's *Much Ado About Nothing* and Sheriff Hartman.[38] Instead, Harris from the outset advertised the play as a newspaper farce, a genre that was already well established on the stage and in motion pictures—and one that was not notably prestigious.[39]

Casting of the play was left to Kaufman, who assigned roles mainly, but not exclusively, to actors and actresses whom he had known earlier in the 1920s. Four roles were of first importance: Hildy Johnson and Walter Burns among the men, Mollie Malloy and Peggy Grant among the women. For Hildy he chose Lee Tracy, a thirty-year-old actor who had appeared in four Broadway plays but had only one previous starring role in 1926, as the dancer Roy Lane in *Broadway* by George Abbott and Philip Dunning. It was widely thought within the theatrical community that Tracy had been chosen only because he was under long-term contract with Harris. Hecht opposed the choice although he was later to consider the actor very fine in the role.[40] Consequently, Tracy had to prove himself beyond ordinary expectations.[41]

For Walter, Kaufman chose Osgood Perkins, thirty-six, who had established a reputation in roles as a glib, malevolent figure in the course of the 1920s. He had appeared in nine plays on Broadway, beginning with Kaufman's collaboration with Marc Connelly, *Beggar on Horseback* of 1924, and had starred as Whittaker in MacArthur's collaboration with Sidney Howard, *Salvation*, for producer Arthur Hopkins earlier in 1928.[42] His role was said to be based on Whittaker Ray, Jed Harris's general manager.[43] Brooks Atkinson wrote of that performance: "The cast includes Osgood Perkins as the type of facile-tongued rogue he plays so easily."[44] Given Perkins's well-established stage persona and his associations with Harris, Kaufman, and MacArthur, one presumes that the play was completed with him envisioned as Walter.

As Mollie, Kaufman chose Phyllis Povah, a University of Michigan alumna who had come to New York late in 1919 and established herself in romantic leads in the early 1920s. She was probably thirty-four. She had made her greatest success in Owen Davis's Pulitzer Prize–winning play of 1922 to 1923, *Icebound*, and in 1924 had starred in Kaufman's collaboration with Edna Ferber, *Minick*.[45] Miss Povah was to be identified with Kaufman's plays well into the 1940s. The romantic lead, Peggy Grant, was assigned to a twenty-year-old actress, Frances Fuller, whose professional experience was limited to three weeks immediately earlier at a stock company in West Chester, Pennsylvania.[46]

The play was successful from the outset. The New York company had its first pre-Broadway trial with a run of four performances in three days at the Apollo Theatre in Atlantic City beginning on May 14, 1928. Harris intended that the company proceed to the Broad Street Theatre in Philadelphia for the following week, but the run was cancelled, reportedly because the local censors objected to the language.[47] Instead, the work was sent to the Broad Street

Theater in Newark, where it was readily accessible to the New York theatrical community.[48] Then, according to plan, the work was withdrawn for the summer but had a further tryout run of a week in Long Branch, New Jersey, beginning on August 6. Reviews from the beginning were highly favorable. The local reviewer in Atlantic City, who did not identify himself, treated the play only as a newspaper farce and mainly devoted himself to praising Lee Tracy as Hildy Johnson, recognizing that the role had been assigned to the actor because of his contract to Harris.[49]

The reviews in Newark were especially favorable to Phyllis Povah. The anonymous reviewer of the *Evening News* wrote:

> One of the best bits of acting, however, in the entire play was Phyllis Povah's depiction of a girl of the street, who, out of pity, has befriended the condemned prisoner. Her tirade against the heartlessness of the reporters toward the end of the first act was one of the high spots of the play.[50]

A reviewer who signed himself "Playgoer" in the *Star-Eagle* considered her second only to Lee Tracy in the cast:

> Phyllis Povah is next in a beautiful array of honest acting. . . . She has a role to delight the heart of any trouper, and troupes it like the grandest trouper of them all.[51]

At the end of the run in Newark it was announced that there would be no cast changes when the play went to Broadway in August.[52]

We know that Hecht, MacArthur, Harris, and Kaufman met continually to discuss the performances, both during rehearsals in New York and during the tryouts in New Jersey. According to Kaufman's biographer, Howard Teichman, their view was that Kaufman had cast the play almost perfectly, except that Povah was not playing an effective prostitute. Kaufman was directed to replace her. Teichman states that the decision was made after five days of rehearsal.[53] Reports in the press bear him out. The specialized racing and entertainment paper, the *Morning Telegraph,* listed the play among rehearsals in progress on July 27 and reported that Povah had been replaced on August 8.[54] This decision is difficult to reconcile with the favorable evaluations of the press to Povah's performances and with the reported enthusiasm of the audiences toward her. Nonetheless, by August 8 Kaufman had hired as a replacement Dorothy Stickney, wife of his friend Howard Lindsay. She had made her Broadway debut in *The Southern Belles* in 1921 and appeared in four subsequent roles of increasing importance. She had recently achieved some fame in the role of Crazy Liz, the demented charwoman in Maurine Dallas Watkins's *Chicago*.[55] Kaufman reported that Stickney, who had what he considered a prim manner, had some difficulty in delivering Mollie's entrance line, "I've been looking for you bastards!" After he assured her that the line had been inserted only to arouse the audience's sympathy for the character, she had no further problems.[56] On the basis of reports of the tryout performances in New Jersey, the play was eagerly anticipated in New York; Robert Benchley stated that the play arrived on Broadway with a reputation that assured its early success.[57]

Harris scheduled the play to open the 1928-to-1929 Broadway season; in particular, he wanted to beat to the boards *Gentlemen of the Press*, a newspaper farce by Ward Morehouse.[58] *The Front Page* opened at the Times Square Theatre on August 14, two weeks before Morehouse's work. Harris called off the performance of his *Coquette* so that Helen Hayes, its star, could attend the first night. In spite of oppressive heat, she sat in the balcony, and when the audience's response to the first act showed that the play was a hit, she rushed out to Hecht and MacArthur, who had gone to sit on the fire escape, to let them know. MacArthur responded by proposing to her, and they were married three days later.[59]

Because of Harris's decision to advertise the play as a farce, the work was in the unusual position of having to rise above its marketing. The tryout in Long Branch evoked the most perceptive and authoritative early review of the play. The *Asbury Park Evening Press* sent its city editor, William S. Conklin, to Long Branch to report his views of the work. He became the first reviewer to note that the play is based on actual events and that it is an attack on William Hale Thompson.[60] Indeed, his review was more insightful than the reviews in the New York papers, which typically treated the play as a farce, summarized the plot, praised the acting of the principals, and discussed the coarseness of the language.[61] Conklin made no mention of the play's profanity in his review but appended a short postscript advising readers to avoid the production if they were offended by the ordinary language of truck drivers. Of the New York reviewers, only S. Jay Kaufman of the *Morning Telegraph* stated flatly, "It is a great play."[62] He also observed, "And a masterpiece of casting was Osgood Perkins as the city editor."

George Jean Nathan in the *American Mercury* expressed the view that Hecht and MacArthur had started to write a straight newspaper play but that it turned farce on them.[63] In part, the authors had to build more farcical elements into the play to accelerate the action working toward the denouement.

In part, Nathan noted what was widely observed, that the first and second acts were more tightly written than the third.

Once the play reached Chicago in November, the delineation of the environment caused reviewers to recognize that the play was not a farce. As long as it was considered simply a farce with fictional characters, the play could not be seen for what it is: a satiric characterization of the actual Republican mayor, William Hale Thompson, and his principal political ally desperately trying to secure the Republicans' one big power base of the pre–New Deal period, the black population, in a city that was otherwise almost wholly Democratic. Robert Morss Lovett, professor of English at the University of Chicago, observed that New York plays about crime were typically set in the habitat of the criminal, but in Chicago they were set in the purlieu of the prosecution, with the press as the regent for the public's right to know. He concluded, "However, the *The Front Page* is a great newspaper play, and destined to run forever."[64] Adversely, Lovett did not consider the mayor an effective delineation of Thompson: "He is not Big Bill the Builder—probably no one could be."[65]

It has always been presumed that the principal purpose of the play was to provide an affectionate retrospective of the Chicago journalism the authors had known and that the plot mainly provides a means for demonstating the journalistic milieu. Certainly the epilogue that Hecht and MacArthur added to the play for its third printing in October 1928 (see pages 187–188) is most consistent with this presumption. The play admits of a rival interpretation, however: that its main thrust is the intellectual assault on William Hale Thompson and Peter M. Hoffman, with the realistic treatment of journalistic life serving as a means for intensifying the attack.

William Hale Thompson was active in Republican politics in Chicago from the late nineteenth century. He became alderman from the Second Ward on the South Side in 1900 and became Cook County Commissioner in 1902. He first allied himself with the political machine of Senator William Lorimer, who was ejected from the United States Senate in 1912 after substantiation of charges of bribery brought by the *Chicago Tribune* on April 30, 1910. Thompson's principal political identification by the time of the play was with the former state senator and one-term congressman, Fred Lundin. The *Tribune* was identified with the rival Republican faction headed by the former governor, Charles S. Deneen. This situation produced a rivalry of almost unequalled acrimony between Thompson and the *Tribune* that far transcended the *Tribune's* traditional Republican loyalties.

Thompson was first elected mayor in 1915 by a margin of 3,591 votes, mainly by virtue of heavy black support in the Second Ward. This ward was then headed by Chicago's pioneer black alderman, Oscar DePriest, who became one of Thompson's principal supporters. The press was almost unanimously hostile to Thompson; only the *Journal* supported him in 1915. In office Thompson was hostile to American participation in World War I and flaunted a demagogic Anglophobia. This stance appealed to the city's some 600,000 residents of German and Austrian extraction and to its Irish population, a mixture that became his second most important constituency. His noninterventionist stance caused the Hearst papers to support him when he successfully sought reelection in 1919; no other Chicago paper did so. Scandals in the school system in 1922, plus a prosecution of his colleague Lundin for graft, caused Thompson not to seek reelection in 1923. After a reform administration of the Democrat William Emmett Dever, which Thompson characteristically disliked intensely, Thompson was reelected mayor in April 1927. Thus, he was again mayor at the time the play was first produced. Because of his conspicuous Anglophobia and general demagoguery during the 1927 election, he had made himself a figure of national reputation—however negatively. Thus, his personality characteristics could hardly have been better known than in 1928. Thompson remained in office until 1931, when scandals in the office of the City Sealer, the municipal department of which Hecht and MacArthur had made such effective use in the play, contributed to his defeat by Anton J. Cermak.

The first reviewer, as far as is known, to state explicitly that the play was not a farce was Frederick Donaghey in the *Chicago Tribune*. He criticized Harris's advertising of the play as a farce, saying, "It is rather, the successful effort of two young men with a mordant outlook on what goes on about them; and among the things that have gone on about them are the incidents and episodes they have put into *The Front Page*."[66] He argued that, instead, the authors had simply used elements of farce—slamming doors, characters flying through the window, concealment in desks—for comedic effect.[67] Farcical elements in comedy—including Shakespearean comedy—are extremely common.

From the outset, performance of the play has been made difficult by the adverse responses to its language. At the time, the ubiquitous profanity and the sexual banter concerning the Mollie Malloy character were widely thought intolerable. Compared with later works, such as Jason Miller's *That Championship Season*, the language is quite mild. The more modern objection is to the ethnic and racial epithets: Polack, nigger, wop, bohunk, turkey, and more. The play could not be the outpouring of intellectual and moral evils the authors imputed to the reporters and, more especially, to the politicians without some representation of ethnic bigotry. The ethnic epithets contribute to the play's standing as a document of its time, not so much for their presence—because such language can be found in society at some level at any time—but rather for their acceptability: no character remonstrates against their use.[68]

By early September 1928, Assistant District Attorney Joab H. Banton in Manhattan had received four complaints against the play. He responded that he was unwilling to censor it but was willing to prosecute if the producers were thought in violation of criminal law.[69] Brooks Atkinson, the *New York Times*'s critic, found the language offensive and considered it a verbal exhibitionism unnecessary for the play's effectiveness.[70] Percy Hammond in the *New York Herald-Tribune* felt "the play would be pleasantly shorter, if less veristic, if the epithets and curses had been left to the imagination."[71] Burns Mantle of the *New York Daily News* in the weekly column on the New York theater that he contributed to the *Chicago Tribune* treated the play as distinguished mainly by profanity, vulgarity, and wisecracks. Arguing that there was no great public interest in newspaper life, profanity, or humor that depends on the proximity of the men's lavatory, he concluded, "I appear to be the only man hereabouts who does not believe in a lasting popularity for 'The Front Page.'"[72] Heywood Broun, although explicitly of the opinion that the work was not a great play, defended its profanity as strengthening the realism of the action. He had considered the lack of profanity among the stokers in Eugene O'Neill's *The Hairy Ape* a vitiation of reality.[73] St. John Ervine, regular reviewer for the *Observer* (London) on leave for a year at the *New York World*, expressed what was for the early reviews a balanced view: "*The Front Page* is an extraordinarily vulgar play, in which there are many brutally humorous lines, some coarse characterizations, a brilliantly swift and well directed production, and uncommonly fine acting. The play is entirely thug."[74] After the play opened in Chicago on November 25, 1928, Reverend Phillip Yarrow of the Illinois Vigilance Association sought a court order to have the cast arrested on the ground that the play was "obscene, indecent and immoral," but Judge Francis Borelli denied his request.[75] When the work opened in Los Angeles on December 30, the language had reportedly been toned down.[76] Those who were affronted by the profanity failed to note that, except by extremely priggish standards, the play is free of obscenities, dirty jokes, or blue humor.

The success of the play in America necessarily generated interest in producing it in Britain, but there its language and general character constituted a far greater impediment to production than at home, for Britain had a long-standing system of censorship of plays by the Lord Chamberlain. The statutory authority for the censorship at the time was embodied in the Theatres Act of 1843 (6 & 7 Victoria, cap. 68), a statute that empowered the Lord

Chamberlain to deny a license for production of a play "whenever he shall be of opinion that it is fitting for the preservation of good manners, decorum, or of the public peace to do so." The act set no guidelines and provided for no review of decisions. The act was so broadly discretionary that the Lord Chamberlain's office necessarily developed its own set of guidelines for licensure of plays. The Lord Chamberlain as of 1928 prohibited representation on the stage of the Deity or Jesus, members of the Royal Family, and actual persons or those who had recently died. Showing couples in bed was specifically prohibited. The manager of the theater in which the play was to be performed was required to apply for a license, providing the Lord Chamberlain with a copy of the text—which, as altered for approval, had to be adhered to—along with the date of the proposed production.

Colonel Robert Loraine, manager of the Apollo Theatre on Shaftesbury Avenue, London, on January 18, 1929, applied to the Lord Chamberlain for a license for the play, enclosing a typescript copy, but stating that he had no specific proposed date for performance. He requested dispatch on the ground that "at the moment I have a very favourable opportunity for its production which may pass if I don't settle soon."[77] As Loraine was about to discover, the play had something to violate each criterion of the Lord Chamberlain for licensure. Every character in the play with one definite exception, and another qualified exception, was a real person. No member of the Royal Family took the stage, but King George was mentioned. No couple was shown in bed, but there is a specific reference to an assignation in the Revere House, with implications of others in the Sherman and Planters Hotels. There were 307 oaths in the text, and more generally the play was a comprehensive outrage to "good manners [and] decorum," though not, admittedly, to public peace.

The typescript was referred to George Slythe Street, an essayist, novelist, editor, and playwright who had been on the Lord Chamberlain's staff since 1914, as reader of plays since 1920.[78] Inevitably, Street's principal objection was to the Mayor's line in Act II, "The slogan I had was all we needed to win, 'Keep King George Out of Chicago.'" This at once introduced a reference to British royalty and unambiguously indentified the Mayor as the actual person, William Hale Thompson. Street also objected to Walter's mock prayer in Act III as offensive to some viewers. He found a phrase in Act III, "You damned hound," unpleasant because it was addressed to a woman. He considered "bitched up" in Act III offensive but noted that it had been allowed in a play of Eden Philpotts. His oddest complaint was against the use of "Gents" in the stage direction and on a sign on the wall of the set; "Gents" is more common in British usage than American and is not usually thought offensive.

To his typescript report he appended some specific directives in manuscript. He required that "Gents" be replaced with "toilet," "bitched up" be altered, and the mock prayer be cut. "You damned hound" might stand, but the number of uses of "God" was excessive and must be reduced. If these changes were made, he wrote, "I very reluctantly agree to allow this unpleasant product of the U.S.A. to pass for licence."[79]

Slightly modifying Street's conditions, Major C. L. Gordon, comptroller of the Lord Chamberlain's office, wrote Loraine agreeing to license the play if a phrase from Act I, "[God] damn your greasy souls," was eliminated, along with "Keep King George Out of Chicago" from Act II, and both the mock prayer and "bitched up" from Act III. Gordon also asked Loraine to specify how many uses of "God" would be eliminated and how many retained. He also requested assurance that none of the names was that of a real person in Chicago.[80] Acceptance of the final condition would have required Loraine to perjure himself. Either for that reason or because he was unable to work out a satisfactory contract with Harris, he abandoned the projected production at the Apollo and requested return of the typescript.[81]

Two efforts were made to produce the play in Britain in the mid-1930s. Herbert Y. Scott, manager of the People's Theatre in Newcastle, apparently after a search of the Lord Chamberlain's correspondence with Loraine in 1929, applied for a license for a production scheduled for November 21, 1935.[82] He submitted a copy of the fifth printing of the Covici-Friede edition, with the proposed excisions marked in red ink. He removed forty-nine references to "God," and nineteen to "Jesus" or "Christ." Most of the other possibly offensive words or phrases were red-lined: bollocks, Hildy's reference to the Last Supper, "Keep King George Out of Chicago," Mollie's "fanny," Endicott's reference to the Sherman Hotel and Walter's reference to the Revere House, plus several minor passages.[83] The Lord Chamberlain was generally satisfied and agreed on November 1, 1935, to license the play for production, provided that the red-lining of the Covici-Friede edition be strictly adhered to, that "Gents" be relettered "Toilet," the number of "Gods" be further reduced by eleven, and assurance be provided that none of the characters bore the names of real people.[84]

For lack of notice in theatrical trade journals and Newcastle newspapers, Scott's proposed production was never mounted. On the basis of Scott's correspondence with the Lord Chamberlain, however, a license was granted on the same terms to the Manchester Repertory Theatre.[85] This brought forth the first British production of the play at Manchester for the week beginning

January 13, 1936. Reviews were generally favorable. A reviewer in the *Guardian* (Manchester) who signed himself "A. S. W." wrote:

> We spend our evening with a company hardened by perpetual concern with murder, rape, arson, gang raids and graft to a callousness about all normal human relationships. But common subservience to a vicious system has not destroyed their individuality. The several portraits in this 'toughs gallery' are drawn with a skill and an intimacy that hold our interest. The full force of the picturesque language of the press room has been tempered for polite English consumption, but at its best it still has a Falstaffian variety in richness in invective and repartee. Here and there a phrase has been altered to suit 1935. A once notorious slogan becomes 'Keep Hitler out of Chicago.' But the pace of the action and the vigour of the character-drawing are not impaired.[86]

No further efforts at a British production are known to have been made before the censorship was abolished in 1968.[87] It was probably the stultifying effect of the censorship, rather than what was rumored, official displeasure with Hecht's Zionism, that delayed the first London production until 1972.

By 1946, when *The Front Page* had its first professional revival on Broadway, the profanity had largely ceased to be shocking. As the reviewer in *Variety* observed, the passage of time and greater liberality in ordinary conversation had weakened the impact of the language.[88] The racial epithets, however, had greatly increased in opprobrium: by the 1940s "nigger" had established itself as the single most offensive word in American English. To the surprise of none, it was the first to be excised. The Blue Network, predecessor of the American Broadcasting Company, on March 29, 1942, produced an adept condensation of the play for radio by Charles Newton. To deal with the problem, Newton expunged the identification of Williams's victim as black, dropped entirely the efforts of the Mayor and Sheriff to assure loyalty of the black electorate, and treated both men merely as candidates attempting to run on a law-and-order platform.[89] Charles MacArthur in the course of directing the 1946 revival was quoted, "We've also dropped the word 'nigger,' which occurred a half dozen times. The plot doesn't hinge on it: So why use it if it's offensive. I also took out a reference to the Redeemer."[90] He also updated some references that he thought had ceased to be recognizable; he reported that he replaced "Clarence Darrow" with "Harold Ickes"—a strange change, one that in retrospect hardly appears logical. Not all of his modifications in language are known, but when the revival opened in Chicago on February 17, 1947, reviewer Claudia Cassidy of the *Tribune* thought the play had been weakened by excessive redrafting, especially in the second act.[91]

Publication of an acting edition by the theatrical publisher Samuel French in 1950 allowed the authors to make their final revisions in the play. MacArthur was to die in 1956 and Hecht in 1964. Surprisingly, "nigger" returns to the text. The principal substantive change is introducing Walter Burns in Act I as an offstage voice on the telephone in his conversations with Mrs. Schlosser, Endicott, and Hildy, probably to deal with an unusual structural characteristic of the play: Walter, although one of the two men with whom the plot is principally concerned, does not take the stage until immediately before the second act climax. In the first New York performance, Osgood Perkins as Walter did not take the stage until 10:27 P.M.[92] This arrangement provided effective suspense for Walter's entry, which his appearance as an offstage voice tends to dissipate. The earlier introduction of Walter entails a considerable amount of additional profanity from him, although some individual oaths by Hildy and the reporters were dropped. Most of the changes occur before Walter makes his appearance in Act II; thereafter the text follows the Covici-Friede edition much more closely. One of the play's most famous lines, Hildy's description of a reporter as "A cross between a bootlegger and a whore" was deleted. Some humor was made explicit that in the original had been based on leaving responses to the imagination. The net effect was to leave the text more prolix than the original and, as critics have noted, weaker.[93] To take a single example, Woodenshoes Eichhorn goes from being "a big, moon-faced, childish and incompetent German policeman" to "a big, moon-faced, optimistic, impressionable German cop." The effect is analogous to W. S. Gilbert's widely criticized redrawing of the illustrations of his early works in 1898: an old man allowed his view of what he conceived to be the excesses of his youth to weaken something generally thought masterful.[94]

Throughout the play's history, there has been a question of how accurately it depicts newspaper life. Frederick W. M'Quigg of Hearst's *Chicago Evening American* in his review of the first Chicago performance wrote of the reporters in the play, "for stage purposes and thrill[,] these playerfolk are admirable. Exploited in a newspaper publication, they are the bunk, for there are not newspaper men like them in the daily grind of getting out your newspaper."[95] M'Quigg's colleague, Harry C. Read, city editor of the *American*, considered the play a "travesty on a profession that all of us who are in it really take seriously . . ."[96] In particular, Read thought the banter of reporters was a veneer, which Hecht and MacArthur took seriously in an effort to build a solid structure for the play. St. John Ervine on the basis of his experience in

British journalism, wrote: "The little group of reporters who form [the] principal characters resemble no reporters I have ever seen, and I have worked on newspapers for about twenty years."[97] Conklin, the reviewer of the *Asbury Park Evening Press*, wrote "Newspaper life has been exaggerated a bit in this play. Undoubtedly this has been done to make the piece more dramatic. It is excusable for in so doing the play has been strengthened." He considered simply falling into a major story, as Hildy Johnson does in the play, unlikely and observed that for authenticity the reporters on stage should have smoked.[98] Hecht and MacArthur strongly defended the depiction of the Criminal Courts pressroom, saying that the play gave a moderate or understated view of what really went on there.[99] Vincent Starrett retrospectively argued, "Citizens who believe that play to be exaggerated know nothing of the newspaper world . . ., especially the Hearst newspaper world. Possibly it is the best newspaper drama ever written, and actually it is not greatly overdrawn."[100] Buddy McHugh in 1974 stated that he considered the play accurate but that it understated the long periods of tedium that police reporting entails.[101]

For whatever reason, all three reviewers of the tryout performances of the Chicago company in Indianapolis in 1928 treated the question of the accuracy of the play at length, and all of them concluded that the work was a faithful representation of newspaper life. Robert G. Tucker of the *Star* wrote, "However, what we like most about *The Front Page* is its sheer honesty, its penetrating and unerring satire in dealing with life as their police reporters find it and its ever present and effervescing humor."[102] Walter Whitworth of the *News* wrote, "The great thing about this play is its faithfulness to the life it portrays. . . . [A] work of art it is, irreverent art, but good art."[103] Walter D. Hickman of the *Indianapolis Times* specifically raised the question of the accuracy of the presentation of life in a pressroom with his city editor, Volney Fowler, and got a very positive response. Hickman concluded a favorable review by saying of the play, "It was so d--- fine that Volney Fowler of my own sheet, told me in the lobby of English's hotel that this play was 'great.' And I will take his word for that."[104]

The perceptive Conklin also observed the play had a generality beyond newspaper life. The conflict between professional obligations and affection for his fiancée presented Hildy with a problem that men in all sorts of activities had faced. Thus, audiences could empathize with the character indefinitely.

The question arises of when the play had finally risen above its initial marketing as a farce. By the time of the first London performance in 1972, most of the reviewers treated the work much as Irving Wardle of the *Times* did in the passage quoted at the outset, but an important critic, Harold Hobson of the *Sunday Times,* could still treat it essentially as trivial: "It is joyous thick-ear stuff, a commercial piece unworthy of a National Theatre with huge sub-sidy, [but] it will delight every infant in the audience, especially those over 40."[105] When the musical version, *Windy City,* was produced in London in 1982, reviewers in all of the major dailies treated *The Front Page* as an Amer-ican classic and divided only on the question whether it could reasonably be improved upon by music—mainly concluding that it could not. Milton Shul-man of the *Evening Standard* expressed the majority view:

> What can music do to enhance the appeal of *The Front Page,* the best play ever written about the newspaper game[?] The answer is nothing. What can music do to detract from the enjoyment of that play? After seeing Windy City . . . a musical adaptation of Hecht and MacArthur's comic masterpiece directed by Peter Wood, the answer is again nothing. I am happy to report this tale . . . is apparently indestructible.[106]

Michael Billington of the *Guardian* (Manchester) wrote:

> Hecht and MacArthur's The Front Page is a classic satirical farce about power, corruption and newspaper life as religion that puts more of America onto the stage than any play of the Twenties. . . . I can't help feeling it needs music like the Sahara needs sand. . . . But although [Windy City] is no disgrace, it leaves one key question unanswered: how can any musical improve on a classic source[?][107]

The minority opinion was stated by Rosalie Horner in the *Daily Express:*

> *The Front Page,* the 1928 stage hit, has become the classic of its kind, the definitive piece on journalism. It endows our profession with just the right blend of cynicism and sentiment. . . . Composer Tony Macauley and writer Dick Vosburgh have done the impossible and turned a great story into a great musical.[108]

She concluded that *Windy City* would supersede *The Front Page* on the boards. When Gregory Mosher became director of the Lincoln Center The-ater of New York in 1986, he chose to begin his inaugural comedy series with *The Front Page.* When asked why he had chosen it, he replied simply that it is "the great American comedy."[109] Consequently, by the 1980s Jed Harris's initial mistake had been undone, and *The Front Page* was recognized for what it is.

The play was not a success that could be duplicated. Because of the use of actual characters and the re-creation of a milieu that the authors had been familiar with for many years, *The Front Page* was unique. Of the four later plays on which Hecht and MacArthur collaborated, the most highly regarded is *Twentieth Century* of 1932, a delineation of a theatrical producer thought to be based on Morris Gest, David Belasco, and Jed Harris.[110]

Of the thousands of people who have seen *The Front Page* over the course of the twentieth century, I suspect that those who enjoyed it most were the audience at its opening in Chicago at the Erlanger Theatre on November 25, 1928. As Ashton Stevens of the *Chicago Herald and Examiner* wrote in his review, "Lines that are merely lines in the New York presentation of Ben Hecht's and Charles MacArthur's epic of the profane and salty reporters were here found to contain matter of singular and mirthful local significance."[111] Jed Harris stated in his autobiography that all the characters were actual but that he had made no effort to match the actual physical types.[112] He wrote, "Indeed, they all turned up at the first night in Chicago and simply wallowed in delight." The ovation at the end of Act I "sounded like the roar of a herd of wild animals panicked by fire at the zoo."[113] The *Post's* reviewer, Clarence J. Bulliet, described the Chicago opening as "one grand party." Many of the references, especially to characters who do not take the stage, were so obscure that only individuals could be expected to recognize them. Bulliet observed this, noting "occasional and raucous shrieks and excited groanings of ecstasy as some point hit home to some newspaper man or other to whom a particular reference had a special cryptic meaning."[114]

In this edition, I have tried to provide the background information that that audience brought to the Erlanger. Given the obscurity of many references that Bulliet noted, a wholly successful effort to identify the people who take the stage and those who are merely mentioned is essentially impossible.

I have rigorously avoided eliminating the offensive material in the text. Because so many people in the early audiences reacted to the play as a gross violation of propriety, a successful re-creation of the emotional impact of that opening night in Chicago should leave some readers offended. Those who are affronted should bear in mind that the denunciation of the denizens of the Criminal Courts pressroom is delivered by the cheap prostitute, Mollie Malloy: "It is a wonder a bolt of lightning don't come through the ceiling and strike you all dead!" Similarly, moral behavior has to be brought in from out of town in the person of the incorruptible Mr. Pincus.

Nonetheless, by the time the famous curtain line is uttered, justice has, in fact, been victorious. For all of Walter Burns's preoccupation with circulation and contempt for intellectual honesty, his *Examiner* has prevented an unspeakable act of political corruption and brought to imminent judgment as contemptible a politician as the nation has ever produced. Perhaps even this work is consistent with W. S. Gilbert's judgment that "virtue is triumphant only in theatrical performances."[115]

NOTES

1. Vincent Starrett, *Born in a Bookshop: Chapters from the Chicago Renascence* (Norman, OK: University of Oklahoma Press, 1965), p. 127.

2. *Times* (London), July 7, 1972, p. 9.

3. Quoted by Michael Blakemore in Barry Norman, "Michael Blakemore: Setting in Motion a Dazzling Machine," *Times*, (London), June 17, 1972, p. 11.

4. Kenneth Tynan, *Show People: Profiles in Entertainment* (London: Weidenfeld and Nicholson, 1977), p. 116.

5. Manuscript note of Tom Stoppard to George W. Hilton, September 2, 1995. In 1996 I did find the quotation in the *Los Angeles Times*, but several months earlier than Tynan remembered, January 20, 1977, sec. IV, p. 12.

6. But, for an argument that their structure is similar, see note 63.

7. On her decision to do Mrs. Grant, see "Helen Hayes Will Play Minor Role in *Front Page*," *New York Times*, August 28, 1969, p. 47.

8. See accounts of by Glenn Lovell in the *San Jose Mercury*, October 1, 1981, p. 1-D, and October 3, 1981, p. 7-C; also by John McClintock in the *Peninsula Times-Tribune*, September 22, 1981, p. C-1, and October 3, 1981, p. C-1. James MacArthur's reasoning was that to have had the variety of adverse experiences necessary to sour him on journalism to the extent of wanting a career change, Hildy would have to be at least thirty-five, but because he himself came through to audiences as young for his age, he should not attempt the role until his early forties. Mr. MacArthur stated that he looked forward to aging enough to play Walter.

9. *The Importance of Being Earnest* had an earlier musical version, a work by Vivian Ellis copyrighted as *So Romantic* in 1950 and as *Half in Earnest* in 1957. (Cards DU26084 and DU44180, respectively, file of U.S. copyright deposits, Library of Congress, Washington.) There are believed to have been additional attempts at fitting music to the play.

10. On their relations, see, in particular, Hecht's biography, *Charlie: The Improbable Life and Times of Charles MacArthur* (New York: Harper & Brothers, 1957); but also the chapter "About MacArthur" in Hecht's *Letters from Bohemia* (Garden City, NY: Doubleday & Co., 1964), pp. 185–201.

11. Jack Gaver, "Front Page Being Staged Without Monkeyshines," *New York World-Telegram*, August 24, 1946, p. 7.

12. An exception to this was the Broadway revival of 1969, in which the casting of the motion picture actress Katharine Houghton as Peggy Grant caused her to be treated as the female lead.

13. *The Spectator*, July 31, 1982, p. 29. Similarly, Benedict Nightingale in *The New Statesman* (July 14, 1972, p. 64) in his review of the 1972 London debut of the play at the Old Vic wrote that Mollie was "the only entirely incredible character in the play, a sentimentally conceived whore who has befriended the doomed man."

14. *Philadelphia Evening Bulletin*, April 6, 1931, p. 24. The reviewer is not identified.

15. Harold Ricklefs, "Hildy Was My Friend," *Press Vet* 24, no. 1 (May 1970),p. 6.

16. "Mr. Murphy Defends His Good Name," *Chicago Journal*, November 27, 1928, p. 4. The letter is reproduced in Appendix B on page 197.

17. In the year before his death, McHugh was a consultant to a production of the play at Fenwick High School in Oak Park, Illinois, held on October 19 to 20, 1974. As the only survivor of the characters in the play, McHugh was treated with great honor at the screening for the Press Veterans of the Lemmon-Mathau film version at the Chicago Theatre on December 21, 1974. (See Bob Greene, "The Real McHugh View: Front Page and the Way It Was," *Chicago Sun-Times*, December 22, 1974, p. 6.)

18. *Chicago Tribune*, December 4, 1928, p. 43.

19. Ben Hecht and Charles MacArthur, *The Front Page: A Play in Three Acts* (New York: Samuel French, 1950), pp. 103, 111, 130.

20. A. A. Dornfeld, *Behind the Front Page* (Chicago: Academy Publishers, 1983), p. 133.

21. On the Hamon, Randall and Fitzgerald cases, see George Murray, *The Madhouse on Madison Street* (Chicago: Follett Publishing Co., 1965), pp. 189–94, 226–31, 312–24.

22. See *Bench and Bar of Illinois* (Chicago: Bench and Bar Publishing Co., 1920), p. 329.

23. The alternative of this reference being to Charles MacArthur's personal history in Chicago is impractical: see footnote 60, following.

24. *Chicago Tribune*, January 3, 1927. For this and the dates immediately following, see the footnotes to the play.

25. *Stagebill* (Chicago), *The Front Page*, sixth week, beginning December 30, 1928, p. 19.

26. William F. McDermott, "Chicago Cleans a Drama by Obliging It to Wear a Hat Unlike Bill Thompson's," *Cleveland Plain Dealer*, December 13, 1928, p. 21.

27. *Chicago Tribune*, November 26, 1928, p. 35. Donaghey, the *Tribune* reported on

November 18 (sec. 7, p. 3), had gone to New Jersey to see one of the tryout performances.

28. *Stagebill, Windy City,* Marriott Lincolnshire Theater, Lincolnshire, Illinois, April 6–June 12, 1994, p. 19.

29. Sidney Zion, "The Scoop from Helen Hayes," *New York Times,* Sunday, November 16, 1986, sec. 2, p. 1. Rose Hecht said that the play was written largely in 1927 in the Hechts' apartment in Beekman Place, New York. Ibid., May 12, 1969, p. 52. Hecht's own account in *Charlie* also states that the play was largely written at the Beekman Place apartment (p. 134).

30. Hecht, *Charlie,* pp. 135–39.

31. Zion, "The Scoop from Helen Hayes."

32. Hecht, *Charlie,* p. 136.

33. Howard Teichman, *George S. Kaufman: An Intimate Portrait* (New York: Athenaeum Press, 1972), p. 131. Harris reportedly accepted the play while his production of *The Royal Family* of Kaufman and Edna Ferber was between rehearsals and tryouts. This narrows the date very closely to the weekend of December 10 to 11, 1927. *The Royal Family* was reportedly still in rehearsal on Friday, December 9, and it opened in Newark on Monday, December 12, 1927. (*The Morning Telegraph,* December 9, 1927, p. 4; December 12, 1927, p. 4.)

34. Jed Harris, *A Dance on the High Wire: Recollections of a Time and a Temperament* (New York: Crown Publishers, 1979), p. 118. Scott Meredith, one of Kaufman's biographers, states that the play already had its title when delivered to Kaufman. (See his *George S. Kaufman and the Algonquin Round Table* [London: George Allen and Unwin, 1977], p. 193.) Harris's account is the more credible: It is a first-person recollection, and because Kaufman and Harris lapsed into lifelong enmity in a dispute of 1929, Harris had no incentive to inflate Kaufman's role in *The Front Page.* (On Harris, see also Martin Gottfried, *Jed Harris: The Curse of Genius* [Boston: Little Brown & Co., 1984].)

There is an additional reason to believe that the name of the play came relatively late. *The Morning Telegraph* made its first mention of the name on April 13, 1928 (p. 3.) The producer Joseph Koehler announced a play entitled *The Front Page* by Edward Goldsmith Riley for fall, 1927, but the brothers Everett and Robert Riskin, who took an option on it, tried it out with a stock company and, in pessimism, let the option lapse, thereby—at least in the opinion of Harris—freeing the name. (See *The Morning Telegraph,* May 1, 1928, p. 3. Riley's play was copyrighted April 19, 1927 [copyright deposit card D25217, Library of Congress].) An earlier play of the same name was copyrighted by Robert L. Dempster on March 8, 1923. (Copyright deposit card D10241, ibid.)

If Kaufman gave *The Front Page* its name, the question arises what Hecht and MacArthur planned to call it, and there is no apparent answer.

35. Garff B. Wilson, *Three Hundred Years of American Drama and Theatre*, 2d ed. (Englewood Cliffs, NJ: Prentice-Hall, 1982), p. 239.

36. Quoted by Walter Whitworth in his review of the play in the *Indianapolis News*, November 23, 1928, p. 20. The statement is undoubtedly based on an interview of Whitworth with Hecht, MacArthur, Harris, and/or Kaufman, all of whom were in Indianapolis for the tryout of the Chicago company of the play on the previous evening.

37. For the text, see Paula R. Backscheider and Douglas Howard, *The Plays of Samuel Foote*, 3 vols. (New York: Garland Publishing Co., 1983). The set is a series of photographic reprints of the originals, with only the individual pagination of the originals. The play, under its original title, *The Mayor of Garret*, appears in volume II. For identification of the principal characters, see Mary Magie Belden, *The Dramatic Work of Samuel Foote* (New Haven: Yale University Press, 1929), pp. 116–18.

38. Ralph Reynaud, reviewing the published edition, found a more comprehensive relation to Shakespeare: "[The language] establishes the etiquette of Mayor Thompson's pineapple plantation and puts the play right into the class of Shakespeare at his merriest and most unabridged. And that isn't such a wisecrack about Shakespeare, either. If the dome-headed old gentleman of Avon . . . ever cooked up a more effective hash of dramatic action, it is buried in the ruins of the Globe (or was it the Swan?) Theatre." (*New York Evening Post*, September 22, 1928, p. 5.) This is the only review of the book version known to me. The other reviews excerpted in *Book Review Digest* prove to be reviews of the the first New York performance.)

39. On the history of the newspaper farce, see Alex Barris, *Stop the Presses! The Newspaper Man in American Films* (South Brunswick, NJ: A. S. Barnes & Co., 1976). A newspaper play, a melodrama rather than a farce, had been a Broadway success as early as 1909: *The Fourth Estate*, by Joseph Medill Patterson and Harriet Ford.

George Jean Nathan stated in *Judge* (September 8, 1928, p. 19) that Harris initially intended to use "a new play" in the billing, but changed to "a new farce." Nathan defended the change, arguing that the former designation would have subjected the play to nit-picking, whereas the latter allowed it simply to be enjoyed. He concluded, "The Hecht-MacArthur manuscript is plainly a farce, and a blamed good one."

40. Harris, *A Dance on the High Wire*, p. 119.

41. More than any of the other principals, Tracy had his career defined by his role in *The Front Page*. He found himself typecast as a hard-bitten reporter both on stage and in films—a situation that, in his later years, he felt he should have resisted.

He also played political figures, notably the ex-president Arthur Hockstader in Gore Vidal's *The Best Man* of 1960. His performance in the motion picture version of that play in 1964 won him an Academy Award nomination. He had reverted to being a song-and-dance man in a revival of Robert Sherwood's *Idiot's Delight* in 1951, and he made his last Broadway appearance in *Minor Miracle* in 1966. Tracy died in Santa Monica, California, on October 18, 1968. See his obituaries in the *New York Times*, October 19, 1968, p. 37, and the *Los Angeles Times*, October 19, 1968, sec.3, pp. 1, 6.

42. See "Osgood Perkins," in William C. Young, *Famous Actors and Actresses of the American Stage* (New York: R. R. Bowker Co., 1975), pp. 914–17. Osgood Perkins never achieved the fame as a mature actor that seemed assured him, for he died abruptly upon the opening of what gave every prospect of being one of his most conspicuous triumphs. On September 20, 1937, at the age of forty-five, he opened in Washington, D.C., opposite Gertrude Lawrence in the pre-Broadway trial of *Susan and God*. Some three hours after the performance, early on September 21, he died of a heart attack in his room at the Willard Hotel. (See the *Washington Post*, September 22, 1937, p. 1.) As a consequence, he is best known to history as the father of actor Anthony Perkins.

43. Arthur Dorlag and John Irvine, *The Stage Works of Charles MacArthur* (Tallahassee: Florida State University Press, 1974), p. 76.

44. *New York Times*, February 1, 1928, p. 31.

45. On Phyllis Povah, see Raymond D. McGill, ed., *Notable Names in the American Theatre*, 2d ed. (Clifton, NJ: James T. White & Co., 1976), p. 1054. She was active on the New York stage until 1954, but continued work in motion pictures, radio, and television thereafter. She lived for forty-five years in Port Washington, Long Island, with her husband, Henry E. Drayton and died on August 7, 1975, in a nursing home in Gainesville, Florida.

The date of her birth is uncertain. The response of her parents to the 1900 census states that she was born in Detroit in July 1893. (1900 Soundex, U.S. Census, 1900, file card, vol. 78, E. D. 31. sheet 9, line 63, National Archives, Washington, D.C.) Her death certificate states that she was born July 21, 1891. (State of Florida, Office of Vital Statistics, File No. 75-053071, Jacksonville.)

46. Frances Fuller was to garner considerable notice as a leading lady both on the stage and in motion pictures. She starred in the Kaufman-Ferber play of 1936 *Stage Door* and played opposite Gary Cooper in the film *One Sunday Afternoon* of 1933. Her greatest success was as a teacher and administrator: She served as president and director of the American Academy of Dramatic Art from 1954 to 1965. She died at her home on the West Side of New York on December 18, 1980. (See her obit-

uaries in the *New York Times*, December 20, 1980, p. 49, and the *Los Angeles Times*, December 29, 1980, p. 21.)

47. *Philadelphia Inquirer*, April 5, 1931, p. SO 6. A program for the projected Philadelphia performances has survived in the theater collection of the New York Public Library's file on *The Front Page*. A touring company was to present the play in Philadelphia in the fall of 1929, but the performances were cancelled because of a musicians' strike. The play was finally presented there by a local resident company on April 4, 1931. (*Philadelphia Record*, April 5, 1931, p. D-3; *Philadelphia Public Ledger*, April 6, 1931, p. 11.)

48. See announcements of the play in the *Newark Evening News*, May 19, 1928, p. 4X; *Newark Star-Eagle*, May 19, 1928, p. 12.

49. *Atlantic City Press*, May 16, 1928, p. 12.

50. *Newark Evening News*, May 22, 1928, p. 11.

51. *Newark Star-Eagle*, May 22, 1928, p. 23.

52. *Morning Telegraph*, May 29, 1928, p. 3.

53. Teichman, *George S. Kaufman*, p. 131.

54. *The Morning Telegraph*, July 27, 1928, p. 5; August 8, 1928, p. 3.

55. Ibid. On Dorothy Stickney, see *Current Biography*, 1942, pp. 518–21. Until her death in New York on June 2, 1998, at age 101, she was the last of the principals to survive.

56. Teichman, *George S. Kaufman*, p. 131; also reported in Samuel L. Leiter, ed., *The Encyclopedia of the New York Stage 1920–1930* (Westport, CT: Greenwood Press, 1985), pp. 293–95. On the basis of what we know of the later careers of the two actresses, the change is even more difficult to explain. Povah matured into roles as comic mother figures, most famously as the chronically pregnant Edith Potter in the stage and screen versions of Claire Booth Luce's *The Women* of 1936 and 1939, respectively. Stickney's best-known later role was as the wife of her actual husband, Howard Lindsay, in *Life with Father*, where her prim manner was well suited to the character. Stickney, who was born in 1900, remained a prominent actress of the New York stage into the early 1970s. She considered Mollie a short part, but a good one. (See Dorothy Stickney, *Openings and Closings* [Garden City, NY: Doubleday & Co., 1979], p. 82.) It is indisputably a difficult role. Vincent Canby, reviewing the 1974 motion picture version in the *New York Times* (December 19, 1974, p. 58), wrote, "This role may well be impossible, however, since it requires the actress to play for straight melodrama while everyone around her is going for laughs."

57. Robert C. Benchley, review of *The Front Page*, *Life* magazine, August 30, 1928, p. 12.

58. Morehouse's play opened at the Henry Miller Theatre on August 27, 1928. Thus, Hecht and MacArthur won the race by about two weeks. The desire to open the

fall season is the presumed reason why there was a delay of three months between the tryout in Atlantic City and the opening in New York. Morehouse retrospectively wrote, "Ben Hecht and Charles MacArthur wrote a rowdy, melodramatic comedy, *The Front Page*, packed with good theater, which outran a gentler newspaper play, *Gentlemen of the Press*, 276 performances to 128," modestly refraining from mentioning that he wrote the latter. (Ward Morehouse, *Matinee Tomorrow: Fifty Years of Our Theater* [New York: Whittlesey House, 1949], p. 229). *Gentlemen of the Press* was not published, but a typescript survives in the New York Public Library's Performing Arts Library in Lincoln Center.

59. Helen Hayes with Katherine Hatch, *My Life in Three Acts* (New York: Harcourt Brace Jovanovich, 1990), pp. 56–57.

60. William S. Conklin, "Mayor Thompson, Et Al.," *Asbury Park Evening Press*, August 7, 1928, p. 3 (reproduced in Appendix B, pp. 196–197).

61. See reviews in the *New York Times* by Brooks Atkinson, August 15, 1928, p. 9, and follow-up story on September 9, 1928, sec. 9, p. 1; Allison Smith, *New York World*, August 16, 1928, p. 11; Burns Mantle, *New York Daily News*, August 19, 1928, p. 51; Wilella Waldorf, *New York Evening Post*, August 15, 1928, p. 16; Percy Hammond, *New York Herald-Tribune*, August 15, 1928, p. 14; Pierre de Rohan, *New York American*, August 15, 1928, p. 15; Gilbert W. Gabriel, *New York Sun*, August 15, 1928, p. 18.

62. S. Jay Kaufman, "*The Front Page* Season's First 2-Year Run," *The Morning Telegraph*, undated review, reprinted by Richard Maney in a folder of reviews submitted to Jed Harris, in papers of Jed Harris, Box 13, Folder 21, Theatre Collection, University of Memphis, Memphis, Tennessee. The review apparently ran in the issue of August 15, 1928, but in a later edition than that microfilmed.

63. *American Mercury* 15, no. 58 (October 1928), 251. Michael Blakemore, director of the first London production in 1972, reached a similar conclusion, holding that the first act was realistic drama, the second comedy, and the third farce. Blakemore believed that Richard Brinsley Sheridan's *The School for Scandal* has the same structure over the course of its five acts. (Barry Norman, "Michael Blakemore," *Times*, (London) June 17, 1972, p. 11.) Bob Gras, director of one of the many centenary productions of *The Importance of Being Earnest* by repertory companies, argued that Wilde's masterpiece has the same progression: "It opens as a comedy of manners — very quietly and sedately. Then it becomes broader comedy, then moves into farce. It moves forward in intensity, while getting funnier and funnier." ("Riverwalk Opens with Wilde Farce," *Lansing (Michigan) State Journal*, September 21, 1995, "What's On" sec., p. 24.)

64. *New Republic*, LVI, No. 718 (September 5, 1928), pp. 73–74. The review antedates the first performance in Chicago; it appears based on the first New York per-

formance. It may have been done from an advance copy of the Covici-Friede book, which was published only six days before the date of the issue.

65. Ibid.

66. Frederick Donaghey, "The Front Page," *Chicago Tribune*, November 26, 1928, p. 35. That the play was not a farce was, of course, implicit in the reviews of Conklin and Lovett earlier in 1928.

67. When I sought the comment on this manuscript of David Eden, a British writer who has done considerable critical and biographical work on W. S. Gilbert, he responded with a cogent case against my argument that the play had to rise above its initial marketing as a farce:

> Obviously I am not acquainted with the critical tradition concerning *The Front Page*, but simply on the basis of my own experience I think farce may be a more honourable title than comedy. Everything you have told me about *The Front Page*, including Hecht's love of brothels and his allegedly obscene novel, suggests that this work belongs to the anti-respectable genre of literature. There are not many classics in this genre—Aristophanes is one, so are Villon and Rabelais, and perhaps Swift. Considering *The Front Page* as a farce brings it within this orbit. Calling it a comedy sanitizes it in order to give it a degree of respectability it does not need. I think Hecht's stage directions are very significant because they show him trying to put a literary gloss on the work as soon as he realized it was successful. If he had anticipated success in advance of production he would surely have done the same to the language of the play itself, weakening its vitality in the process. He would have done the same if he thought he was writing comedy—it is the irresponsible nature of the scurrilous that permitted the vitality of *The Front Page*. Technically speaking I think it is easier to deal with the fate of Mollie in terms of farce than if she is a character in comedy. In farce, as in a cartoon, people can be thrown out of a window and nobody minds what happens to them on landing. In comedy you are dealing with persons, which means it is wrong to hurt them in a casual way. (Letter of David Eden to George W. Hilton, April 9, 1995.)

68. This was noted, for example, by the producers of the Shaw Festival's production of the play at the Shaw Theatre, Niagara-on-the-Lake, Ontario, in 1994. See Denis Johnston, ed., *1994 Shaw Festival: A Study Guide for Teachers: The Front Page* (Niagara-on-the-Lake, Ontario: Shaw Festival, 1994), p. 35.

69. *New York Times*, September 6, 1928, p. 23; September 7, 1928, p. 16.

70. Ibid., September 9, 1928, sec. 9, p. 1. Pierre de Rohan of the *New York American* was of the same view. (*New York American*, August 15, 1928, p. 15.)

71. *New York Herald-Tribune*, August 15, 1928, p. 14.

72. "'The Front Page' Is Sordid and Profane," *Chicago Tribune*, August 26, 1928, sec. 7, p. 1.

73. "It Seems to Heywood Broun," *The Nation*, no. 3298 (September 19, 1928), p. 262.

74. *The Saturday Review of Literature* 5, no. 31 (February 23, 1929), pp. 706–7.

75. *New York Times*, February 26, 1929, p. 30.

76. *Los Angeles Times*, December 30, 1928, p. 13.

77. Typescript letter of Colonel Robert Loraine to the Lord Chamberlain, January 18, 1929, Lord Chamberlain's correspondence, British Museum, manuscript room, Deposit No. 14280, "The Front Page." On Loraine, see Malcolm Morley, "Robert Loraine," *Enciclopedia dello Spettacollo* VI (1959), p. 1651.

78. On Street (1867–1936), see entries in his name in *Harmsworth's Universal Encyclopedia* IX (no date), 7379; and *Who Was Who* III (1941), p. 1305.

79. Typescript Reader's Report of G. S. Street, January 19, 1929; manuscript additions dated January 21, 1929. "The Front Page" file, Deposit No. 14280, British Museum, manuscript room.

80. Typescript letter of C. L. Gordon to Colonel Robert Loraine, January 23, 1929. Ibid.

81. Typescript letter of Colonel Robert Loraine to C. L. Gordon, December 4, 1929. A manuscript note on the letter states that the typescript of the play was returned to Loraine on December 5. The correspondence of the Lord Chamberlain reveals another effort in this period to mount a production in London. Charles B. Cochrane from a Bond Street address wrote on March 1, 1929, requesting information on the proposed alterations in the play on the ground that a syndicate of which he was a member was interested in producing it. He wrote a week later to say that his group did not now anticipate being interested in a production. (Letters of Charles B. Cochrane to C. L. Gordon, March 1 and 7, 1929.) Ibid.

82. Typescript letter of Herbert Y. Scott to the Assistant Comptroller of the Lord Chamberlain, October 26, 1935. Ibid.

83. Ibid., Deposit No. 1069.

84. Lord Chamberlain's Plays Correspondence Index, Deposit No. 14280. Ibid.

85. Application by Angela Broughton, Secretary, Manchester Repertory Theatre, to C. L. Gordon, December 10, 1935, stating a proposal to produce the play on January 13, 193[6]. The application was granted in a letter of G. S. Titman to Ms. Broughton, December 31, 1935, under the same conditions as required of the People's Theatre, Newcastle. Ibid.

86. *Manchester Guardian*, January 14, 1936, p. 11.

87. On the censorship, see John Johnston, *The Lord Chamberlain's Blue Pencil* (London: Hodder & Stoughton, 1990).

88. *Variety*, September 11, 1946, p. 58: "What was hot stuff in a rowdy Volsteadian era now emerges as somewhat diluted." The reviewer signed himself "Abel," presumably the longtime editor, Abel Green.

89. Charles Newton, "The Front Page," by Ben Hecht and Charles MacArthur, Blue Network adaptation, broadcast March 29, 1942. Mimeographed script in New York Public Library, Performing Arts Library, Lincoln Center, New York.

90. Gaver, "Front Page Being Staged Without Monkeyshines."

91. *Chicago Tribune*, February 18, 1947, p. 19.

92. Young, *Famous Actors and Actresses*, p. 915.

93. For example, Glenn Lovell, writing in connection with the Stanford Community Theater's 1981 production, described the acting edition as "watered down." *San Jose Mercury*, October 1, 1981, p. 1D.

94. See Leslie Baily, *The Gilbert & Sullivan Book* (London: Cassell & Co., Ltd., 1952), pp. 371–72.

95. *Chicago Evening American*, November 26, 1928, p. 27.

96. "'Front Page' Iis Good Play but Distorted," ibid. p. 22.

97. *The Saturday Review of Literature*, V, no. 31 (February 23, 1929), 706–7. This was the general view of British journalists. A man who signed himself J. F. G., reviewing the first British performance in 1936, wrote, "To a play of newspaper life every critic necessarily looks with keener interest at the technicalities of his own job, and in this respect one finds many absurdities in 'The Front Page.'" (*Manchester Evening Chronicle*, January 14, 1936, p. 2.) The reviewer who wrote under the initials E. C. C. observed of the same production, "Asking a British reporter to review 'The Front Page' is like asking a cricketer to write on baseball. It makes him want to stand and shout 'We are not a bit like this.' You should enjoy this play . . . but don't come away with the idea . . . that you have learned anything about the production of English newspapers." (*Manchester Evening News*, January 14, 1936, p. 10.)

98. Claudia Cassidy in her review for the *Chicago Journal of Commerce*, remarked that Lloyd Nolan, the actor who played Ernie Kruger, the reporter assigned to her paper, was deficient for not lighting a Murad cigarette. (November 26, 1928, p. 14.)

No reviewer appears to have noted what seems to me the most unrealistic element in the play: the reporters never lapse into talking about baseball. For a group of Chicago journalists to sit around wasting time without turning to some discussion of the Cubs and White Sox—during the season or out of it—borders on the inconceivable. There is no evidence that either Hecht or MacArthur was a baseball fan, but it would be strange if no one pointed out this lacuna to them. For an extremely realistic treatment of the way in which the baseball teams drift in and out of conversation in Chicago, see the various mystery novels of the author, Sara Paretsky.

99. Hecht, *Charlie*, esp. p. 49.

100. Starrett, *Born in a Bookshop*, p. 97.

101. Bob Greene, "The Real McHugh View: Front Page and the Way It Was," *Chicago Sun-Times*, December 22, 1974, p. 6. Robert Benchley in his review of the initial Broadway performance in *Life* magazine had expressed the same view.

102. *Indianapolis Star*, November 23, 1928, p. 7.

103. *Indianapolis News*, November 23, 1928, p. 20.

104. *Indianapolis Times*, November 23, 1928, p. 12. The performances were held in English's Opera House.

105. *Sunday Times*, July 9, 1972, p. 29.

106. London *Evening Standard*, July 21, 1982, p. 20.

107. *Guardian* (Manchester), July 21, 1982, p. 9. A less favorable review by Russell Davies in *Plays and Players* reached a similar conclusion, ". . . the music in this musical is ultimately disposable. As we knew, all along, that it would be." *Windy City, Plays and Players* no. 348 (September 1982), pp. 24–25.

108. *Daily Express* (London), July 22, 1982, p. 13.

109. *Chicago Tribune*, November 24, 1986, II, p. 1.

110. *The Stage Works of Charles MacArthur*, p. 174.

111. *Chicago Herald and Examiner*, November 27, 1928.

112. *A Dance on the High Wire*, p. 119. He somewhat overstated this. He chose a short actor, William Foran, for McCue in the first New York company; Buddy McHugh was only five feet, four inches.

113. Ibid., p. 119.

114. *Chicago Evening Post*, November 26, 1928, p. 6.

115. From *The Mikado, Plays and Poems of W. S. Gilbert* (New York: Random House, 1932), p. 389.

PRODUCER'S
INTRODUCTION

B efore I began to work in the theater, I thought that playwrights were the most glamorous fellows in the world. I pictured them strolling into the palatial offices of great impresarios, or into heady boudoirs of famous stars, always imperturbable and epigrammatic—exquisites to the tips of their fingers. Where I got this cock-eyed idea I don't know.

But I do know that authors are rarely as arresting as their plays. And I have learned from experience that a pretty good play can be written by an idiot. In fact, I can assure you that in a group of successful playwrights you are likely to discover as distinguished a body of men as you might find at an Elks' outing.

All the more pleasant then to devote these lines to such brilliantly unorthodox gentlemen as the authors of *The Front Page*.

For here is a play which reflects miraculously the real as well as the literary personalities of the playwrights. Every line of it glows with a demoniacal humor, sordid, insolent and mischievous to the point of downright perversity, in which one instantly recognizes the heroic comic spirit of its authors.

Ben Hecht and Charlie MacArthur are the *Katzenjammer* kids of the theater. At once sophisticated and artless, they desire little more than to upset "der Kaptain" occasionally. "Der Kaptain" is anyone who aspires to authority, dignity, or any other pretenses which our heroes regard as bogus. In the slightly exaggerated but all too human character of the Sheriff in *The Front Page* they have achieved a comic portrait in the Shakespearian manner of low comedy and, I think, the best of its kind since the boards of the old Globe first creaked under the official boots of the hallowed Dogberry.

Both Hecht and MacArthur owe their literary origins to the newspapers of Chicago. Famous crime reporters, their talents were first cradled in the recounting of great exploits in arson, rape, murder, gang war and municipal politics. Out of a welter of jail-breaks, hangings, floods and whore-house raidings, they have gathered the rich, savory characters who disport themselves on the stage of the Times Square Theatre.

And though they would be the last to acknowledge it, because they are terrified of the word "charm," they have nevertheless written *The Front Page* with a more innocent and unsynthetic charm than I have ever found in Barrie. In an original manuscript almost devoid of stage directions I found this: "Jennie, the scrublady enters. The reporters rise and give her an ovation."

And in an age when the theater is imprisoned in a vise of literal and superficial realism, a paradise for the journeymen and hacks who infest the Authors League of America, and in a day when the successful portrayal of a newspaper reporter is accomplished by attaching to the person of the actor a hip-flask and a copy of the American Mercury, it is soothing and reassuring to stumble on a stage reporter who begins an interview in this innocent fashion: "Is it true, Madame, that you were the victim of a Peeping Tom?"

—Jed Harris, from the 1928 Covici-Friede edition of *The Front Page*. (Jed Harris produced *The Front Page* at the Times Square Theatre, New York, August 14, 1928; staged by George S. Kaufman.)

NOTES ON THE TEXT

A n editor would, if possible, begin with the draft of *The Front Page* submitted by Ben Hecht and Charles MacArthur to Jed Harris under his option to produce the play. Neither this nor any other manuscript of the play is known to have survived. As noted in the introduction, Harris hired George S. Kaufman for very extensive rewriting and condensation of Hecht's and MacArthur's draft. In particular, Harris objected to an incursion of gangsters into the pressroom in the third act and required Kaufman to excise them. Kaufman's draft, which went into rehearsal, did not contain the gangsters' incursion, but it did contain another character subsequently excised, Alderman Willoughby, a black member of the city council who entered the pressroom on several occasions in connection with transactions for gin—another indication that the play was set during Prohibition.

In absence of the manuscript drafts, it would be preferable to use the typescript submitted for the copyright deposit of May 10, 1928, but this, like the manuscripts, has apparently been destroyed. The copyright office of the Library of Congress has not retained the deposit copies of works filed before 1950 if the works were published, as *The Front Page* was, seventeen days after its first Broadway performance.[1] This is most unfortunate, for the loss of both the manuscript and the copyright deposit copy prevent our knowing what the text was before the deletion of Alderman Willoughby.

The character of Alderman Willoughby could only have been modeled on Chicago's pioneer black alderman and—later—congressman, the Republican Oscar DePriest. Because DePriest was Thompson's principal lieutenant in Thompson's main stronghold, the Second Ward on the South Side, a character to represent him was logically a part of the play. Willoughby was to be played by Charles Gilpin, an actor who had established his reputation in Eugene O'Neill's *The Emperor Jones* in 1920. Gilpin was advertised as a member of the cast for the opening in Atlantic City and is shown as Willoughby in the program for the stillborn run in Philadelphia scheduled for the following week.

Gilpin appears to have ruined his prospects in the play, although there are rival accounts of how he did so. Richard Maney, the play's publicist, wrote that Gilpin arrived at the dress rehearsal unable to deliver his lines, apparently besotted with gin.[2] Hecht reported that the actor simply disappeared into Harlem and was discovered there "kicking the gong around."[3] They agree that the character was written out of the play in a day, but they do not state which day that was. Nellie Revell in her column "Remarks at Random" in *Variety* stated, probably correctly, that Gilpin was dropped on May 14, 1928, the eve of the opening in Atlantic City.[4]

Alderman Willoughby's elimination is difficult to explain. Even if Hecht, MacArthur, Harris, and Kaufman were unwilling to give Gilpin a second chance, there was a gap of nearly three months between the tryout in Atlantic City and the tryout in Long Branch immediately before the opening in New York, during which it should have been easy to recruit another actor for the role. Hecht in his account reported that the alderman—presumably because of racial sensitivities—had to be treated with a degree of dignity, not as a comic figure.[5] Because the other Republicans, the Mayor and the Sheriff, are treated savagely, any courtesy or restraint shown toward Willoughby would have created an imbalance in the play. All concerned may have concluded that the Willoughby character was flat and that the comedy was stronger without him. This may have been true in some superficial sense, but his elimination weakened the logic of the plot and reduced the effectiveness of the satire on William Hale Thompson, for Oscar DePriest was more important to Thompson's electoral successes than Sheriff Hoffman was.

It is not clear what changes were made in the text between the Atlantic City and Long Branch tryouts, but Malcolm Goldstein in his biography of George S. Kaufman states that Kaufman cajoled the authors into making cuts, apparently at this time.[6] The summary of the play published in *Theatre* magazine in its August 1928 issue, necessarily antedates the opening in New York in the middle of that month, and several quotations that the magazine printed are presumably from the script as the play was performed in Atlantic City.[7] The summary does not mention Alderman Willoughby. A comparison with the text in the book version published by Covici-Friede on August 31, 1928, which probably represents the approximate text of the first Broadway performance, shows a limited number of changes, but the quotations are only a small fraction of the play's dialogue.[8] The reviewer in the *Newark Star-Eagle* stated that eighty-six words had been dropped between the Atlantic City and

Newark tryouts, but added, "You will never learn from this family journal what the expurgated eighty-six were."[9]

The typescript that Colonel Robert Loraine submitted to the Lord Chamberlain in anticipation of a production of the play in London in 1929 differed in some respects from the Covici-Friede edition, although it was probably done too late to include Alderman Willoughby. The Lord Chamberlain required excision of two short passages, both of which show some degree of difference from the Covici-Friede edition. He objected to Mollie's "Damn your greasy souls" from Act I, a line that reads "God damn your greasy souls" in the book. More important, he took offense at "You damned hound" from Act III, a phrase that does not appear in the Covici-Friede edition. As noted in the introduction, Loraine requested return of the typescript after the projected production had been dropped, and his papers are not known to have survived.

I have necessarily taken the first book version published by Covici-Friede in August 1928 as the earliest surviving text, but I have provided interpolations from earlier drafts where such can be identified and where the excisions or substitutions from the earlier draft seem to me to have weakened the text. Where the changes were trivial, or appear to have strengthened the text, I have noted the earlier text in footnotes.

I have not attempted to provide comprehensive comparisons with the 1950 acting edition. The changes in phrasing were very numerous, but most are on the level of deleting profanity—or, less frequently, adding it. With the exception of the three specific references to Duffy Cornell, the changes did not affect the identifications of individuals and the re-creation of the milieu being attempted in the present edition. In addition, as I have observed in the introduction, the net effect of the changes made for the 1950 edition is to weaken the play. I have noted only major changes that represent reversions to earlier drafts than the Covici-Friede edition, or appear to indicate some re-evaluation of the text by the authors, or particularly exemplify the weakening of the text.

The characters will be identified at their first appearance or, in the case of the reporters, the first reference to them. In italics is the name in full as given in the play, even though only the last name is typically mentioned at the first reference.

NOTES

1. Copyright deposit card for Ben Hecht and Charles MacArthur, *The Front Page*, D 83856, May 10, 1928, Library of Congress, Room 401. Series D is of dramas subsequently published.

2. Richard Maney, *Fanfare: The Confessions of a Press Agent* (New York: Harper & Bros., 1957), p. 133.

3. Ben Hecht, *Charlie: The Improbably Life and Times of Charles MacArthur* (New York: Harper & Brothers, 1957), p. 139.

4. *Variety*, May 23, 1928, p. 54. She also stated that Gilpin was dropped but replaced by someone else, and then the part was eliminated. The local review and *Variety's* own review (May 16, 1928, p. 48) do not provide evidence to support this portion of her account.

5. Hecht, *Charlie*, p. 139.

6. Malcolm Goldstein, *George E. Kaufman: His Life, His Theater* (New York: Oxford University Press, 1979), p. 149.

7. The excerpts in *Theatre* for the condemned man use the spelling "Earle Williams," which we know was used in Atlantic City on the basis of the review of the performance there in *Variety*, May 16, 1928, p. 48.

8. "The Play That Is Talked About—The Front Page," *Theatre*, August 1928, pp. 24–26, 50, 62.

9. *Newark Star-Eagle*, May 22, 1928, p. 23.

NOTES ON THE
PRINCIPAL CHARACTERS

THE REPORTERS

ROY V. BENSINGER, *Chicago Tribune*. Albert F. Baenziger, police reporter for the *American*. Baenziger was born on August 4, 1882, and went to work for the *Inter Ocean* on August 1, 1905. He joined the *American* on November 19, 1906, and remained active with the paper and its successor, the *Herald-American,* until retiring on March 27, 1953. He was one of the most distinguished police reporters, active in major cases, including the investigations of Richard Loeb and Nathan Leopold for the murder of Bobby Franks in 1924 and of the multiple murderer William Heirens in 1946. For the *American* he also covered golf and yachting, two of his own avocations. Richard Philbrick of the *Chicago Tribune*, who served early in his career as Baenziger's chauffeur for trips out of Chicago—Baenziger was consistently afraid to drive outside the city—reports that Hecht and MacArthur, who disliked Baenziger's abstemious behavior, accurately portrayed Baenziger's neurasthenic characteristics. Baenziger, Philbrick reported, as late as the 1940s was offended by the treatment, feeling that the authors were a couple of irresponsible drunks hostile to him. When Baenziger retired, a celebration was held in his honor at the Criminal Court Building. He died on September 20, 1955, at age seventy-three. (See "Al Baenziger, H-A Reporter Retires: 50-Year News Career Ends," *Chicago Herald-American.* March 28, 1953, City/Turf Edition, p. 4; obituaries in *New York Times,* September 22, 1955, p. 31; *Chicago Tribune,* September 22, 1955, sec. 3, p. 4; *Chicago Daily News,* September 22, 1955, p. 58.)

Alternatively, Ben Hecht in his book *Gaily, Gaily* (p. 189) states that the character was actually Roy C. Benzinger of the *Tribune,* but that the neurasthenic characteristics were those of LeRoy "Spike" Hennessey of the *American,* who was interested only in retirement to Florida, and had no desire for

39

fame. Hecht also attributed the neurasthenic personality traits and desire to retire to Florida to Hennessey in his reminiscences in the *Chicago Literary Times* (vo.l 1, no. 20 [December 15, 1923], p. 8.) Albert Baenziger is well documented, but there is no evidence of a Roy C. Benzinger on the *Tribune* or elsewhere in Chicago journalism. Hecht's autobiographical writing is not accurate; his two autobiographical books appear to have been written from memory without significant research. George Murray in conversation states that the hostility between Baenziger and Hecht extended to Baenziger's once slugging Hecht in front of the *Tribune's* building.

The name "Bensinger" was well known in Chicago from the pool halls and bowling alleys of Louis A. Bensinger, who by coincidence died at age seventy on May 2, 1928, shortly before the play's first performance in Atlantic City.

MURPHY, *Chicago Journal of Commerce.* James Francis Murphy, a police reporter with whom Hecht worked on the *Journal* in his early years in Chicago. The *Journal*, which dated from 1844, was the city's oldest active newspaper at the time of the play, but it was in very weak condition. Murphy, who was born on June 4, 1876, went to work in 1892 for one of the component organizations of the City News Bureau as a messenger boy. He was typical of the reporters of the generation of the play in having a high school education— or less. In 1896 he joined the Navy because he had been told he could play a lot of baseball there. Instead, he found himself in the Spanish-American War as the writer on Admiral Dewey's flagship in the Battle of Manila Bay. He returned to the City News Bureau to cover crime on the West Side, and then became a reporter for the *Inter Ocean* and *American* before joining the *Journal.* When the *Journal* ceased publication in August 1929, he shifted to the *Chicago Times*, which was founded in the following month to utilize the *Journal's* physical plant. He died on Christmas Day in 1947, still an active reporter for the *Chicago Times.* (See obituaries in the *New York Times*, December 26, 1947, p. 15; *Chicago Daily Times* December 26, 1947, p. 3.) For his views on use of his name in the play, see Appendix B, page 197.

MIKE ENDICOTT, *Chicago Post.* There is no record of a reporter of this name in the Chicago journalism of the period, and none with a name that could have been altered by the authors' usual methods of minor spelling differences and changes of suffixes into "Endicott." On the other hand, for Endicott to be a fictional character would be inconsistent with the statements of the authors and Jed Harris that all the reporters were actual. The apparent reason for "Endicott" is that the actual reporter had a name that was impractical to alter in the authors' customary fashion. The most probable explanation is that the reporter for the *Post* whom they chose was named Johnson. Use of his name, even if altered, would have confused him with the hero (Hildy Johnson). The authors then fabricated a name based on the Endicott Johnson Corporation, the major shoe producer of the time based in Binghamton, Endicott, and Johnson City, New York. This suggests that the prototype for the character was Edwin C. Johnson, brother of Hilding Johnson, and a career employee of the *Post*. Apart from the problem of duplicating of surnames, a sibling relation between this character and Hildy Johnson would have served no purpose in the plot.

Edwin C. Johnson was born in Sweden and came to America with his parents at age seven. He began newspaper work as a copyboy at the *Post*, and progressed through reporter to assistant city editor before the paper ceased publication in 1932. He was then a reporter for the *Herald and Examiner* from 1933 to 1939. He joined the *Chicago Sun* on its formation in 1941 and again rose to assistant city editor. He continued with the *Chicago Sun-Times* after the merger of the *Sun* and *Times* early in 1948. He died in Swedish Covenant Hospital in Chicago on October 2, 1948, at age fifty-two. (See obituaries in *Chicago Herald-American,* October 3, 1948, p. 32; *Chicago Sun-Times,* October 3, 1948, three-star final only, p. 48; *Chicago Tribune,* October 4, 1948, sec. 3, p. 10; *Chicago Daily News,* October 4, 1948, p. 24. None of the obituaries suggests that he was the prototype for Endicott.)

As usual with people named Johnson, there is a degree of ambiguity. Richard Philbrick suggests an alternative in Enoch M. Johnson, who covered the Criminal Court Building for the *Chicago Daily News* for twenty-five years, from the mid-1920s to his retirement in January 1949. Following Hilding Johnson's death in 1931, he was the dominant figure in the pressroom. Before joining the *News,* he worked for the City News Bureau and the *Journal.* He has no known associations with the *Post*, and he began his coverage of the criminal courts for the *News* about the time Charles MacArthur left Chicago. He died at age sixty-three in Grant Hospital, Chicago, on July 14, 1950. (See his obituaries in the *Chicago Daily News,* July 14, 1950, p. 3; *Chicago Tribune,* July 15, 1950, sec. 2, p. 5; *New York Times,* July 15, 1950, p. 13. Again, the obituaries contain no suggestion that he appears in the play as Endicott.)

ED SCHWARTZ, *Chicago Daily News.* The character is based on a reporter named Jack Schwartz. He is not well documented, but he is believed to have been Jacob V. Schwartz, who applied for a position at the City News Bureau at age twenty-one on March 28, 1907, and was hired on March 22, 1908. A possible alternative is Jacob Schwartz, twenty-four, who applied to the City News Bureau on January 27, 1913. There is no evidence that the latter Schwartz was hired. Jack Schwartz is known to have spent most of his career on the *Chicago Daily News* and the *Minneapolis Tribune*. By the time the play was produced, he appears to have gone to Minneapolis.

The *Daily News* was Chicago's most prestigious evening paper, the traditional choice of affluent suburbanites for the afternoon train trip back to the suburbs. The rise of automobile commutation, inauguration of the national evening telecasts of news, and other factors caused it to cease publication in 1978.

WILSON, *Chicago Evening American*. If this represents a writer for the *American*, the only known candidate is Herbert C. Wilson, the longtime automotive and travel editor. (See *The Working Press of the Nation* 1 [1955], p. 66.) This is a peculiar choice, for he had no known background in police reporting and on the basis of retrospective accounts lacked the flamboyance suitable to the play.

The *American* was Hearst's evening paper in Chicago, the lowest in intellectual quality of any represented in the play. Hecht wrote his view of the paper in 1923: "Mr. Hearst's *Chicago Evening American* is a refreshingly honest newspaper. Its sly editors are calmly aware that ninety percent of their readers are subnormal servant girls, bridge-tenders, soda-water clerks and bellicose illiterates. They cater with an unflagging altruism to the furtive obscenities and arrested mental development of a grateful lower middle class." (*Chicago Literary Times* 1, no. 10 [July 15, 1923], p. 1.)

ERNIE KRUGER, *Chicago Journal of Commerce*. The name is an amalgam of two Chicago reporters, Ernest Larned Pratt and Jesse Krueger. Pratt began as a reporter with the *Tribune* in 1899, but became a career Hearst journalist, serving variously as assistant managing editor of the *Chicago Evening American*, city editor of the *Herald and Examiner*, editor-in-chief of Hearst's International News Service and manager of the Hearst papers' bureau in Washington. He also worked for the Hearst Publishing Co. in New York and operated an advertising agency there. He returned to Chicago about 1943 and worked as a copy editor on the *Tribune* until 1953, when he retired to Claremont, California. He died at his home there at age seventy-six on November 18, 1954. Pratt was a virtuoso on the banjo, and his favorite song was indeed

"By the Light of the Silvery Moon." (See Vincent Starrett, *Born in a Bookshop: Chapters from the Chicago Renascence* [Norman: University of Oklahoma Press, 1965], p. 98.; Ben Hecht, *Gaily, Gaily,* p. 192; obituaries in the *New York Times,* November 27, 1954, p. 13; and the *Chicago Tribune,* November 27, 1954, sec. 3, p. 7.)

The last name is adapted from Jesse Krueger of the *American.* He joined the *American* as a high school student in 1910 and retired in 1962 after fifty-two years as a reporter, rewrite man, war correspondent, motion picture critic, columnist, editor, and promotional executive for the Hearst papers nationally. He died in New York, his home in his later years, on September 14, 1967, at age seventy-three. (See obituary in the *New York Times,* September 16, 1967, p. 33.)

As far as is known, neither of these men wrote for the *Journal of Commerce.* This newspaper reported the escape of Tommy O'Connor, but as its reviewer, Claudia Cassidy, said in her review of the first Chicago performance, the paper did not maintain a police reporter. (*Chicago Journal of Commerce,* November 26, 1928, p. 14.) There is some reason to believe that in earlier drafts of the play Kruger was assigned to the German-language newspaper, the *Illinois Staats-Zeitung.* Percy Hammond, in the course of reviewing the opening performance in the *New York Herald-Tribune* (August 15, 1928, p. 14), stated that one of the reporters, whom he did not identify, represented the *Staats-Zeitung.* This is consistent with the authors choosing a Germanic surname for the character based on Ernie Pratt. The *Staats-Zeitung* gave up daily publication on February 6, 1922, possibly rendering it unattractive to the authors. There are problems with this interpretation, however. Hammond also mentioned the *Journal of Commerce* as one of the papers the reporters represented, and all the reviews and programs of the play, from the first performance in Atlantic City, assign Kruger to the *Journal of Commerce.* Hammond may have read an earlier draft of the play. For further reason to suspect this, see the footnote on 222 on page 183.

MCCUE, *City News Bureau.* Leroy F. "Buddy" McHugh, who went to work for the City News Bureau as a copyboy in 1906, quickly rising to reporter. As mentioned in the introduction, he shifted to the *American* in 1915. He remained active as a police reporter for this newspaper and its successors until his retirement in 1963. He died in Chicago on May 15, 1975, at age eighty-four. (See his obituaries in the *Chicago Tribune,* May 16, 1975, sec. 2, p. 12; and the *New York Times,* May 17, 1975, p. 30.)

Hilding Johnson, drawn by William Rolig from the halftone that accompanied Johnson's obituary in the Chicago *Herald and Examiner* of March 24, 1931 (p. 10).

JOHN HILDING JOHNSON, leading crime reporter of the *Chicago Herald and Examiner*. Johnson was an obvious, almost inevitable, figure to be the hero of the play. He was well established as the dominant figure among the reporters.

Johnson was born in Sweden about 1889. He began his career in journalism with the City News Bureau in March 1908 and left to join the *Chicago Examiner* in 1916. Like the rest, he was a "legman" who phoned his stories into a rewrite desk, without customarily getting a byline. He only occasionally visited the newspaper; his paychecks were sent to the pressroom at the Criminal Court Building. A later passage in which Hildy says he is waiting in the pressroom for his paycheck is consistent with his practice. The description of him on this page is at least superficially accurate, including his appearance, sense of humor, and the implication of alcoholism. Meyer Levin in reviewing the first Chicago performance for the *Daily News* objected, however, that the delineation of Johnson's personality in the play did not accord with the prototype. (*Chicago Daily News*, November 26, 1928, p. 7.) The relations of Johnson with his editor are mainly based on the experiences of Charles MacArthur.

Johnson, while cold sober, was hit by a taxicab in front of the Criminal Court Building in 1928 and confined to the hospital for seven months. He voiced the opinion that the accident would never have occurred if he had been drunk as usual and swore to avoid sobriety in the future—a vow he appears to have kept singlemindedly. On his release from the hospital, he returned to work but with the admonition of his physician, Dr. Orlando F. Scott, that he might die at any time. After working in his customary fashion, he became ill on Saturday, March 21, 1931. Scott induced him to enter Auburn Park Hospital, where Johnson died at age forty-two of a stomach hemorrhage at 3:30 A.M. on Monday, March 23. He was survived by his wife, Marjorie, and his son, Louis, eight.

Chief Justice John P. McGoorty ordered trials suspended, and the Criminal Court Building closed on the afternoon of Wednesday, March 25, for his funeral. His chair and his phone in the pressroom were draped with black. A large throng attended the service at the Sparbaro Mortuary at 708 N. Wells Street in the area to which the play has so many references. The funeral was said to have brought out the largest assembly of old Chicago reporters ever observed. Buddy McHugh was one of the pallbearers, and Helen Hayes, who was performing in Chicago in *Petticoat Influence* (see play footnote 109), attended the service. Johnson was buried in Rosehill Cemetery.

Photograph by Sophie Baker for the National Theatre, from a print in the archive of the Theatre Museum, Covent Garden. Copyright 1972 by Sophie Baker. Photograph used by arrangement with Sophie Baker, with permission of Maureen Lipman, the Royal National Theatre and the Theatre Museum.

MAUREEN LIPMAN, who played Mollie Malloy in the first London production of *The Front Page,* staged by the National Theatre at the Old Vic, was the most highly praised member of the cast. She became a prominent comic actress in British television and on the London stage and also a successful autobiographical writer. Lipman was kind enough to write me of her considerations in playing Mollie:

> I think my overwhelming memory of playing Mollie was that it was written in such a way that Mollie simply reacts, so there was no need to act, and since she was a very simple soul whose thoughts came from her guts rather than from any complex mental process, I could literally react nervously to the situation and to the pressure put upon me by the various newsmen in the office. Thinking slowly, but on your toes, is a very exciting way of working, particularly for me, because I tend to think very quickly as a person—so I had to adapt to a new rhythm without losing any of the pace of the scene.
>
> I played the scene with Clive Merrison as Earl with a mixture of self-deprecation and sensitivity because it seemed to me, and Michael [Blakemore] agreed, that Mollie was acting instinctively because this was the first man who'd ever been kind to her. She therefore showed fierce loyalty but the word heroism didn't come into her scale of reference. She became a wounded creature who hadn't the intelligence or skill to deceive or justify

her defence of Earl, so she did the only the only thing she'd ever known how to do, she sacrificed her body.

Blakemore's direction was very detailed and he encouraged me to use a lot of body language, hence the twitching feet which several members of the audience remarked upon, and which left me in the curious position of being an actress looking at her own feet and wondering what they were going to do next.

In a sense I was in my element in *The Front Page*, playing a cameo role of great comic and tragic depth, and I count it as one of my happiest and most fulfilling stage experiences. (Letter from Maureen Lipman to George W. Hilton, September 5, 1995.)

Vote for Big Bill the Builder
He Cannot Be Bought, Bossed or Bluffed

The Mayor: A campaign poster of William Hale Thompson (Chicago Historical Society).

WILLIAM HALE THOMPSON was born on May 14, 1869, and entered Republican politics in Chicago in the late nineteenth century. Establishing an early base of support in the South Side black community, he served as alderman from the Second Ward from 1900 to 1902. He then served as Cook County Commissioner from 1902 to 1904 and was elected mayor on April 6, 1915.

Thompson's relations to the press were not as shown in the play. Although the Hearst papers were Democratic, the *Herald and Examiner* was the only Chicago daily to support Thompson in the election of 1919. Most of the Chicago journalistic community had the contempt for him evident in the text. The *Tribune* particularly loathed him, to the point of prohibiting use of his name by the 1930s: its readers quickly learned what was meant by "a former Republican mayor of Chicago." Thompson died at age seventy-four on March 18, 1944. A biography of Thompson is Lloyd Wendt and Herman Kogan, *Big Bill of Chicago* (Indianapolis: Bobs-Merrill Co., 1953). See also Andrew K. Prinz, "William Hale Thompson," in Melvin G. Holli and Peter d'A. Jones, eds., *Biographical Dictionary of American Mayors* (Westport, CT: Greenwood Press, 1981), pp. 362–63.

Samuel E. Pincus, assistant attorney general of Illinois. The photograph is from the delegates' manual of the Illinois Constitutional Convention of 1920, in which Pincus represented a Chicago West Side constituency (Chicago Historical Society).

SAMUEL E. PINCUS was a lawyer of considerable distinction. Born in Chicago on October 10, 1889, Pincus took his LL.B. at Northwestern University Law School in 1912 and was admitted to the Illinois bar in the same year. The reasons for his inclusion in the play are complicated, but it would have been difficult to the point of impossibility to find a man who could serve the authors' purposes better.

Basically, Pincus was an active Democrat throughout his career. The text gives the impression that he was from downstate and unfamiliar with Chicago, but this is the reverse of truth. Pincus was a Chicagoan not only by birth, but also by political identification. Notably, he was elected on November 4, 1919, to represent a West Side district in the constitutional convention that sat in Springfield from January 20, 1920, to October 10, 1922. At issue was the State of Illinois' chronic problem of division of political power between Cook County and the downstate counties, specifically in this instance, relative allocation of seats in the legislature and on the Supreme Court. Pincus uniformly voted in the interest of Chicago. The proposed constitution was rejected by the electorate on December 12, 1922.

Pincus's service in the constitutional convention of 1920 to 1922 occurred during his tenure as assistant attorney general of Illinois. This was a title given to a large number of lawyers subordinate to the attorney general. Pincus was appointed to this office by Attorney General Patrick J. Lucey, a Democrat, in 1915. He continued under the anti-Thompson Republican Edward J. Brundage, who served two consecutive terms from 1917 to 1925; Brundage was the only anti-Thompson Republican elected to statewide office in the 1920 general election. As the convention wound down, Pincus announced his intention to seek a six-year term as municipal judge in Chicago in the election of November 7, 1922, but he was defeated. The appointment as assistant attorney general apparently ended when Pincus became city prosecutor of Chicago on April 17, 1923, under Democratic Mayor William Emmett Dever, a reform candidate elected earlier in that month. As far as can be determined, Pincus retained his law office, private practice, and legal residence in Chicago throughout his appointment as assistant attorney general and his membership in the constitutional convention, although both required him to spend a great deal of time in Springfield. There is no logical relation between his membership in the constitutional convention and delivery of the reprieve, but as assistant attorney general, he would be the appropriate officer for such a duty. Thus, the reprieve comes from the hand of a Democrat in the office of a Republican of the Deneen faction, both hostile to Thompson.

Pincus served as city prosecutor of Chicago until 1927 and was appointed assistant corporation counsel of Chicago in 1931, a post he held until his death in 1956. (See his obituary in the *Chicago Tribune*, February 26, 1956, part I, p. 35; brief biographies in Louis L. Emmerson, ed., *Blue Book of the State of Illinois, 1921–1922* [Springfield, 1921], p. 228; *The Bench and Bar of Illinois* [Chicago: Bench & Bar Publishing Co., 1920], p. 329; Hyman L. Meites, *History of the Jews of Chicago* [Chicago: Chicago Jewish Historical Society, 1990— reprint of the original of 1924, p. 431]).

Pincus was neither a small man nor the ineffectual character delineated here. He was 5 foot 10 inches and at least moderately athletic; he played baseball as a young man and golf in his mature years. The Chicago Bar Association's evaluation of him when he declared for the municipal judgeship in 1922 was "a conscientious lawyer and fairly well qualified." (*Chicago Tribune*, April 2, 1922, p. 6.) His position as city prosecutor put him in the position of being the chief legal officer in the Mayor Dever's effort to rid Chicago of prostitution, pornography, and related activities. In his first annual report as city prosecutor, Pincus stated, "We have been relentless in the prosecution of crooked bondsmen, keepers of immoral hotels, panderers and others who have offended against the . . . morals of the people of Chicago." (City of Chicago, Law Department, Annual Report, 1923, p. 58.) In his third report, he wrote: "I also wish to report that we have conducted a special investigation and drive against indecent and lewd magazines, totaling 19 cases." (*Annual Report,* 1925, p. 72.) Finally, in 1926 he reported: "We have continued our investigations and drive against indecent and lewd magazines, and have been successful in the prosecution of 51 cases; this persistent campaign has caused the distributors and publishers of these magazines to withdraw distribution in Chicago." (*Annual Report,* 1926, p. 68.)

At the outset of this cleansing campaign, Hecht was publishing, in association with Maxwell Bodenheim, a newspaper, the *Chicago Literary Times.* Hecht took a strong editorial position against what he viewed as the puritanism of the Dever administration. He referred to the reformers as "sinister numbskulls who are depriving us of our God-given liberties" in "Are Our Reformers Knaves or Idiots?" (*Chicago Literary Times*, 1, no. 16 [October 15, 1923], p. 1.) See also "A Terrible Parable," (*Chicago Literary Times 1*, no. 13, [September 1, 1923], p. 1.) The parable recounts the effort of the despot Ali Dever Hassan to clean up Baghdad. The despot, failing in milder measures, beheads the entire youth of the city, leaving Baghdad to the elderly. Hecht in 1923 and 1924 was also defending himself—unsuccessfully, as it proved—in a federal action for placing obscene material, his novel *Fantazius Mallare*, in the U.S. mail. Hecht, his illustrator Wallace Smith, and his publishers Pascal Covici and William McGee were fined $1,000 each. (See *Chicago Daily News*, February 5, 1924, p. 3; *Chicago Tribune*, February 7, 1924, p. 20.)

Accordingly, Pincus provided the authors with a public official who had been in a position to deliver the reprieve important to the plot, and a figure identified with a puritanism they were eager to attack. Equally important, they undoubtedly evaluated him as what he was: an honorable lawyer who would have rejected the sort of bribe offered to him in the play.

The Chicago Police Department's mug shots of Tommy O'Connor, prototype for Earl Williams. Note how closely the description of Williams approximates O'Connor's actual appearance. He was a small man, 5 foot 8 inches and 138 pounds (Chicago Historical Society).

TOMMY O'CONNOR was not the sympathetic character of the play. Rather, by the time of the escape he had established himself as the archetypal desperate criminal. He had a record for robbery dating back to 1907, was thought to have engaged in kidnapping, and was suspected of two previous murders before the sequence of events leading to his incarceration on death row. That sequence began with a robbery at the Illinois Central Railroad suburban station at Randolph Street on February 1, 1918, in which ticket collector Dennis Tierney, a former city policeman, was killed. O'Connor on January 21, 1919, killed Jimmy Cherin, one of his accomplices in Tierney's murder, after failing to induce Cherin to go into the Stateville penitentiary to kill Harry Emerson, another of the accomplices, who was prepared to testify that O'Connor had been the triggerman. O'Connor was tried for the murder of Tierney in April 1919, but was acquitted, in spite of positive identification by Emerson. O'Connor was indicted for the murder of Cherin and was to be tried on September 10, 1920, but he skipped bail.

On March 22, 1921, a police party headed by Sergeant Patrick O'Neill was sent to arrest O'Connor at the home of O'Connor's brother-in-law on the South Side. O'Connor appeared at the back door and fired on O'Neill, who died half an hour later at St. Bernard's Hospital. O'Connor and a man wanted for another murder endeavored to escape to Minneapolis, but in attempting to rob a porter on the Chicago Great Western Railway, they were subdued by the train crew, arrested, and jailed in St. Paul. O'Connor was returned to Chicago and put on trial on September 6 for the murder of O'Neill. He was found guilty on September 24, 1921, and sentenced by Judge Kickham Scanlan to be hanged on Thursday, December 15.

The escape was not, as in the play, on the eve of the execution. On Sunday morning, December 11, O'Connor was being held in an ordinary cellblock of the jail; he was to be moved to the condemned cell on the thirteenth. Along with four fellow prisoners, all convicted robbers, O'Connor made a mass escape by use of a pistol allegedly smuggled into the jail in a pork chop sandwich. Other prisoners began streaming out of the cell block, but Emil Bairie, a clerk in the jail office, called out, "Bring out the rifle squad quick and pot some of these birds." This caused one of O'Connor's partners in the escape attempt to turn back, along with the prisoners who had followed them.

The four remaining escapees made their way to the roof of a shed at the west fence of the yard behind the jail. One of their number broke both ankles jumping from the shed and could not proceed. The other three ran north into Illinois Street, where they commandeered the Model T Ford of a city light inspector who was making his daily rounds. O'Connor pushed his pistol into the man's face and told him, "Start driving and drive like hell!" As a murderer facing execution in four days, O'Connor spoke with an authority out of desperation that came through clearly to his victims.

The light inspector got only as far as Illinois and Clark Streets, where he killed his engine. O'Connor's two remaining companions stole away unobtrusively, and O'Connor, now acting alone, comandeered a series of three automobiles, the last of which was an Overland touring car driven by an unidentified man who had two women passengers. This car was observed going west on Division Street and north on Clybourn Avenue, but O'Connor was never seen again.

From the direction O'Connor had taken, the police presumed he was heading northwest toward the Grass Lake–Fox Lake area immediately south of the Wisconsin border. They endeavored to search the northwestern suburban area, but the episode demonstrated the inadequacy of policing in outlying Cook County. By December 13, the police had received alleged sightings of O'Connor from twenty towns and several hundred points in Chicago itself. A reported 5,000 police were engaged in the search. The police and sheriff's personnel made themselves look as foolish in chasing down the vast number of disparate rumors as the play indicates. In particular, five Chicago detectives pursuing a lead to Hartford, Wisconsin, were injured, one seriously, when their touring car skidded off an icy road near Menominee Falls. The chase ended with all five in a Milwaukee hospital.

What happened to O'Connor remains a mystery. A body found under a bridge three miles north of Palmyra, Wisconsin, was suspected of being the driver of a car O'Connor commandeered on his way north. He was thought to have gone to the Twin Cities area and from there into Canada. He was rumored in the Chicago Irish community to have made his way back to Ireland and to have died there in the upheavals of the 1920s. (Account based on stories of the escape in the *Chicago Tribune, Chicago Herald and Examiner,* and *Chicago Daily News,* December 12–14, 1921, plus verification of earlier dates. A fuller account, with identifications of the escapees and the other persons involved is in Richard C. Lindberg, *To Serve and Collect: Chicago Politics and Police Corruption from the Lager Beer Riot to the Summerdale Scandal* [New York: Praeger, 1991, pp. 219–25]).

Osgood Perkins, as Walter, holds firmly onto Walter Baldwin, as Bensinger, while he works out his plot with Duffy Cornell on the phone (New York Public Library).

Walter Howey, drawn by William Rolig from the halftone that accompanied Howey's obituary in the *New York Times* (March 22, 1954, p. 27). The name is that of Walter Noble Burns, author of *The Saga of Billy the Kid,* but the character is universally recognized to represent Walter Crawford Howey, editor of the *Herald and Examiner.* MacArthur in drawing the character is believed also to have drawn on his experience with Frank Carson, city editor of the *Herald and Examiner.*

WALTER CRAWFORD HOWEY came to Chicago from his home town of Fort Dodge, Iowa, where he had some limited newspaper experience. In Chicago he was first a reporter for the *American,* but rose to city editor of the *Inter Ocean* and then to city editor of the *Tribune.* After a dispute in 1917 with Joseph M. Patterson, copublisher of the *Tribune,* he went to the *Herald and Examiner* to begin a career as rather a quintessential Hearst editor. William Randolph Hearst sent him to Boston in 1922 to be editor of the *Boston American,* and in 1924 he went to New York to help set up the *Mirror.* He later served as personal assistant to Hearst, but was posted to Boston as editor of the *Record-American* in 1939. In 1942 he returned to Chicago as editor of the merged *Herald-American.* He also served as supervising editor of Hearst's *American Weekly.* His final post was as executive editor of the *Boston American, Daily Record,* and *Sunday Advertiser.* He and his wife, Gloria, were severely injured in an automobile accident on January 14, 1954. Mrs. Howey died of pneumonia about ten days later before leaving the hospital, but Howey managed to return home, where he died in his sleep on March 21 at age seventy-two. (See his obituary in the *New York Times,* March 22, 1954, p. 27.)

Howey was consistently a great enthusiast for pictorial journalism and made advances in reproduction and transmission of photographs. In particular, he held a patent on transmission of halftones over ordinary telephone wires.

Views of Howey range widely. After Howey lost his left eye, it was said that it was easy to tell which eye was glass — the warmer one. (Alex Barris, *Stop the Presses! The Newspaperman in American Films* [South Brunswick, NJ: A. S. Barnes & Co., 1976], p. 14.) Harry C. Read, city editor of the *Chicago American,* in his article on the play took particular offense at this characterization of Howey, saying that it "is a deliberate distortion of a great and able original [that] smacks of personal venom." (*Chicago American,* November 26, 1928, p. 22.)

The Front Page

Courtesy of Chicago Historical Society

CAST OF CHARACTERS

WILSON, *American*
ENDICOTT, *Post*
MURPHY, *Journal*
McCUE, *City News Bureau*
SCHWARTZ, *Daily News*
KRUGER, *Journal of Commerce*
BENSINGER, *Tribune*
MRS. SCHLOSSER
WOODENSHOES EICHHORN
DIAMOND LOUIE
HILDY JOHNSON, *Herald and Examiner*
JENNIE
MOLLIE MALLOY
SHERIFF HARTMAN
PEGGY GRANT
MRS. GRANT
THE MAYOR
MR. PINCUS
EARL WILLIAMS
WALTER BURNS
TONY
CARL
FRANK
POLICEMEN, CITIZENS

SCENE

The scene is the pressroom in the Criminal Courts Building, Chicago.

ACT I
Eight-thirty on a Friday night.
ACT II
Shortly afterward.
ACT III
A few minutes later.

ACT I

This is the pressroom in the Criminal Courts Building,[1] Chicago; a chamber set aside by the City Fathers for the use of journalists and their friends. It is a bare, disordered room, peopled by newspapermen in need of shaves, pants pressing, and small change. Hither reporters are drawn by an irresistible lure, the privilege of telephoning free. There are seven telephones in the place, communicating with the seven newspapers of Chicago. All are free.

An equally important lure is the continuous poker game that has been going on now for a generation, presumably with the same pack of cards. Here is the rendezvous of some of the most able and amiable bums in the newspaper business; here they meet to gossip, play cards, sleep off jags, and date up waitresses between such murders, fires, riots, and other public events as concern them.

The furniture is the simplest; two tables, an assortment of chairs, spittoons, and wastebaskets, a water cooler, etc.—two dollars worth of dubious firewood, all told.

There is one elegant item, however; a huge, ornate black walnut desk, the former property of Mayor Fred A. Busse, deceased about 1904.[2] It now belongs to

---

[1]*Criminal Courts Building.* This structure at the northwest corner of Dearborn Street and Austin Avenue—the present 54 Hubbard Street—was designed by Otto H. Matz, a leading architect of the city, who had been active since the 1850s. It is one of the best examples of his work and one of the last surviving. Contrary to the text, the building was begun in 1891 and completed in 1893. Matz made use of elements of the Richardsonian Romanesque style of the time, notably in the building's impressive doorway. The Cook County Jail was immediately to the north. The office building was still in use for the criminal courts at the time the play appeared, but its replacement was nearing completion, the present complex of criminal courts and jail at 26th Street and California Avenue, which opened in 1929. Upon vacating the Criminal Court Building—its correct name—the Cook County government conveyed it to the City of Chicago, which used it principally to house the Health Department. The Chicago Police Department and some lesser municipal bodies also maintained offices in it.

In 1986 the building was acquired by J. S. Friedman & Associates, who beautifully restored it as Courthouse Place, an office building mainly housing architects, consulting engineers, and others in independent professional practice. The interior was greatly modified, but the pressroom is believed to have been on the fourth floor, just east of the elevator shafts, an area currently occupied by the building's suite 402. The set for the original production, designed by Richard Sovey, was fairly universally considered both authentic and effective.

[2]*Fred A. Busse.* Fred Adolph Busse, mayor of Chicago from 1907 to 1911. Born on March

ROY BENSINGER, feature writer for the Chicago Tribune *and a fanatic on the subject of hygiene.*

Despite MR. BENSINGER's views, his desk is the repository for soiled linen, old sandwiches, empty bottles, and other items shed by his colleagues. The two tables serve as telephone desks, gaming boards, and (in a pinch) as lits d'amour.

The electric lights are naked of shades.

The walls, unpainted since the building was erected in 1885, sport a frieze of lithographs, hand-painted studies, rotogravure cuttings, and heroic pencil sketches, all on the same theme: Woman. The political unrest of the journalists is represented by an unfavorable picture of Kaiser Wilhelm II, hand drawn.

At stage left is a door, labeled "Gents."[3]

At the back is a double door, opening on the main corridor of the building.

At the stage right are two high, old-fashioned windows overlooking the Cook County Jail.

It is eight-thirty at night.

Four men are playing poker at the main table in the center of the room. They are MURPHY of the Journal, *ENDICOTT of the* Post, *SCHWARTZ of the* News, *and WILSON of the* American; *four braves known to their kind as police reporters. Catatonic, seedy Paul Reveres, full of strange oaths[4] and a touch of childhood. Off by himself in a chair sits ERNIE KRUGER, a somnolent reporter for the* Journal of Commerce. *Ernie is gifted beyond his comrades. He plays the banjo and sings. He is dreamily rendering his favorite piece, "By the Light of the Silvery Moon," as the poker game progresses.*

3, 1866, he was active in Republican politics on the North Side from a relatively early age. His single term as mayor coincided with the later years of the great Edwardian prosperity. Upon completion of the term, Busse retired from public life and, contrary to the text, died on July 10, 1914. Although a Republican in an office generally held by Democrats, Busse continues to be regarded within the city government and also by academic observers as one of the most effective mayors in the history of Chicago. (See *National Cyclopedia of American Biography* XV [1916], p. 67.) Busse's desk was, in fact, a fixture of the pressroom. After Cook County vacated the building, the desk was taken to the pressroom of the Chicago Police Department's headquarters at 11th and State Streets. The desk served there until the pressroom was refurnished in 1959 to 1960, and then is believed to have been destroyed. (Letter of Police Officer Michael T. Sullivan to George W. Hilton, June 19, 1995.)

[3] *Gents.* For the objections of the Lord Chamberlain's office to this line and to the sign on stage, see the introduction.

McCUE of the City News Bureau[5] is telephoning at BENSINGER's desk through the gamblers' chatter. He is calling all the police stations, hospitals, etc. on behalf of his companions, in a never-ending quest for news. His reiterations, whined in a manner intended to be ingratiating, have in them the monotonous bally-hoo wail of the press.

And so:

THE CARD PLAYERS: Crack it for a dime. . . . By me. . . . I stay. . . . Me too. . . . I'm behind again. . . . I was even a couple of minutes ago. . . . Papers?. . . Three. . . . Two. . . . Three to the dealer.

McCUE: *(Into phone.)* Kenwood three four hundred[6]. . . . *(Another telephone rings.)* Hey, take that, one of you guys. Ernie, you're not doing anything. *(They pay no attention. With a sigh, McCue props one telephone receiver against his ear; reaches over and answers the other phone.)* What's the matter with you guys? Are you all crippled or something? *(Into second phone.)* Pressroom! *(Suddenly he gives attention to the first phone.)* Hello, Sarge[7] . . . McCue. Hold the line a minute. *(Back to second phone.)* No, I told you it was the pressroom. *(Hangs up; takes first phone again.)* Anything doing, Sarge? All right. Thank you, Sarge. *(Hangs up.)*

THE CARD PLAYERS: What are you waiting for? How'd I know you were out? Two Johns. Ladies. *(Etc.)*

McCUE: Robey four five hundred.

MURPHY: Ernie! Take that mouth organ in the can and play it! *(The music swells a little in reply.)*

ENDICOTT: These cards are like washrags.

---

[4]*full of strange oaths.* The reference is to the speech of Jaques in Act II, Scene VII, of Shakespeare's *As You Like It*, beginning "All the world's a stage . . .":
Then a soldier,
Full of strange oaths, and bearded like the pard. . . .

[5]*City News Bureau.* An organization that reported local news for the city's newspapers to avoid duplicative reporting on minor items—mainly routine police actions, minor court cases, and high school athletic results. The bureau took shape in a merger of 1890, incorporating predecessor organizations that dated from 1881. It was founded by eight newspapers as a nonprofit cooperative, but all ten papers active in 1890 joined as charter members. It reached its peak with fifteen members, including the Associated Press, in 1894. The bureau was long identified as a training ground—at low salary—for young journalists. At the time of the play, it occupied an office in the Ashland Block at 155 N. Clark Street. It survived until March 1, 1999, jointly owned at the end by the *Tribune* and *Sun-Times*. The *Tribune* then

WILSON: Let's chip in for a new deck.

SCHWARTZ: These are good enough—I'm eighty cents out already!

McCUE: *(Into phone.)* Is this the home of Mrs. F. D. Margolies?[8]

MURPHY: I'd like a deck with some aces in it.

McCUE: *(Cordially, into phone.)* This is Mr. McCue of the City News Bureau. . . . Is it true, Madame, that you were the victim of a Peeping Tom?[9]

KRUGER: Ask her if she's worth peeping at.

WILSON: Has she got a friend?

McCUE: *(Into phone.)* Now, that ain't the right attitude to take, Madame. All we want is the facts. . . . Well, what did this Peeping Tom look like? I mean, for instance, would you say he looked like a college professor?

ENDICOTT: Tell her I can run up for an hour.

KRUGER: I'll accommodate her if she'll come down here.

SCHWARTZ: By me.

McCUE: *(Into phone.)* Just a minute, Madame. Is it true, Mrs. Margolies, that you took the part of Pocahontas in the Elks' Pageant seven years ago?[10] . . . Hello. *(To the others.)* She hung up.

MURPHY: The hell with her! A dime. *(The fire-alarm box, over the door, begins to ring.)*

ENDICOTT: Where's that fire?

WILSON: Three-two-one!

SCHWARTZ: Clark and Erie.

KRUGER: *(Wearily as he strums.)* Too far.[11]

McCUE: *(Into phone.)* Harrison four thousand.

---

replaced it with a smaller, similar body, the New City News Service, serving itself and the city's broadcast media. (See *City News Centennial 1890–1990* [Chicago: City News Bureau, no date]; A. A. Dornfeld, *Behind the Front Page* [Chicago: Academy Chicago Publishers, 1983].)

[6]*Kenwood 3400.* None of the phone numbers in the play is actual.

[7]*Sarge.* Not identifiable.

[8]*Mrs. F. D. Margolies.* Diana Frutkin Margolies, wife of a prominent rabbi, Joseph Hayim Margolies of the South Side Hebrew Congregation. Rabbi Margolies's home phone number (1923) was Normal 5287; this is one of the most unambiguous indications that the phone numbers in the play are not actual. See also footnote 185.

[9]*Is it true, Madame, that you were the victim of a Peeping Tom?* This famous line was actually delivered by Buddy McHugh in a phone interview from the pressroom of the police department's detective bureau while McHugh worked for the City News Bureau. Overheard by the reporters, it became an oral tradition among them and was picked up secondhand by Hecht and MacArthur, who decided to use it unaltered in

(SCHWARTZ rises; stretching; ambles over and looks out the window.) Oh, Christ!—what time is it, anyway?

WILSON: Half past eight. *(Rises; goes to the water cooler.)*

MURPHY: *(Drawing cards.)* One off the top.

WILSON: How's the wife, Ed? Any better?

SCHWARTZ: Worse.

WILSON: That's tough.

SCHWARTZ: Sitting here all night, waiting for 'em to hang this bastard! *(A gesture toward the jail.)*

KRUGER: It's hard work, all right.

McCUE: *(Into phone.)* Hello, Sarge? McCue. Anything doing? . . . Yeah? That's swell. . . . *(The players pause.)* A love triangle, huh? . . . Did he kill her? . . . Killed 'em *both!* Ah! . . . Was she good-looking? . . . *(A pause. With vast disgust.)* What? Oh, niggers! *(The players relax.)*

KRUGER: That's a *break.*

McCUE: No, never mind—thank you, Sarge. *(Jiggles receiver.)* Englewood, six eight hundred. *(The* Examiner[12] *phone rings. It is on the main table. Endicott answers.)*

ENDICOTT: *(Into phone.)* Criminal Courts pressroom. . . . No, Hildy Johnson ain't here. . . . Oh, hello, Mr. Burns. . . . No, he ain't here yet, Mr. Burns. *(Hangs up.)* Walter Burns again. Something must have happened.

SCHWARTZ: I'm telling you what's happened. Hildy quit.

MURPHY: What do you mean, quit? He's a fixture on the *Examiner.*

KRUGER: Yeah! He goes with the woodwork.

---

the play. (See John J. McPhaul, *Deadlines and Monkeyshines: The Fabled World of Chicago Journalism* [Englewood Cliffs, NJ: Prentice-Hall, Inc., 1962], pp. 1–2.) This may explain why the play anachronistically places McHugh at the City News Bureau, thirteen years after he left it.

[10]*The Elks' Pageant.* The reference is probably to the Elks' Day at the second Pageant of Progress, a promotion of William Hale Thompson held at the Municipal Pier (Navy Pier) on August 18, 1922. If so, this is an anachronism, for at no time that could be assigned to the play could the Elks' Day have been seven years in the past.

[11]*Too far.* Clark and Erie intersect only five blocks north of the Criminal Court Building.

[12]*The Examiner.* The *Chicago Herald and Examiner*, lead newspaper of the Hearst chain in Chicago. The paper was founded as the *Chicago Morning American* on May 2, 1902, and was renamed the *Chicago Examiner* on March 31, 1907. Upon merger with the *Chicago Record-Herald* on May 2, 1918, it became the *Herald and Examiner*. The time of the play is explicitly after the merger; Hildy is identified in the cast of characters

SCHWARTZ: I got it from Bert Neeley.[13] I'm *telling* you—he's gettin' married.

MURPHY: Walter wouldn't let him get married. He'd kidnap him at the altar.

McCUE: *(Into phone.)* Hello, Sarge. McCue. Anything doing?

ENDICOTT: Remember what he did to Bill Fenton,[14] when he wanted to go to Hollywood? Had him thrown into jail for arson.

MURPHY: Forgery.

McCUE: Shut up! . . . *(Into phone.)* Anybody hurt? . . . Oh, fine! What's his name? . . . Spell it. . . . S . . .C . . . Z . . . J . . . Oh, the hell with it. *(Hangs up.)*

ENDICOTT: A guy ain't going to walk out on a job when he's drawing down seventy bucks a week.

SCHWARTZ: Yeah? Well, if he ain't quit, why ain't he here covering the hanging?

McCUE: *(Into phone.)* Give me rewrite.

ENDICOTT: Walter sounded like he was having a hemorrhage.

McCUE: *(Into phone.)* Hello, Emil.[15] Nothing new on the hanging. But here's a big scoop for you.

SCHWARTZ: I wish to God *I* could quit.

KRUGER: You'd think he'd come in and say good-bye.

MURPHY: That Swede bastard!

McCUE: Shut up, fellas. *(Into phone.)* Ready, Emil? *(He intones.)* Dr. Irving

---

as a member of the *Herald and Examiner*, not of the *Examiner* alone. Nonetheless, the authors were almost certainly accurate in having all concerned refer to the journal as the *Examiner*. The paper, rather a quintessential example of Hearst journalism, was reportedly never highly profitable, but it vied at the time of the play with the *Tribune* as leader in the city's morning circulation. The rivalry with the *Tribune* was increasingly unsuccessful in the 1930s; improvements in educational levels tended to work strongly against it. The *Herald and Examiner* was merged with Hearst's evening paper, the *American,* on August 28, 1939, into the *Chicago Herald-American.* The combined paper's competitive position was no better, and it was sold to the *Tribune* on October 21, 1956. The *Tribune* operated it as an evening paper, *Chicago's American* until April 27, 1969, and then as *Chicago Today* until September 13, 1974, when it was discontinued. The Hearst papers were housed at 215 W. Madison Street until November 5, 1912, and subsequently at 326 W. Madison at the corner of Madison and Market Streets. For a history of the newspaper, see George Murray, *The Madhouse on Madison Street* (Chicago: Follett Publishing Co., 1965).

[13]*Bert Neeley*. The context is that Neeley was a contemporary thoroughly familiar with the reporters—presumably as a drinking companion. There are several prospects, the most likely of whom is Bertrand J. Neely, a salesman based at 300 W. Lake Street during Hecht's early years in Chicago journalism. By 1923 he was listed in the city directory as assistant manager of Jenkins & Co., a manufacturer of valves and other

Zobel[16]—Z for Zebra—O for onion—B for baptize—E for anything and L for Lousy—

CARD PLAYERS: Pass. . . . By me. . . . Crack it for a dime. . . . Stay.

McCUE: *(Into phone.)* Yes, Zobel! That's right! With offices at sixteen-o-eight Cottage Grove Avenue. Well, this bird was arrested tonight on complaint of a lot of angry husbands. They claim he was treating their wives with electricity for a dollar a smack.

MURPHY: Is the Electric Teaser in again?

McCUE: *(Intoning into phone.)* He had a big following, a regular army of fat old dames that was being neglected by their husbands. So they was visiting this Dr. Zobel in their kimonas to get electricity.

ENDICOTT: I understand he massages them too.

McCUE *(Into phone.)* Anyhow, the doctor is being held for malpractice and the station is full of his patients who claim he's innocent. But from what the husbands say it looks like he's a Lothario. All right. *(Hangs up; jiggles receiver.)*

MURPHY: Hey, Ernie, why don't you go in for electricity instead of the banjo? *(BENSINGER enters. He is a studious and slightly neurotic fellow who stands out like a sore thumb owing to his tidy appearance.)*

KRUGER: It's got no future.

---

industrial rubber products. Alternatives are Albert R. Neely, a piano salesman; Albert E. Neely, a salesman for W. C. Ritchie & Co.; and the least likely, Albert Neely, a janitor resident at 615 E. 36th Street.

Alternatively, this may be a reference to Albert E. Neely (1835–1898), a prominent commission merchant, grain dealer, and, as partner in the firm of Neely & Ham, operator of one of the city's principal grain elevators of the nineteenth century. (See his obituary in the *Chicago Tribune*, August 8, 1898, p. 5.) If this is the prototype, Neely had nothing to recommend him to the authors except being dead, but for other uses of unrelated names of deceased persons, see footnotes 14 on Bill Fenton and 135 on Earl Williams.

[14]*Bill Fenton, Examiner.* Probably William T. Fenton, president of the National Bank of the Republic, who committed suicide by drowning in Lake Michigan on March 31, 1922 (See the *Chicago Tribune*, April 2, 1922, p. 9). By application of the authors' usual calculations, his death allowed his name to be used without alteration. William Fenton was a common name, however, so that there are various possible alternatives, none of whom is known to have been a reporter of the *Herald and Examiner*. The passage may recount an effort of Howey to retain a reporter of an unrelated name.

[15]*Emil.* Emil F. Hubka, an employee of the City News Bureau from March 16, 1902, to 1926. He became assistant day editor in 1908 and city editor in 1913, his post at the time of the play. Thus, he was the correct man for McCue to phone. Hubka served

McCUE: *(Into phone.)* Sheridan two thousand.

BENSINGER: *(With horror.)* What the hell, Mac! Is that the only telephone in the place!

McCUE: It's the only one with a mouthpiece on it. *(This is true.)*

MURPHY: *(Putting down his hand.)* Read 'em and weep. *(Takes the pot. Prepares to deal.)*

BENSINGER: *(Howling.)* How many times have I got to tell you fellows to leave my phone alone? If you've got to talk through a mouthpiece, go *buy* one, like I did!

MURPHY: Aw, shut up, Listerine.

McCUE: *(At another phone.)* Sheridan two thousand.

BENSINGER: My God, I'm trying to keep this phone clean and I'm not going to have you fellows coughing and spitting in it, either, or pawing it with your hands!

SCHWARTZ: What is this—a hospital or something?

ENDICOTT: How's that pimple coming along, Roy?

BENSINGER: *(Pulling a suit of dirty underwear from a drawer of his desk.)* And you don't have to use this desk for a toilet!

MURPHY: Yeah? Well, suppose you quit stinking up this place with your goddamn antiseptics for a change! *(Removing a moldy piece of pie from a desk drawer.)*

BENSINGER: *(Wailing.)* Ain't you guys got any self-respect?

McCUE *(Into phone.)* Hello, Sarge! . . . Congratulations on that Polack capture, Sarge. I hear you're going to be promoted. Anything doing?

---

as city editor of the *Herald and Examiner* in 1926 and 1927. He became night city editor of the *Daily News* and was recruited as the first night city editor of the *Chicago Sun* in anticipation of its beginning publication in 1941. In 1948 he became Chicago editor of *Billboard* magazine and retired after losing sight in one eye in 1956. He became legally blind in 1960 and according to records of the Chicago Press Veterans died in February 1969. A requiem mass was said for him at St. Theresa Church in Palatine, Illinois, on February 25, 1969.

[16]*Dr. Irving Zobel.* Not identifiable. The address, 1608 Cottage Grove Avenue is nonexistent; Cottage Grove Avenue begins at 2201. The name does not appear to accord with any actual physician. It may be an adaptation of the name of Solomon Zobel, a bartender. The use of electrical and electromechanical devices for sexual stimulation of women was common in the late nineteenth and early twentieth centuries. See Rachel P. Maines. *The Technology of Orgasm* (Baltimore: The Johns Hopkins University Press, 1999).

[17]*Grand Crossing.* Once a major railroad junction on the South Side at approximately

THE CARD PLAYERS: Nickel. . . . Up a dime. . . . Drop. . . . Stay.

McCUE: *(Into phone.)* Yeah? . . . Just a second, Sarge. . . . *(To the players.)* Nice little feature, fellas. Little kid, golden curls, everything, lost out near Grand Crossing.[17] The cops are feeding her candy.

MURPHY: What else are they doing to her?

McCUE: Don't you want it?

SCHWARTZ: No!

ENDICOTT: Stick it!

WILSON: All yours. *(Starts to deal a new hand.)*

McCUE: *(Into phone.)* Never mind, Sarge. Thank you, Sarge. *(McCue hangs up.)*

SCHWARTZ: Anything new on the hanging, Bensinger?

WILSON: *(Dealing.)* My deal, ain't it?

MURPHY: Hey! Zonite![18]

BENSINGER: What is it?

MURPHY: Question before the house: Gentleman wants to know what's new on the hanging.

BENSINGER: Nothing special.

KRUGER: *(With a yawn.)* Did you see the sheriff?

BENSINGER: *(Bitterly.)* Why don't you get your own news?

KRUGER: *(Philosophically.)* Somebody ought to see the sheriff.

ENDICOTT: Anyhow, this looks like the last hanging we'll ever have to cover.

SCHWARTZ: Yeah. Can you imagine their putting in an electric chair?[19] That's awful.

ENDICOTT: Going to toast them, like Lucky Strikes.

75th Street and Woodlawn Avenue, the crossing of the Pennsylvania, New York Central, and Nickel Plate Road with the Illinois Central main line. By the time of the play, the railroads had been elevated and grade-separated, ending the junction's importance in railroading, but it had long since given its name to the surrounding neighborhood.

[18]*Zonite!* An antiseptic and vaginal douche, a commercial adaptation of the Carrel-Dakin Solution, developed as a medication for wounds in World War I. It was produced in New York by the Zonite Products Co., later by the pharmaceutical firm of Smith, Kline & French. In the acting edition of 1950, this expletive becomes a meaningless "Zenita," an example of the euphemistic quality of the changes in the acting edition.

[19]*putting in an electric chair.* Illinois converted from hanging to electrocution by a bill signed into law by Governor Len Small on July 6, 1927, while the play was being written. Electric chairs were to be installed in the state prisons at Stateville (Joliet) and Menard and in the Cook County jail. (See the *New York Times,* July 7, 1927, p. 12.)

MURPHY: Who opened?

SCHWARTZ: What's the matter? Got a hand?

(MRS. SCHLOSSER[20] enters. She is the wife of Herman Schlosser, of the Examiner. MRS. SCHLOSSER once used to go to dances, movies, and ice cream parlors, and she is still pretty, although shopworn. If she is a bit acidulated, tight-lipped, and sharp-spoken, no one can blame her, least of all these braves of the pressroom, who have small respect for themselves or each other as husbands, fathers, and lovers.)

ENDICOTT: (As guiltily as if he were the errant Mr. Schlosser.) Hello, Mrs. Schlosser. Herman hasn't been in yet.

McCUE: Hello, Mrs. Schlosser. Have you tried the Harrison Street Station?[21] (Helpfully.) He may be sleeping in the squad room.

SCHWARTZ: (Bitterly.) What became of that rule about women coming into this pressroom?

MURPHY: Yeah—I don't let my *own* wife come in here.

MRS. SCHLOSSER: (Inexorably.) Did he have any money left when you saw him?

McCUE: Well, I didn't exactly see him. Did you, Mike?

ENDICOTT: No, I didn't really see him either.

MRS. SCHLOSSER: (Like twenty wives.) Oh, you didn't? Well, was he still drinking?

McCUE (With unconvincing zeal.) I tell you what, I'll call up the grand jury room if you want. Sometimes he goes to sleep up there.

The act went into effect immediately, but criminals already condemned to death by hanging were still to be hanged. This created the anomaly, mentioned in connection with the escape of Tommy O'Connor, that if O'Connor had been reapprehended, he would have had to be hanged.

This passage is a good demonstration of the impossibility of assigning a single date to the play. If the execution being awaited is that of O'Connor in December 1921, the reporters could hardly be treating the conversion to electrocution as so imminent that this would be their last hanging.

[20]*Mrs. Herman Schlosser.* Herman Schlosser was a printer during Hecht's early years in Chicago. The name of his wife—or even whether he had a wife—is unknown. He—or they—had apparently left Chicago permanently before World War I. Note that the authors assign no first name to Mrs. Schlosser. The stage directions for the character's entry in the acting edition of 1950 (p. 14) give her the first name of "Myrtle," but there is no presumption that this was the actual name of the prototype. Myrtle, which was the name of Al Baenziger's wife, may have been transferred to this character.

MRS. SCHLOSSER: Don't trouble yourself! I notice Hildy Johnson ain't here either. I suppose the two of them are out sopping it up together.

SCHWARTZ: Now, you oughtn't to talk that way, Mrs. Schlosser. Hildy's reformed—he's gettin' married.

MRS. SCHLOSSER: Married? Well, all I can say is, God help his wife!

MURPHY: Come on—are we playing cards or aren't we?

MRS. SCHLOSSER: I suppose you've cleaned Herman out.

WILSON: *(A nervous husband in his own right.)* Honest, Mrs. Schlosser, we ain't seen him.

MRS. SCHLOSSER: *(Bitterly.)* He can't come home. I kept dinner waiting till eleven o'clock last night and he never even called up.

ENDICOTT: *(Into phone.)* Hildy ain't showed up yet.

ENDICOTT: Well, why pick on us?

KRUGER: Yeah—we're busy.

(A phone rings.)

ENDICOTT: *(Answering it.)* Pressroom!

MRS. SCHLOSSER: You know where he is. You're covering up for him.

McCUE: Honest to God, Mrs. Schlosser—

ENDICOTT: *(Into phone.)* . . . No, Mr. Burns, Hildy ain't showed up yet.

MRS. SCHLOSSER: Is that Walter Burns? Let me talk to him!

ENDICOTT: *(Into phone.)* Just a minute, Mr. Burns. Herman Schlosser's wife wants to talk to you.

MRS. SCHLOSSER: *(Taking the phone, honeyed and polite.)* Hello, Mr. Burns.

MURPHY: Come on—who opened?

ENDICOTT: Check it.

MURPHY: A dime.

MRS. SCHLOSSER: This is Mrs. Schlosser. . . . Oh, I'm very well, thank you. . . . Mr. Burns, I was just wondering if you knew where Herman

---

Mrs. Schlosser is frequently dropped from the play. She did not appear in the 1969 Broadway revival, and she was not written into *Windy City*.

[21]*Harrison Street Station*. The actual Harrison Street Station was the headquarters of the First Division and the Second Precinct of the Chicago Police Department located at the intersection of Harrison and LaSalle Streets, but it was closed in July 1911. It was responsible for the First Ward brothel area and the rest of the South Side immediately below the Loop. The name was carried over to its replacement of 1912, a new station at 625–627 South Clark Street that served the same area. Because the structure housed the South Clark Street Police Court, it was a place where one of the reporters might reasonably be found. This building served until 1928 and was razed in 1935. (See the *Chicago Tribune*, October 28, 1935, pp. 9, 28.)

was. He didn't come home last night, and you know it was payday. . . . *(Tearfully.)* But it won't be all right. I'm just going crazy. . . . I've done that, but the cashier won't give it to me. . . . So, I thought maybe if you gave me some sort of order—oh, will you, Mr. Burns? That's awfully nice of you. . . . I'm sorry to have to do a thing like that, but you know how Herman is about money. Thank you ever so much. *(Hangs up; turns on the reporters viciously.)* You're all alike, every one of you! You ought to be ashamed of yourselves!

MURPHY: All right, we're ashamed. *(To WILSON.)* A dime's bet.

MRS. SCHLOSSER: Sitting around like a lot of dirty, drunken tramps! Poker! *(She grabs MURPHY'S cards.)*

MURPHY: *(Leaping up in fury.)* Here! Gimme those! What the hell!

MRS. SCHLOSSER: You know where he is, and I'm going to stay right here till I find out!

MURPHY: He's at Hockstetter's,[22] that's where he is! Now give me those cards!

MRS. SCHLOSSER: Where?

WILSON: The Turkish Bath on Madison Street!

ENDICOTT: In the basement!

MURPHY: Give me those!

MRS. SCHLOSSER: So! You did know. *(MURPHY nervously awaits his cards.)* Liars! *(She throws the cards face up on the table.)*

MURPHY: *(As she throws them.)* Hey! *(They spread out on the table.)*

MRS. SCHLOSSER: You're a bunch of gentlemen, I must say! Newspapermen! Bums! *(Exits.)*

MURPHY: *(Almost in tears.)* Look! The second straight flush I ever held.

ENDICOTT: Jesus!

MURPHY: Eight, nine, ten, jack, and queen of spades. If I was married to that dame I'd kick her humpbacked.

BENSINGER: *(Having cleansed his telephone with a dab of absorbent cotton and a bottle of antiseptic: into phone.)* City Desk!

---

[22]*Hockstetter's Turkish Bath.* A fictional institution, making use of the name of Benjamin "Barney" Hochstadter, a sportswriter of the *Post*. In the declining years of the *Post* he turned his attention increasingly toward bowling, writing extensively about the sport, and finally leaving journalism to devote himself to it full time. He inaugurated the Hochstadter Classic for bowlers with averages below 186 and jointly with Louis P. Petersen organized the unrestricted Petersen Classic. Hockstadter with his wife Bee formed a leading husband-and-wife bowling team. He was also proprietor of a bowling alley. He died in Chicago at age sixty-five on May 24, 1960. (See his obituary in the *Chicago Daily News*, May 25, 1960, p. 60.)

ENDICOTT: *(Gathering the cards together.)* I don't know what gets into women. I took Bob Brody[23] home the other night and his wife broke his arm with a broom.

BENSINGER: *(Having collected his notes and thoroughly protected himself from contagion by wrapping a piece of paper around the handle of his telephone.)* Shut up, you fellows! *(Into phone.)* This is Bensinger. Here's a new lead on the Earl Williams hanging. . . . Yeah, I just saw the sheriff. He won't move the hanging up a minute. . . . I don't care *who* he promised. . . . All right, I'll talk him again, but its no use. The execution is set for seven o'clock in the morning.

KRUGER: *(To the tune of "Three o'Clock in the Morning," sings.)* Seven o'clock in the morning—

BENSINGER: Shut up Ernie. . . . *(Into phone.)* Give me a rewrite man.

KRUGER: *(Morose.)* Why can't they jerk these guys at a reasonable hour, so we can get some sleep.

BENSINGER: *(To the room.)* I asked the sheriff to move it up to five, so we could make the City Edition.[24] Just because I asked him to, he wouldn't.

MURPHY: That guy wouldn't do anything for his mother.

KRUGER: He gives a damn if we stay up all night!

---

[23]*Bob Brody.* Remarkably, there appears to have been no one named Robert Brody in Chicago in the period of the play. By application of the authors' practice in altering names, this should be Bob Brodie. The only candidate is Robert Brodie, a carpenter who lived at 6833 S. Justine Street, but this appears an improbable identification. More likely, it may be a reference to Alexander Lewis Brodie, chief clerk to the coroner in the 1920s, and himself the coroner from 1940 to 1952. His name was, in fact, "Brody," but he began spelling it "Brodie" to conform to a paycheck issued to him in 1912. (See his obituary in the *New York Times*, August 24, 1952, p. 88.)

[24]*the City Edition.* More formally known as the City Final, this was the *Tribune*'s basic edition, the last one of the day. It circulated in the metropolitan area only; the *Tribune* served its extensive readership in smaller cities and in the rural Midwest with earlier editions. Working on the presumption that the readership arose at 6:00 A.M., the publishers endeavored to have the City Edition available by that hour, either by home delivery for the breakfast table or, alternatively, at the newsstands for reading on the trip to work. Normally, the City Edition went to press about 4:30 A.M., but it could be delayed. Bensinger was correct in presuming it could be held for a hanging at 5:00, but not for one at 7:00. (For information on the *Tribune*'s sequence of editions, I am indebted to Richard Philbrick.)

ENDICOTT: You've got no kick coming. I've had two dinners home in the last month.[25]

BENSINGER: *(Into phone.)* Hello. Jake?[26] . . . New lead on the Williams hanging. And listen—don't put Hartman's name in it. Just say "the Sheriff." *(The reporters listen.)* Ready? . . . The condemned man ate a hearty dinner. . . . Yeah, Mock turtle soup, chicken pot pie, hashed brown potatoes, combination salad, and pie à la mode.

KRUGER: Make mine the same.

BENSINGER: *(Into phone.)* No—I don't know *what* kind of pie.

MURPHY: Eskimo!

McCUE: *(Wistfully.)* I wish I had a hamburger sandwich.

BENSINGER: *(Into phone.)* And, Jake, get this in as a big favor. The whole dinner was furnished by Charlie Apfel[27]. . . . Yeah—Apfel. A for adenoids, P for psychology, F for Frank, E for Eddie, and L for—ah—

MURPHY: Lay an egg.

BENSINGER: Proprietor of the Apfel-wants-to-see-you-restaurant.

WILSON: That means a new hat for *some* body. *(A soft cadenza from the banjo.)*

MURPHY: I better catch the fudge, fellas.[28] *(Without dropping his cards, MURPHY picks up a telephone. He pantomimes for three cards.)*

---

[25] In the acting edition this sentence is followed by "Worked on my day off three weeks running."

[26] *Jake.* Because "Jake" is a nickname, not invariably a contraction of Jacob, it is impossible to fit the name to a specific rewrite man of the *Tribune.* Vern E. Whaley, a retired reporter whose experience in Chicago journalism goes back to 1921, believes this to be an unambiguous reference to Alfred "Jake" Lingle, a police reporter for the *Tribune* who was assassinated on June 9, 1930, in the passage leading to the Illinois Central suburban station in one of the most publicized criminal cases of the Prohibition era. Lingle was quickly revealed to have ties to the Capone mob, and the police attributed the murder to the rival gang of Bugs Moran. A St. Louis gunman, Lee Brothers, was convicted of the crime and given a ten- to fourteen-year sentence. Dennis E. Hoffman in his *Scarface Al and the Crime Crusaders* (Carbondale: Southern Illinois University Press, 1993) argues that the assassination was of major importance in galvanizing Colonel Robert R. McCormick to put the *Tribune*'s authority into the effort to bring down the Capone organization. Lingle would be an unlikely figure for a rewrite man. He was reportedly semiliterate, but a very effective legman in gathering facts. He invariably phoned in his stories, depending on the *Tribune*'s rewrite desk to deal with his limitations in exposition.

[27] *Charlie Apfel.* Charles Louis Appel, proprietor of the North Side Turner Hall at 820 N. Clark Street about half a mile north of the Courts Building and jail. The restaurant was the dining room of the Turner Hall. Appel was born in Coblin, Germany, as

BENSINGER: *(Into phone.)* Now here's the situation on the eve of the hanging. The officials are prepared for a general uprising of radicals at the hour of execution, but the Sheriff still refuses to be intimidated by the Red menace.

MURPHY: *(Into his phone, while accepting three cards.)* Give me a rewrite man, will you?. . . Yeah. Some more crap on the Earl Williams hanging.

BENSINGER: *(Into phone, as two reporters listen.)* A double guard has just been thrown around the jail, the municipal buildings, railroad terminals, and elevated stations. Also, the Sheriff has just received four more letters threatening his life. He is going to answer these threats by a series of raids against the Friends of American Liberty[29] and other Bolshevik organizations. Call you later. *(Hangs up.)*

SCHWARTZ: Bet a dime.

MURPHY: *(Into phone.)* Ready? . . . Sheriff Hartman has just put two hundred more relatives on the payroll to protect the city against the Red army, which is leaving Moscow in a couple of minutes. *(Consults his hand.)* Up a dime. *(Back to phone.)* And to prove to the voters that the Red menace is on the square, he has just wrote himself four more letters threatening his life. I know he wrote them on account of the misspelling.

Carl Apfel in 1872, but at an early age he was brought to the United States, where he anglicized his name and became a leading figure in the Chicago German-American community. As a supporter of the Thompson-Lundin political clique, he was appointed by Thompson to the Chicago Public Library Board in 1922. He achieved some national fame from his adoptive daughter, Augusta Appel, who, under the name of Lila Lee, became a leading actress of silent motion pictures.

The appearance of Appel in the play as provider of the last meal of a prisoner awaiting execution is accurate. Appel's obituary in the *Chicago Tribune* states: "Known as a genial host at the North Side Turner hall, Appel was regarded as 'little Santa Claus' in the old county jail. Many free meals were sent from his kitchens to prisoners in the jail, and condemned men were always served their last supper by him."

His benefactions to the prisoners and the rest of his operations in Chicago were abruptly ended by some major legal problems in the fall of 1923. He was indicted for embezzlement and operation of a confidence game, allegedly defrauding friends and associates of about $250,000 for a scheme to provide whiskey to pharmacists and to acquire an illicit brewery. While on bail in mid-October, he went to Los Angeles ostensibly to visit Lila Lee. The trip was interpreted as a bail violation, causing him to be indicted also for larceny by a bailee. He fled to Mexico and reportedly lived subsequently in Dresden, Germany, and in New York. He was unwilling ever to return to Chicago. The case against him was never brought to trial, leaving the exact

ENDICOTT: Drop.

MURPHY: *(Into phone.)* That's all, except the doomed man ate a hearty dinner. As follows: Noodle soup, rustabiff, sweet a-potat', cranberry sauce, and pie à la mud.

SCHWARTZ: I raise another dime.

MURPHY: *(Consults his cards.)* Wait a minute. Up again. *(Back to phone.)* Statement from who? The Sheriff? . . . Quote him for anything you want—he can't read. *(Hangs up. BENSINGER's phone rings.)*

THE CARD PLAYERS: Call. . . . Three bullets. . . . Pay at this window. . . . Shuffle that deck. . . . I get the same hand every time.

BENSINGER: *(Answering his phone.)* What? *(To McCUE, as SCHWARTZ starts to shuffle.)* Didn't you send that in about the new alienist?

McCUE: *(Flat on his back on the smaller table.)* I got my hands full with the stations.

BENSINGER: *(Into phone.)* All right, I'll give you what I got. Dr. Max J. Eglehofer.[30] From Vienna. There's a dozen envelopes on him in the morgue. . . . Well, he's going to examine Williams at the request of—ah—wait a minute— *(Shuffles through his notes.)* —United Federation for World Betterment.[31]

---

nature of his alleged plot unclear. In 1933 he went to Elyria, Ohio, to live with his other daughter, Mrs. Leonard Tuffer. He died in Elyria at age sixty-three on November 29, 1935. (See obituaries in the *New York Times*, November 30, 1935, p. 15, and the *Chicago Tribune*, November 30, 1935, p. 22. On his legal involvements, see also the *Chicago Tribune*, October 16, 1923, p. 3; October 19, 1923, p. 12, October 24, 1923, p. 10; November 9, 1923, p. 17.)

[28]*the fudge.* In the acting edition this line is followed by "Is it open?" The "fudge" is a small area in a newspaper, typically on the front page, left open when the rest of the paper is set, so that very brief accounts of last-minute news can be inserted immediately before the press run. In British journalism, it is known as the "stop press." Necessarily, fudges were mainly indentified with evening papers, which had chronic problems of dealing with news that broke late in the day; morning papers had all night to process such items. The *Journal*, which variously used a seven- or eight-column format, regularly used most of the right-hand column on the front page as a fudge for racing results, baseball scores, and late-breaking items, in particular military news during World War I. An evening paper such as the *Journal* endeavored to have its principal edition ready for newsstand sale to commuters on the homeward trip. This implied a press run about 2:30 P.M. to reach Loop news stands at least by 4:30. If Murphy were concerned with his fudge, his action should have been around 2:00 P.M., not as here, after 8:30 at night. Thus, although Bensinger's concern with making the City Edition of the *Tribune* was plausible, Mur-

KRUGER: I'm for that.

BENSINGER: Sure—He's one of the biggest alienists in the world. He's the author of that book, *The Personality Gland.*[32]

McCUE: And where to put it.

BENSINGER: *(Modestly into phone.)* He just autographed it for me.

MURPHY: Did he bite his initials in your pants, too ? . . . Nickel.

KRUGER: *(Into phone lazily.)* Give me the City Desk!

BENSINGER: *(Into phone.)* All right. He's going to examine him in about fifteen minutes. I'll let you know. *(He hangs up and resumes his study of* The Personality Gland.*)*

KRUGER: *(Very tired.)* Kruger calling! Nothing new on the hanging.

SCHWARTZ: Say, how about roodles on straights or better?[33] I want to get some of my dough back.

WILSON: Hey, I thought we weren't going to give them alienists any more free advertising.

ENDICOTT: That's the fourteenth pair of whiskers they called in on this god-damned case.

MURPHY: Them alienists make me sick. All they do is goose you and send you a bill for five hundred bucks.

---

phy's trying to make the fudge on the *Journal* was not.

[29]*Friends of American Liberty.* Probably, but not assuredly, the authors' version of the American Civil Liberties Union. If so, the reference is some ur-McCarthyism.

[30]*Dr. Max J. Eglehofer.* The name is adapted from Jacob Egelhoff, a reporter mainly for German-language newspapers in Chicago. He was born in Germany and emigrated to the United States about 1888. He began his career with the German-language press shortly before the Columbian Exposition of 1893. He joined the City News Bureau in 1918, but became court reporter for the *Chicago Abendpost* in 1919. Still in that capacity, he died of a stomach ailment on June 2, 1931. (See his obituary in the *Chicago Tribune*, June 4, 1931, p. 25.) The character of Dr. Eglehofer is thought to be based on Wilhelm Stekel, the Viennese psychoanalyst whom Hecht interviewed in Chicago in 1913. From the interview Hecht apparently developed the low opinion of psychiatrists evident in the play. (See Hecht's *A Child of the Century*, p. 155; *Gaily, Gaily*, pp. 62–85.)

Hecht seems to have been extremely fond of the name. Slightly altered to "Eggelhoffer," the character reappears as a Viennese medical specialist in radium poisoning in Hecht's film *Nothing Sacred* for David O. Selznick in 1937.

[31]*United Federation for World Betterment.* Apparently a fictional organization.

[32]*The Personality Gland.* None of Stekel's various books has a title as simplistic as this. The book is apparently fictional.

[33]*roodles.* A roodle is a token, such as a beer cap, placed in a poker pot, which when

McCUE: *(Into phone.)* This is McCue. . . . Looks like the hanging's coming off at seven all right. . . . Yeah, the Governor's[34] gone fishing and can't be found. . . . No, fishing. *(From the direction of the jail comes a sudden whirr and crash.)* They're testing the gallows now. . . . Yeah—testing 'em, with sandbags. . . . Maybe you can hear 'em. *(He holds up phone toward window and laughs pleasantly. Then, bitterly.)* What? The same to you! *(Hangs up. Another whirr and crash.)*

SCHWARTZ: I wish they'd quit practicing. It makes me nervous.

WILSON: Up a dime.

KRUGER: *(Yelling out of window.)* Hey, Jacobi![35] Quit playing with that gallus! How do you expect us to do any *work?*

VOICE FROM JAIL YARD: Cut that yelling, you goddamned bums!

McCUE: Ain't much respect for the press around here. *(The fire alarm sounds the same number as before.)*

McCUE: That's a second alarm, ain't it?

MURPHY: Who cares?

KRUGER: *(Motionless.)* Probably some orphanage.

MURPHY: Maybe it's another cathouse. Remember when Big Minnie's[36]

---

won gives the holder the right to choose the type of poker to be played in the next hand.

[34]*the Governor.* The reference is almost certainly to Lennington "Len" Small (1862–1936) of Kankakee. Small had been active in downstate Republican politics from the beginning of the twentieth century, serving as state treasurer twice, 1904 to 1908 and 1917 to 1919. He was elected governor at the general election of 1920 and took office on January 10, 1921. He was considered a very servile member of Thompson's political clique, consistently with the ire the Mayor shows to him in the play for a reprieve that might ruin the Republicans. Shortly after taking office as governor, Small was indicted by an action of the anti-Thompson Republican attorney general, Edward J. Brundage, for embezzlement and conspiracy for acts during his second tenure as state treasurer. Small was found not guilty, but was forced to pay $650,000 in a civil suit. Small's principal positive accomplishment was bringing to fruition Illinois's initial system of concrete-surfaced roads. By the time he left office on January 14, 1929, he could claim responsibility for a network of some 7,000 miles of hard-surfaced roads, the largest in the country.

Small was governor of Illinois at almost any time to which the play could be assigned. If the play is assigned to an earlier date than January 10, 1921, the governor was Frank E. Lowden (1861–1943), a Republican who took office on January 8, 1917. A considerably more reputable politician than Small, Lowden devoted himself mainly to fiscal reform and to improvement of race relations following the

burned down, and the Mayor of Galesburg came running out? *(A phone rings.)*

THE CARD PLAYERS: Dime. . . . I call. . . . Two sixes. *(Etc.)*

McCUE: *(Answering phone.)* What? The Mayor's office! *(To the rest.)* Maybe a statement.

KRUGER: Tell 'em we're busy.

McCUE: *(Into phone.)* Hello. *(Then exuberantly.)* Hello, you goddamn Swede! *(To the others.)* It's Hildy.

MURPHY: What's he doing in the Mayor's office?

McCUE: *(Into phone.)* What? What's that? What? *(To the others.)* He's stinko! *(Into phone.)* What are you doing with the Mayor!

MURPHY: If he's got any left, tell him to bring it over.

McCUE: *(Into phone.)* Huh? Kissing him good-bye?

ENDICOTT: Tell him to come over and kiss us.

MURPHY: I'm getting ready.

McCUE: *(Into phone.)* Well hurry up. *(To the room.)* He's stepping high.

MURPHY: What did he say?

KRUGER: Is he coming over?

McCUE: That's what he said.

THE CARD PLAYERS: Pass. . . . By me. . . . Take a deal. *(Etc.)*

(WOODENSHOES EICHHORN enters.[37] He a big, moon-faced, childish, and incompetent German policeman.)

Chicago riots of 1919. Lowden, who was more independent than Small, was fre quently overtly hostile to Thompson.

[35] *Jacobi.* Edward L. Jacoby, a career guard in the Cook County Jail. As the text states, he was assistant jailer in the early 1920s, subordinate to Chief Jailer George F. Lee.

[36] *Big Minnie's cathouse.* This brothel is not identifiable, but the implication is that it was a lower-class one. Names such as this were typically of black madams who operated on the South Side. Herbert Asbury, the historian of red light districts, notes that about the time of the Columbian Exposition of 1893, one such woman, called Big Maud, operated a brothel known as the Dark Secret on Clark near 12th Street. (*Gem of the Prairie: An Informal History of the Chicago Underworld* [New York: Alfred A. Knopf, 1940], p. 106.)

Vern E. Whaley believes that Big Minnie's was an actual brothel near the Club de Lisa, the leading black night club of the period. This implies that the brothel was in the vicinity of Garfield Boulevard (55th Street) and State Street.

[37] *Woodenshoes Eichhorn.* Based on Herman F. "Wooden Shoes" Scheuttler, superintendent of Police during World War I. Scheuttler was born in Chicago on July 14, 1861, joined the police force on July 12, 1883, and became superintendent on January 11,

BENSINGER: Hello, Woodenshoes. Got any news?

WOODENSHOES: *(Solemnly.)* I just been over to the death house. Did you hear what Earl Williams said to the priest?

ENDICOTT: Aw, forget it!

MURPHY: The paper's full of the hanging now. We ain't got room for the ads.

BENSINGER: *(Looking up from his book.)* What did he say, Woodenshoes?

WOODENSHOES: *(Awed.)* He says to the priest that he was innocent.

MURPHY: Do you know any more jokes?

WOODENSHOES: Well, I'm just telling you what he says.

MURPHY: I suppose that copper committed suicide. Or maybe it was a love pact.

WOODENSHOES: Well, Williams has got a very good explanation for that.

ENDICOTT: *(Derisively, to the reporters.)* He'll start crying in a minute. *(To WOODENSHOES.)* Why don't you send him some roses, like Mollie Malloy?

SCHWARTZ: Yeah. She thinks he's innocent, too.

WOODENSHOES: You fellas don't understand. He admits killing the policeman, but he claims they're just using that as an excuse to hang him, on account he's a radical. But the thing that gets me—

McCUE: Before you go on, Woodenshoes, would you mind running down to the corner and getting me a hamburger sandwich?

WOODENSHOES: *(Patiently.)* Personally, my feeling is that Earl Williams is a dual personality type on account of the way his head is shaped. It's a typical case of psychology. *(The card game goes on.)* Now you take the

---

1917. He died in office at Alexian Brothers Hospital on August 22, 1918. (See the *Chicago Tribune*, August 23, 1918, p. 1.)

[38]*the nigger vote is important.* The play occurs before the massive conversion of the African-American population from Republican to Democratic early in the administration of Franklin D. Roosevelt. Thus, the preoccupation of the Republican politicians in the play with maintaining loyalty of the South Side ghetto is realistic: without that loyalty they could not elect a Republican mayor—and after losing it they never again did so.

[39]Presumably because the Holocaust had intervened, this entire speech is deleted from the acting edition of 1950.

[40]*Diamond Louie.* There were two gangsters to whom this name might apply. The more likely is "Diamond" Louis Alterie, one of the most prominent thugs of the period. He was born in California in 1885 as Leland Deveraigne; the family contracted the surname to "Varain." He adopted the name "Louis Alterie" from a boxer whom he admired. After some early experiences in California including, remarkably, a short

events leading up to the crime; his hanging a red flag out of the window on Washington's Birthday. That ain't normal, to begin with. The officer ought to have realized when he went up there that he was dealing with a lunatic. I'm against having colored policemen on the force, anyway. And I'll tell you why—

ENDICOTT: *(Suddenly.)* Make that two hamburgers, will you, Woodenshoes, like a good fellow?

WOODENSHOES: *(Hurt.)* I thought you fellas might be interested in the psychological end of it. None of the papers have touched that aspect.

MURPHY: *(Profound, but casual.)* Listen, Woodenshoes, this guy Williams is just a bird that had the tough luck to kill a nigger policeman in a town where the nigger vote is important.[38]

KRUGER: Sure! If he'd bumped him off down south they'd have given him a banquet and a trip to Europe.

McCUE: Oh, the South ain't so bad. How about Russia, where they kill all the Jews and nobody says anything?[39]

MURPHY: Williams was a bonanza for the City Hall. He gets hung—everybody gets elected on a law and order platform.

ENDICOTT: "Reform the Reds with a Rope." *(WILSON makes an unprintable sound.)*

MURPHY: When that baby drops through the trap tomorrow, it's a million votes. He's just a divine accident. Bet a dime.

WOODENSHOES *(Blinking through the above.)* That's it—an accident. He didn't know it was a policeman, even. Why, when this officer woke him up—

McCUE: *(Tolerantly.)* Sure. You're right, Woodenshoes. And ask 'em to put a lot of ketchup on one of them sandwiches, will you!

WILSON: *(Sore.)* I haven't filled a hand all night. *(DIAMOND LOUIE,[40] a*

---

period as a policeman in Venice, he moved to Chicago, where he became active in labor racketeering, identifying himself with Dion O'Banion and thereby establishing himself as an anti-Capone hoodlum. About 1920 Alterie organized Local 25 of the Office, Theater & Amusement Janitors Union, which he had separated from the established Motion Picture Operators Union. Hostility from the Capone mob, which looked upon him as an irresponsible blowhard, caused Alterie to withdraw from Chicago to operate a dude ranch near Glenwood Springs, Colorado. He married Erma Rossi, daughter of Mike Rossi, a leading figure in Denver crime. Alterie shot two salesmen in a Denver hotel room in 1932, incurring a sentence of one to five years in a Colorado penitentiary, to be suspended on condition that he leave Colorado. He returned to Chicago in 1933, where the end of Prohibition and the incarceration of Al Capone diverted organized crime's attention to the labor racketeering in *ham gunman, enters. He is sleek, bejeweled, and sinister to everybody but the caballeros of the pressroom, who knew him when he ran a fruit stand. He is greeted with unction.)*

LOUIE: Hello, fellows.

SCHWARTZ: Well, well, well! Diamond Louie!

MURPHY: If it ain't the Kid himself! Oooh! Look at the pop bottles!

McCUE: Hurry up, Woodenshoes! I'm starving!

KRUGER: Get one for me, Woodenshoes!

BENSINGER: Make mine a plain lettuce—on gluten bread.

WOODENSHOES: *(Blinking.)* Where am I gonna get the dough for all these eats!

McCUE: Charge it.

MURPHY: You got a badge, ain't you? What's it good for?

WOODENSHOES: *(Shuffling out.)* Four hamburgers and a lettuce.

DIAMOND LOUIE: Where's Hildy Johnson?

ENDICOTT: *(Rudely.)* Up in Minnie's room.

MURPHY: Who wants to know?

KRUGER: Say Louie, I hear your old gang is going to bump off Kinky White.[41]

---

which Alterie specialized. Alterie was assassinated in front of his apartment building at 922 Eastwood Avenue in the Uptown area on the morning of July 18, 1935. Two men shot him with a total of nineteen bullets and shotgun pellets from an apartment across the street that they had engaged for the purpose. The attack was variously attributed to Alterie's attempts to muscle in on the Motion Picture Operators Union, or an effort of the Capone mob, now headed by Frank Nitti, to move in on the Janitors Union. At the time of his death Alterie was three weeks short of his fiftieth birthday. In the grand tradition, the murder was never solved. (See the *Chicago Tribune*, July 19, 1935, p. 1, with follow-up news items throughout July.) Although the use of thugs to intimidate newsdealers was practiced in this period, Alterie is not known to have worked for a newspaper, and there is no evidence whether he once ran a fruit stand.

The less likely prospect is "Diamond Lou" Cowen, a secondary figure in the Capone organization. A tiny man, only five feet tall, Cowen was a news vendor outside the office of the *Cicero Tribune* during Al Capone's takeover of Cicero about 1923. Capone vested title to some $500,000 worth of apartment buildings in Cowen's hands and made him the bail bondsman for the organization. When Capone ousted Robert St. John as publisher of the *Cicero Tribune*, he installed Cowen as publisher, giving Cowen his only known newspaper connection. Locally, he was considered the slot machine king of the western suburbs. On October 27, 1933, while on his way home from the Sportsman's Park race track, in which he held an equity, Cowen was as-

DIAMOND LOUIE: *(With sinister reticence.)* Is that so?

MURPHY: Better wait till after election[42] or you won't make the front page.

ENDICOTT: Yeah. We had to spike that Willie Mercer[43] killing.

DIAMOND LOUIE: Well, I'll tell you. I'm off that racket. I don't even associate with them fellas anymore.

MURPHY: Go on! You gotta kill somebody every day or you don't get any supper.

DIAMOND LOUIE: No. No kiddin'. I'm practically retired, you know what I mean?

SCHWARTZ: Retired from what! You never carried anything but a bean blower![44]

DIAMOND LOUIE: All joking aside. Honest. I'm one of you fellas now. I'm in the newspaper game.

MURPHY: *(With scorn.)* You're what?

ENDICOTT: He's gettin' delusions of grandeur.

DIAMOND LOUIE: Yeah. That's right. I'm a newspaperman . . . working for Walter Burns.

WILSON: What!

ENDICOTT: *(Very politely.)* What you doin' for Burns? A little pimping?[45]

---

sassinated in his automobile on Roosevelt Road in Cicero. Again, the murderers were not apprehended. Partly because of his small stature, Cowen is an unlikely prototype for the Diamond Louie of the play. His operations were almost entirely in the Cicero area, he had no known associations with the major Chicago newspapers, and he came to prominence only in the mid-1920s, too late for the authors' tenure in Chicago. (See the account of Cowen's assassination in the *Chicago Tribune*, October 28, 1933, p. 1; Laurence Bergreen, *Capone: The Man and the Era* [New York: Simon & Schuster, 1994], pp. 119–24, 359.)

[41]*Kinky White.* If this reference is to a gangster of the time, there are several alternatives, none of whom is known to have been called "Kinky." The best known, and the most likely, is William "Three Finger Jack" White, a Capone mobster active in the Chicago Teamsters Union. On the basis of photographs, he did have curly hair. He began his career with the gang of William "Klondike" O'Donnell on the West Side but progressed to the Capone organization as it came to dominate the area. Alternatively, "Bud" White was operator of the gambling ship *City of Traverse*, and "Pudgy" White was a North Side hoodlum active in the Weiss-O'Banion-Moran mob. Because of Alterie's identification with the O'Banion interests, logically the speech should not refer to "Pudgy" White.

Alternatively, if this was one of Hecht's and MacArthur's known associates in Chicago, the best prospect is Martin A. White, a reporter for the *Tribune* and *American* around the turn of the century. He began his career with the *Tribune* in 1895,

MURPHY: He's marble editor.

DIAMOND LOUIE: *(With dignity.)* I'm assistant circulation manager for de nort' side.

WILSON: Got a title and everything.

ENDICOTT: Burns'll be hiring animal acts next.

SCHWARTZ: What d'ye want Hildy for? Tailing him for Walter?

ENDICOTT: What do you know about that, Louie. We hear he's quit the *Examiner.*

McCUE: Yeah. What's the dope, Louie?

DIAMOND LOUIE: Well, I don't think it's permanent, you know what I mean?

SCHWARTZ: What the hell happened?

ENDICOTT: They must of murdered each other, the way Walter sounded.

DIAMOND LOUIE: Naaaa! Just a little personal argument. Nothin' serious.

McCUE: Come on . . . what's the dirt?

DIAMOND LOUIE: I don't know a single thing about it.

McCUE: Should we tell Hildy you were lookin' for him?

DIAMOND LOUIE: *(With affected nonchalance.)* No. Never mind. *(Again the whirr and crash of the gallows. LOUIE looks.)* What's that?

---

but left local journalism to join the Associated Press in 1908. He rose to general news editor of AP, but resigned in 1931 to become general manager of King Features and Universal Services, a post he held until 1937. He then became director of information for the Federal Trade Commission and assistant to the chairman. Still holding these positions, he died in Washington at age seventy-three on April 30, 1946. (See his obituary in the *Washington Post,* May 1, 1946, p. 16.)

[42]*the election.* Although the prospect of an imminent election is basic to the plot, it cannot be identified as any actual election. To satisfy the internal logic of the play, it would have to be held with both Mayor Thompson and Sheriff Hoffman in office and seeking reelection, but there was never such an election. The closest approximation was the mayoralty election of April 3, 1923, when both men were in office, but Thompson had declined to run because of irregularities in the Chicago school system. That election is consistent with the Mayor's viewing the prospects as very insecure for the Republicans, for Democrat William Emmett Dever defeated the anti-Thompson Republican Arthur C. Lueder.

[43]*Willie Mercer.* Probably either William Mercer, 3258 Vernon, or William D. Mercer, 3661 S. Wabash, both waiters.

[44]*You never carried anything but a bean blower!* This is probably a reference to one of the frustrations of Alterie's life: He wanted to be called "Two-Gun Louie," but he could not convince the press he was that lethal and thus could never escape the

ENDICOTT: They're fixin' up a pain in the neck for somebody.

DIAMOND LOUIE: *(With a genteel lift of his eyebrows.)* Hah! Mr. Weeliams!

MURPHY: They'll be doing that for you some day.

DIAMOND LOUIE: *(Very flattered.)* Maybe. *(To the players.)* Well—keep your eye on the dealer. *(He starts to leave.)*

MURPHY: *(Turning from the card game for the first time.)* Wait a second, Louie. *(DIAMOND LOUIE pauses politely.)* Come here. *(As DIAMOND LOUIE approaches.)* Where do you keep your cap pistol? . . . Here? *(He gooses DIAMOND LOUIE.)*

DIAMOND LOUIE: *(With a leap.)* Hey! For God's sake! Look out, will you! Jesus, that's a hell of a thing to do! . . . *(He exits angrily.)*

ENDICOTT: *(Calling after him.)* Call again, Louie.

MURPHY: Any time you're in the building.

KRUGER: And don't bump off anybody before election day.

MURPHY: *(Sadly.)* Louie hasn't got much self-control.

ENDICOTT: What do you know about Hildy? Looks like he's quit, all right.

WILSON: Yeah . . . What do you think of that?

ENDICOTT: There won't be any good reporters left after a while.

MURPHY: *(Gently.)* No. Mossie Enright[46] getting stewed and falling down the elevator shaft. And poor old Larry Malm.[47]

---

nickname "Diamond Louie." (See William T. Moore, *Dateline Chicago: A Veteran Newsman Recalls Its Heyday* [New York: Taplinger Publishing Co., 1973], p. 171.)

[45]In the acting edition "A little pimping?" is replaced by "Writing the Society colmun?" [sic].

[46]*Mossie Enright.* Maurice E. "Mossy" Enright, one of the major hoodlums of the era. A pioneer in labor racketeering, he was murdered in front of his home, 1110 W. Garfield Boulevard, by Sunny Jim Cosmano at dusk on February 3, 1920. (See the *Chicago Tribune*, February 4, 1920, p. 1.) The use of this name for a reporter is strange, for much of the audience would inevitably recognize the actual Enright. Hecht in 1923 stated that this event occurred to a reporter named Jack Lawson, who rose from a poker game at the Press Club and stepped smilingly into the elevator shaft. If so, I have failed to find any substantiation. (*Chicago Literary Times*, no. 17 [November 1, 1923], p.1.)

[47]*Larry Malm.* Lawrence Y. Malm, a reporter for the *Chicago Daily News*, the *Journal*, and the City News Bureau in the early years of the century. He began his career as a copyboy for the *Daily News* about 1895. A lifelong bachelor, he worked for the *Journal* from about 1911 to 1917, thereby becoming acquainted with Hecht. In 1923 Hecht stated that Malm, who he said looked like a Swedish cherub after a hard night, while drunk was placed as a practical joke in a wagon between two piles of corpses from the Iroquois Theatre fire of 1903. Upon awaking with a hangover, Hecht said,

SCHWARTZ: And Carl Pancake that disappeared.[48] *(A phone rings.)*

ENDICOTT: *(Answering it.)* Hello. . . Oh hello, Mr. Burns. Why, he was in the mayor's office a few minutes ago . . .

(HILDY JOHNSON[49] enters. He is a happy-go-lucky Swede with a pants-kicking sense of humor. He is barbered and tailored like a normal citizen—a fact that at once excites the wonder and mirth of his colleagues. Hildy is of a vanishing type—the lusty, hoodlumesque, half-drunken caballero that was the newspaperman of our youth. Schools of journalism and the advertising business have nearly extirpated the species. Now and then one of these boys still pops up in the profession and is hailed by his editor as a survivor of a golden age. The newspapermen who have already appeared in this pressroom are in reality similar survivors. Their presence under one roof is due to the fact that Chicago is a sort of journalistic Yellowstone Park offering haven to a last herd of fantastic braves that once roamed the newspaper offices of the country. Mr. Johnson carries a new suitcase, two paper parcels, and—a cane! A rowdy outburst succeeds his entrance.)

MURPHY: *(Loudly.)* Ooh! Lookit the cane! What are you doing? Turning fairy?

McCUE: Yum, yum! Kiss me!

WILSON: Where the hell you been?

ENDICOTT: Walter Burns on the wire, Hildy.

HILDY: What's that?

McCUE: What's the matter, Hildy? My God! He's got a shave!

SCHWARTZ: Jesus! Look at the crease in his pants!

ENDICOTT: It's Walter Burns, Hildy. Will you talk to him for God's sake!

Malm was so unstrung by the episode that he remained drunk for three years. Malm, sent by the City News Bureau to cover a suicide attempt at City Hall in 1918, raced up five flights of stairs, incurring a condition reported as "dilation of the the heart." Pneumonia set in, and he died on January 6, 1918, at age thirty-eight. (*Chicago Literary Times* 1, no. 17 [November 1, 1923], p. 8. See also Hecht, *A Child of the Century*, p. 137. Obituaries of Malm appear in the *Chicago Daily News*, January 7, 1918, p. 16, and the *Chicago Tribune*, January 10, 1918, p. 15.)

[48]*Carl Pancake that disappeared.* Karl Darling Pancake, a reporter who began his career at age sixteen on the *Inter Ocean* in 1894. He served as a crime reporter on the *Tribune* but shifted to the Hearst papers and was last reported in the Chicago City Directory as rewrite editor of the *American* in 1911. Pancake does, in fact, disappear from the directory thereafter. Sent to Los Angeles to cover the trial in 1911 of the brothers John J. and James B. McNamara for the bombing of the *Los Angeles Times* on October 1, 1910, he developed a fondness for Southern California and moved there in 1913. Pancake surfaces in the *Los Angeles City Directory* in 1924 as

HILDY: Tell that paranoiac bastard to take a sweet kiss for himself! . . . Come on Ernie! . . . *(Sings.)* "Good-bye, forever . . ."[50]

ENDICOTT: Say, listen, Hildy. Will you do me a personal favor and talk to Walter! He knows you're here.

McCUE: He's calling up about nine million times.

KRUGER: All we do is answer that goddamn phone . . .

MURPHY: What's the matter? Scared of him?

HILDY: I'll talk to that maniac—with pleasure. *(Into phone, with mock formality.)* Hello, Mr. Burns. . . . What's that, Mr. Burns?. . . Why your language is shocking, Mr. Burns. . . Now, listen, you lousy baboon. Get a pencil and paper and take this down: Get this straight because this is important. It's the Hildy Johnson curse. The next time I see you—no matter where I am or what I'm doing—I'm going to walk right up to you and hammer on that monkey skull of yours until it rings like a Chinese gong. . . .

McCUE: Oh, boy!

ENDICOTT: That's telling him!

HILDY: *(Holding sizzling receiver to the nearest reporter.)* Listen to him! *(Into phone.)* No, I ain't going to cover the hanging! I wouldn't cover the last supper for you! Not if they held it all over again in the middle of Clark Street. . . . Never mind the Vaseline, Jocko! It won't do you any good this time! Because I'm going to New York like I told you, and if you know what's good for you, you'll stay west of Gary, Indiana! A Johnson never forgets! *(He hangs up.)* And that, boys, is what is known as telling off the managing editor. *(The reporters agree loudly.)*

BENSINGER: Can't you guys talk without yelling?

HILDY: *(His song rising again.)* "Good-bye Forever!"

(Voice from jail yard.) Hey cut the yodeling! Where do you think you are!

HILDY: *(Moving toward window, takes out his pocket flask.)* Hey, Jacobi!

---

an apartment owner and real estate operator. He had a continuous residence in Los Angeles at various addresses thereafter and beginning in 1937 was listed as a writer. He is reported among Chicago press veterans to have been active in photojournalism. He died in Los Angeles on October 29, 1943, at age sixty-five. (See his obituary in the *Los Angeles Times*, November 2, 1943, p. 9, printed without change in the *Chicago Tribune*, November 2, 1943, p. 18.)

[49] *Hildebrand Johnson.* John Hilding Johnson. See pp. 44–45.

[50] *Good-bye, forever.* Possibly "Good-bye Forever, Tomorrow We Part," by Tony Stanford (1901), but there were several songs with similar titles, notably the nineteenth-century ballad, "Farewell Forever" of Michael Connelly and H. B. Farnie.

Pickle-nose! *(He takes a final drink from the flask, then aims and throws it out the window. A scream of rage arises from the jail yard. HILDY smiles and salutes his victim.)* On the button! *(Turns to ERNIE, resumes his song.)*

BENSINGER: *(Pleading.)* Oh, shut up!

WILSON: What did you quit for, Hildy?

SCHWARTZ: We hear you're going to get married?

HILDY: I'm getting married, all right. *(Shows tickets.)* See that! Three tickets to New York! Eleven-eighteen tonight![51]

WILSON: Tonight!

McCUE: Jesus, that's quick!

MURPHY: What do you mean three?

HILDY: Me and my girl and her goddamn ma!

ENDICOTT: Kinda sudden, ain't it?

SCHWARTZ: What the hell do you want to get married for?

HILDY: None of your business!

MURPHY: Ooooh! He's in love! Tootsie-wootsie!

McCUE: Is she a white girl?

ENDICOTT: Has she got a good shape?

WILSON: Does Walter know you're getting married?

HILDY: Does he know I'm getting married? He congratulated me! Shook hands like a pal! Offered to throw me a farewell dinner even.

ENDICOTT: That's his favorite joke—farewell dinners.

MURPHY: He poisons people at them.

HILDY: He gets me up to Polack Mike's[52]—fills me full of rotgut—I'd have been there yet if it hadn't been for the fire escape!

SCHWARTZ: That's what he done to the Chief of Police!

HILDY: Can you imagine? Trying to bust up my marriage! After shaking hands! . . . *(Anxiously.)* Say, my girl didn't call up, did she, or come in looking for me? What time is it, anyway?

---

[51] *eleven-eighteen tonight.* The reference is almost certainly to the New York Central's train 90, the all-Pullman overnight express to Cleveland known successively as the Chicago-Cleveland Special and as the Forest City. The train left La Salle Street Station during the 1920s at times between 11:00 and 11:30 P.M., though never at 11:18. In the summer of 1927, when the play was written, the train left at 11:10. By connection with train 60 at Cleveland and train 50 at Buffalo, Hildy's party could have been in New York by 10:10 the following evening. The only alternative—a very inferior one—would have been train number 28 at 11:25 P.M., which would have provided only a second-morning arrival in New York. There were no later departures.

[52] *Polack Mike's.* Presumably an actual speakeasy but unidentifiable.

SCHWARTZ: Quarter past nine.

McCUE: Eighteen minutes after.

HILDY: *(Starting to take off his coat.)* I got to be at this house at seven.

ENDICOTT: What house?

HILDY: Somebody giving a farewell party to my girl.

WILSON: At seven tonight?

HILDY: Yeah?

MURPHY: You got to run like hell.

HILDY: Oh, that's all right. Fellow doesn't quit a job every day. Especially when its Walter Burns. The lousy baboon —

ENDICOTT: When's the wedding, Hildy?

HILDY: It's in New York, so you guys ain't going to have any fun with it. None of them fake warrants or kidnapping the bride, with me! *(HILDY folds his old shirt and puts it in BENSINGER'S drawer.)*

BENSINGER: Aw, for God's sake! Cut that out! *(Throws the shirt on the floor.)*

WILSON: Everybody's getting this New York bug. It's just a rube town for mine.[53]

SCHWARTZ: I was on a New York paper once—the *Times*. You might as well work in a bank.

MURPHY: I hear all the reporters in New York are lizzies.[54]

McCUE: Remember that fellow from the New York World?

ENDICOTT: With the derby?

MURPHY: *(Presumably mimicking a New York journalist.)* Could you please instruct me where the telegraph office is? *(Makes a rude noise.)* You'll be talking like that, Hildy.

HILDY: Yeah?

ENDICOTT: Which one of them sissy journals are you going to work for?

HILDY: None of them! Who the hell wants to work on a newspaper? A lot of crumby hoboes, full of dandruff and bum gin they wheedle out of nigger aldermen.[55]

---

[53] *a rube town.* A hick town, a strange epithet for New York.

[54] *lizzies.* Early twentieth-century slang for effeminate males. See Lester V. Berrey and Melvin Van Den Bark *The American Thesaurus of Slang*, 2d ed. (New York: Thomas Y. Crowell Co., 1953), p. 360.

[55] *nigger aldermen.* This characteristic passage is all that remains of Alderman Willoughby, a character based on William Hale Thompson's ally, alderman Oscar De-Priest, to be played by Charles Gilpin, but excised from the play immediately after the dress rehearsal. (See the introduction and Notes to the Text.) The English librettist Dick Vosburgh restored Alderman Willoughby to the characters who take the stage in his *Windy City* of 1982.

MURPHY: That's what comes of stealing a cane.

ENDICOTT: What are *you* going in for—the movies?

HILDY: I am not. Advertising business. One hundred and fifty smackers a week.

McCUE: Yeah?

ENDICOTT: One hundred and fifty *what?* [56]

SCHWARTZ: *(A sneer.)* A hundred and fifty!

HILDY: Here's the contract. *(Hands it to McCUE, who starts to look through it. They crowd around this remarkable document.)* I was just waiting to get it down in black and white before I walked in and told Walter I was through.

McCUE: *(With contract.)* Jesus, it *is* a hundred and fifty!

WILSON: Was Walter sore?

HILDY: The lousy snake-brain! The goddamn ungrateful ape! Called me a traitor, after ten years of sweating my pants off for practically nothing. Traitor to what! What did he or anybody else in the newspaper business ever do for me except try to make a bum out of me! Says "You can't quit without notice!" What the hell does he think I am? A hired girl? Why, one more word and I'd have busted his whiskey snout for him!

KRUGER: Why didn't you?

MURPHY: Who's going to cover the hanging for the *Examiner?* [57]

McCUE: Why the hell didn't you tell a fellow?

WILSON: Yeah—instead of waiting till the last day?

HILDY: And have Walter hear about it? I've always wanted to walk in and quit just like that! *(A snap of the fingers.)* I been planning this for two

---

[56] In the acting edition, Murphy simultaneously delivers a line, "Go tell Aunt Rhody!" The line is the opening of a folk song:

Go tell Aunt Rhody
That the old grey goose is dead.
The one she's been savin'
To make a feather bed.
She died in the millpond
A-standin' on her head.

[57] *Who's going to cover the hanging for the* Examiner? This is a conspicuous flaw in the plot. As important as the hanging is delineated, it is inconceivable that the *Herald and Examiner* would not have made a definite arrangement for a reporter to be at courthouse in the face of the uncertainty of Hildy's being there. In the 1974 motion picture version a young reporter called Rudy Keppler was written into the script to deal with the problem.

months—packed up everything yesterday, and so did my girl! Furniture and all. *(The fire signal has been sounding through the last few words. HILDY looks up.)* Hey, fellows, that's Kedzie and Madison ain't it? The Washington Irving School's out there.[58]

MURPHY: Who the hell's in school this time of night?

McCUE: What do you care, anyhow? You've quit.

HILDY: *(Laughs, chagrined.)* Just thought it might be a good fire, that's all. *(Again the whirr and crash of the gallows.)*

KRUGER: For Christ's sake! *(At the window.)* Ain't you got anything else to do? Hey! You Jacobi!

BENSINGER: Hey, fellows. I'm trying to read.

WILSON: *(Also near window.)* They're changing the guards down there. Look—they've got sixteen of them. *(Voices come from the courtyard—"Hey!" "Hurry up." "Get a move on, Carl!" etc.)*

McCUE: *(Hands back the contract.)* You're going to miss a swell hanging, Hildy.

HILDY: Yeah? You can stick it.

MURPHY: So you're going into the advertising business, eh? Writing poetry about Milady's drawers.

ENDICOTT: Going to wear an eyeshade?

WILSON: I'll bet he has a desk with his name on it, and a stenographer.

MURPHY: You'll be like a fire horse tied to a milk wagon.

ENDICOTT: *(To Murphy.)* I don't know what gets into these birds. Can you imagine punching a clock and sitting around talking like a lot of stuffed shirts about statistics?

HILDY: Yeah—sour grapes, that's all it is. Sour grapes.

MURPHY: I got a dumb brother went in for business. He's got seven kids and a mortgage and belongs to a country club. He gets worse every year. Just a fathead.

HILDY: Listen to who's talking. Journalists! Peeking through keyholes! Running after fire engines like a lot of coach dogs! Waking people up in the middle of the night to ask them what they think of companionate marriage.[59] Stealing pictures off old ladies of their daughters that get raped

---

[58]*Washington Irving School.* An actual grammar school at 2140 W. Lexington Avenue.

[59]*companionate marriage.* This reading is found in the excerpts published in *Theatre.* Companionate marriage was a proposed marital relation in which the couple agreed to forego parenthood until they had established compatibility. If they proved incompatible, and no children had been born to them, they could divorce simply by mutual consent without either party having a financial obligation to the other. The

in Oak Park. A lot of lousy, daffy, buttinskis, swelling around with holes in their pants, borrowing nickels from office boys! And for what! So a million hired girls and motormen's wives'll know what's going on.

MURPHY: Your girl must have handed you that line.

HILDY: I don't need anybody to tell me about newspapers. I've been a newspaperman fifteen years.[60] A cross between a bootlegger and a whore.[61] And if you want to know something, you'll all end up on the copy desk— gray-headed, humpbacked slobs, dodging garnishees when you're ninety.[62]

SCHWARTZ: Yeah, and what about you? How long do you think you'll last in that floozie job!

ENDICOTT: You'll get canned cold the minute your contract's up, and then you'll be out in the street.

KRUGER: Sure—that's what always happens.

HILDY: Well, it don't happen to me. And I'll tell you why, if you want to know. Because my girl's uncle owns the business, that's why.

WILSON: Has he got a lot of jack?

HILDY: It's choking him. You know what he sent us for a wedding present!

MURPHY: A dozen doilies.

---

proposal was at its peak of interest at the time the play was produced, for its principal advocate, Judge Benjamin Barr Lindsey of Denver (with a coauthor, Evans Wainright), in the previous year had produced a book advocating the arrangement, *The Companionate Marriage* (New York: Boni & Liveright, 1927). Necessarily, the proposal was highly controversial, for it entailed both birth control and divorce, to which ethical opposition was still widespread. A hostile commentary by a leading official of the Anti-Saloon League was Noah C. Gause, *Companionate Marriage?* (Newark, NJ: Victory Letter Shop, 1928). Unfortunately, the only known copy of Gause's book is the copyright deposit in the Library of Congress, which was reported stolen or lost in 1984. Possibly because of the subject's controversial nature, "companionate marriage" in the Covici-Friede edition is replaced with "Mussolini." Surprisingly, "companionate marriage" returns in the acting edition of 1950, even though the concept had largely passed out of currency. No-fault divorce has superseded it in modern law.

[60] *I've been a newspaperman fifteen years.* Hilding Johnson became a newspaperman in 1908. Thus, the statement places the action in 1923, within the time period in which the majority of events in the play occurred. If the line is attributed to Charles MacArthur, the action would have to be set in 1930, two years after the play appeared.

[61] *A cross between a bootlegger and a whore.* This line, one of the most widely quoted from the play, is dropped from the acting edition—one of the least defensible bowdlerizations of the text.

HILDY: I wouldn't tell you bums, because it's up in high finance and you wouldn't understand it.

ENDICOTT: Probably gave you a lot of stock in the company that you can't sell.

KRUGER: I know them uncles.

HILDY: The hell he did! He gave us five hundred cash, that's what he gave us.

McCUE: Go on!

SCHWARTZ: There *ain't* five hundred in cash.

HILDY: Yeah? *(Pulling out a roll.)* Well, there it is—most of it, except what it costs to get to New York.

McCUE: Jeez, let's see.

HILDY: Oh, no!

MURPHY: How about a finif[63] till tomorrow!

HILDY: *(Mimicking an androgyne.)* I won't be here tomorrow. And that reminds me. *(Takes out a little book.)* It comes to *(Consults book.)* eight dollars and sixty-five cents altogether, Jimmie. Eight dollars and sixty-five cents.

MURPHY: What does?

HILDY: That includes the four bucks in front of the Planters Hotel,[64] when you were with that waitress from King's.[65]

MURPHY: I thought I paid that.

---

[62]This passage succinctly states a chronic fear of reporters. No one, most of them felt, wanted an old reporter, producing the adverse progression that Hildy describes.

[63]*finif.* A five dollar bill. See Berry, *The American Thesaurus of Slang*, pp. 16, 423, 458, 525. The term was mainly identified with racetracks, where it was used for the number five in odds, as well.

[64]*Planters Hotel.* A moderately priced hotel at 19 N. Clark Street, nine stories tall, immediately north of Hecht's favorite intersection, Madison and Clark. The hotel was designed by architect J. E. O. Pridmore and opened early in 1912. It contained two hundred rooms and was integral with a theater, originally called the Columbia. The hotel was closed about 1974 and razed to provide land for the present First National Bank plaza. (See "The New Planters Hotel, Chicago," *Hotel Monthly* 20, no. 230 [May, 1912], 58–59.)

[65]*King's.* An inexpensive restaurant at 32 N. Wells Street, purported originator of chicken à la king. Its modest prices made it a favorite of the reporters, and its location on the strip of restaurants along Wells Street made it convenient to their offices. Like many of the traditional Loop restaurants, King's was unable to survive Prohibition and closed in the early 1920s.

HILDY: No. *(Reading from notes.)* Herman Schlosser . . . altogether twenty dollars and . . .

McCUE: Ha! Ha! Ha!

ENDICOTT: Ho! Ho! Ho!

HILDY: All right. I guess I might as well call it off, all around. I should have known better than to try to collect, anyhow. *(Tears out the page and throws it at Murphy.)* You might say thanks.

MURPHY: Not after that waitress.

SCHWARTZ: About that fifty bucks, Hildy. If you want a note —

HILDY: What fifty bucks? Aw, forget it.

SCHWARTZ: You see, it wasn't only the wife taking sick, but then besides . . . *(JENNIE,[66] a slightly idiotic scrubwoman, enters. She receives an ovation. "Yea, Jennie!" "Jennie!" "Well, if it ain't Jennie," all delivered in various dialects with intended comedy effect.)*

KRUGER: I hear you just bought another apartment house, Jennie!

MURPHY: I hear you've fallen in love again, Jennie!

JENNIE: *(Giggling.)* Can I wash up now, please?

BENSINGER: Yeah, for God's sake do! This place smells like a monkey cage.

HILDY: Go on! You don't want to wash up on a night like this! This is a holiday! I'm going away, Jennie! Give us a kiss! *(He embraces her.)*

JENNIE: *(Squealing.)* Now you Hildy Johnson, you keep away from me! I'll hit you with this mop! I will!

HILDY: *(Tickling her.)* What's the matter? Ain't I your fellow any more? I'll tell you what we'll do, Jennie! You and I'll go around and say good-bye! Everybody in the building!

McCUE: Hey, the warden called you up! Wants to see you before you go!

HILDY: There you are Jennie! We're *invited!* He invited Jennie, didn't he? You bet he did!

JENNIE: Now you know he didn't!

HILDY: *(Lifting pail of water.)* Only we can't carry this all over! *I* know! *(At window.)* Hey! Jacobi! Look! *(Throws water out. Jennie giggles hysterically.)*

---

[66]*Jennie.* Unfortunately, personnel records of the Cook County Sheriff's Department before 1945 have not survived, making it impossible to search for janitorial employees such as this woman. Of the known personnel of the correctional institutions with whom the authors were presumably in contact in the course of their duties, the only apparent candidate is Jennie Armbruster, a matron in the Chicago city jail. (See "Pay Rolls of the City of Chicago for the Month of May, 1915," printed copy in Municipal Reference Collection, Chicago Public Library, p. 228.)

VOICE: *(Off.)* Who did that?

SCHWARTZ: Better shut off them lights. Somebody's liable to come up.

HILDY: *(To Jennie.)* Come on, Jennie! We'll say good-bye to the warden! *(He embraces her again.)*

JENNIE: *(Struggling.)* No, no! You let go of me! The warden'll be mad! He'll *do* something!

HILDY: To hell with him! *I* own this building! Come on! *(Pausing in the door.)* If my girl calls up, tell her I'm on my way! *(Exits with JENNIE, singing "Waltz Me Around Again, Jennie."*[67] *Coy screams from JENNIE, and the banging of a pail as it is kicked down the corridor.)*

BENSINGER: Thank God *that's* over!

KRUGER: What's the *Examiner* going to do with Hildy off the job?

WILSON: It must be great to walk into a place and quit.

McCUE: Yeah. *(He moves sadly away and uses one of the phones on the long table.)* Diversey three two hundred.

ENDICOTT: *(Sentimentally.)* I got an offer from the publicity department of the stockyards last year. I shoulda took it.

SCHWARTZ: What I'd like would be a job on the side.

McCUE: *(A lump in his throat.)* A desk and a stenographer. That wouldn't be so bad. I wouldn't mind a nice big blonde.

MURPHY: *(Outlining a voluptuous bust.)* With a bozoom! *(Phone on small table rings.)*

McCUE: *(Sighs, then into his own phone.)* Hello, Sarge. McCue. Anything doing?

WILSON: *(Answering other phone.)* What's that? *(His tone becomes slightly formal.)* Yes, ma'am. . . . No, Hildy ain't here just now, madam. He left a message for you, though. . . . Why, he said he was on his way. . . . No, he didn't say where—just that he was on his way. . . . All right, I'll tell him, ma'am. *(Hangs up.)* Oooh! Is *she* sore!

SCHWARTZ: Hildy oughtn't to do that. She's a swell kid.

McCUE: *(Into phone.)* All right! Thank you, Sarge! *(Hangs up.)* A hundred and fifty bucks a week! Can you imagine?

KRUGER: Probably gets Saturdays and Sundays off, too.

WILSON: *(Sadly.)* And Christmas.

McCUE: I wonder who Walter'll send over here in Hildy's place.

---

[67] *Waltz Me Around Again, Jennie.* An adaptation of the popular song, "Waltz Me Around Again, Willie," by Will D. Cobb and Ren Shields, from "His Honour the Mayor" (1906).

(MOLLIE MALLOY[68] *enters. She is a North Clark Street tart, cheap black sateen dress, red hat and red slippers run over at the heels. She is a soiled and gaudy houri of the pavement. Despite a baleful glare on MOLLIE'S part, the boys brighten visibly. They are always glad to see whores.*[69])

MURPHY: *(Warmly.)* Hello, Mollie!

ENDICOTT: Well, well! Nookie!

WILSON: Hello, kid! How's the old tomato can?

McCUE: *(Feeling himself to be a Chauncey Olcott.*[70]) Shure, and how are yez, Mollie?

MOLLIE: *(In a tired, banjo voice.)* I've been looking for you bastards![71]

MURPHY: Going to pay a call on Williams?

SCHWARTZ: He's just across the courtyard!

KRUGER: Better hurry up—he hasn't got all night.

McCUE: Yes, he has!

ENDICOTT: *(Formally.)* Say, Mollie, those were pretty roses you sent Earl. What do you want done with them tomorrow morning?

MOLLIE: *(Tensely.)* A lot of wise guys, ain't you? Well, you know what I think of you—all of you.

MURPHY: Keep your pants on, Mollie.

---

[68]*Mollie Malloy.* Given Hecht's pride in his thorough acquaintance with prostitution in Chicago, this character was either the portrayal of an unidentified individual streetwalker, or a representative type based on various women the authors had known. As noted in the introduction, she is, unfortunately, stereotypical. The designation of her as a "North Clark Street tart" is actually a courtesy to differentiate her from inmates of the South Clark Street brothels of an earlier period. On the basis of reported police cases, streetwalkers of the time worked out of the Normandie and other North Clark Street hotels. The area continued to be identified with prostitution until well after World War II, though mainly with B-girls operating in strip joints and other local bars.

There seems no prospect that the authors would have neglected to give Mollie the surname of someone they wanted to identify with her. Her name is most probably based on John Anthony "Jack" Malloy, whom they knew as city editor of the *Herald and Examiner* in the early 1920s. Malloy was to rise to a director's post in the Hearst empire. Malloy was born in Chicago, and in his mid-teens became a property boy at Powers Theatre. There an actor, Arnold Daly, suggested he take up journalism. He went with the *Chicago Day Book*, a tabloid that accepted no advertising, in 1915. He joined the *Daily News* in 1918 and the *Herald and Examiner* in 1920. He associated with both Hecht and MacArthur in news coverage in the early 1920s. Hecht considered Malloy a hypocrite with respect both to liquor and prostitution: "For instance the crack vice and bootlegging investigators who from day to day star-

MOLLIE: *(To Murphy.)* If you was worth breaking my fingernails on, I'd tear your puss wide open.

MURPHY: What you sore about, sweetheart? Wasn't that a swell story we give you?

MOLLIE: You cheap crumbs have been making a fool out of me long enough!

ENDICOTT: Now what kind of language is that?

BENSINGER: She oughtn't to be allowed in here! I caught her using the drinking cup yesterday!

MOLLIE: *(Flaring.)* I never said I loved Earl Williams and was willing to marry him on the gallows! You made that up! And all that other crap[72] about my being his soul mate and having a love nest with him!

McCUE: Well, didn't you?

ENDICOTT: You've been sucking around that cuckoo ever since he's been in the death house! Everybody knows you're his affinity!

MOLLIE: *(Blowing up.)* That's a lie! I met Mr. Williams just once in my life, when he was wandering around in the rain without his hat and coat on like a sick dog. The day before the shooting. And I went up to him like any human being would and I asked what was the matter, and he told

---

tle the readers of the town with their pious revelations of graft and viciousness are as a rule such men as Jack Malloy . . . hearty drinkers of moonshine, and carefree lovers of the life that goes on in the 'low dives' they righteously expose." (Ben Hecht, "What a Newspaper Reporter Remembers," Part I, *Chicago Literary Times* 1, no. 17 [November 1, 1923], p. 8.) Malloy became sports editor of the *New York American*, but returned to Chicago as city editor of the *American* in 1929. In 1930 he began eight years of service with the Hearst papers in Boston. In May, 1939, he was made managing editor of the *Chicago American*, and in 1942 became executive editor of the merged *Chicago Herald-American*. He remained in that position when he died abruptly of a heart attack in Chicago on March 19, 1943, at age forty-seven. (See his obituary in the *New York Times*, March 20, 1943, p. 15.)

Alternatively, this may be a reference to Larry Mulay, an employee of the City News Bureau from 1919. He was city editor of the bureau for thirty years until his retirement in 1974. He died in Sun City, Arizona, at age eighty-three in 1988. At the time of his retirement, he stated that he was the prototype for one of the characters in *The Front Page*, and it is difficult to find an alternative to this one. (See Bob Weidrich, "Being Educated by Larry L. Mulay," *Chicago Tribune*, June 2, 1974, sec. I, p. 5.) Mulay had a stolid, conventional personality that presented no particular reason for the authors to identify him with Mollie. In addition, it is unlikely that Mulay would have been prominent enough in Chicago journalism by the time Hecht and MacArthur left the city to have warranted inclusion in the play.

me about bein' fired after working at the same place twenty-two years and I brought him up to my room because it was warm there.

ENDICOTT: Did he have the two dollars?

MURPHY: Aw, put it on a Victrola.

MOLLIE: Just because you want to fill your lying papers with a lot of dirty scandal, you got to crucify him and make a bum out of me!

ENDICOTT: Got a match, Mollie?

MOLLIE: *(Heedless.)* I tell you he just sat there talking to me . . . all night . . . just sat there talkin' to me . . . and never once laid a hand on me! In the morning he went away and I never saw him again till the day at the trial!

ENDICOTT: Tell us what you told the jury! *(They laugh reminiscently.)*

MOLLIE: Go on, laugh! God damn your greasy souls![73] Sure I was his witness—the only one he had. Yes, me! Mollie Malloy! A Clark Street tart! I was the only one with guts enough to stand up for him! And that's why you're persecuting me! Because he treated me decent, and not like an animal, and I said so!

ENDICOTT: Why didn't you adopt him instead of letting him run around shooting policemen?

SCHWARTZ: Suppose that cop had been your own brother?

Finally, the name may be adapted from Captain Dennis E. Malloy of the Chicago Police Department, who as chief of the Sheffield Station in 1929 was indicted for accepting gambling payoffs. (See *Chicago Daily News*, May 13–15, 1929, passim.)

[69]*They are always glad to see whores.* Alan Brien, a British journalist, in an exceptionally perceptive review of the first London production, pointed out a more basic reason why the reporters should have warmed to a prostitute:

Work in a newspaper office and work in a brothel have a lot in common[:] Frenzied bouts of quite enjoyable activity interrupting long, lazy periods of niggling, card-playing, drinking, boasting and reminiscing. On the lowest level, a willingness to take on all comers, to treat all contacts as equal, venturing out in every kind of weather to bring back a succession of one-night stands. At the higher level, the chance to specialise, to be able to refuse unsuitable assignments, eventually even of earning a flat with a maid or a desk with a secretary. And whipping you along, the retired hooker, the Editor or Madam (rarely called upon to perform personally between the sheets except for crowned heads, Prime Ministers and millionaires), by a mixture of bullying and flattery, with an occasional bonus for overtime. For both the aim is to get everything safely 'to bed' by 3 A.M. You could even cite the proprietor in the background who owns the property, and foots the bills, but is careful not to reveal too much knowledge of what goes on behind this facade. The money earned may not be all that rewarding—but at least it is paid for natural talents which education would only spoil. And how many of your school-fellows and neighbours could say the same?

MOLLIE: I wish to God it had been one of you!

MURPHY: *(Finally irritated.)* Say, what's the idea of this song and dance, anyhow? This is the pressroom. We're busy.

SCHWARTZ: Go on home!

MURPHY: Go and see your boyfriend, why don't you?

McCUE: Yeah—he's got a nice room.

ENDICOTT: *(With a wink at the rest.)* He won't have it long. He's left a call for seven A.M.

MOLLIE: *(Through her teeth.)* It's a wonder a bolt of lightning don't come through the ceiling and strike you all dead! *(Again the sound of the gallows.)* What's that? Oh, my God! *(She begins to cry.)*

BENSINGER: *(Rising.)* Say, what's the idea?

MOLLIE: Talking that way about a fellow that's going to die.

ENDICOTT: *(Uncomfortable at this show of grief.)* Don't get hysterical.

MOLLIE: *(Sobbing.)* Shame on you! Shame on you!

McCUE: *(To the rest.)* It wasn't my fault. I didn't say anything.

MOLLIE: *(Hysterically.)* A poor little crazy fellow that never did any harm. Sitting there alone this minute, with the Angel of Death beside him, and you cracking jokes.

MURPHY: *(Getting up meaningly.)* Listen, if you don't shut up, I'll give you something *good* to cry about!

MOLLIE: *(Savage.)* Keep your dirty hands off me!

MURPHY: *(In a short and bitter struggle with her.)* Outside, *bum!*

MOLLIE: *(Shooting through the door.)* You dirty punks! Heels! Bastards! *(Exits.)*

MURPHY: *(Slams the door. A pause.)* The nervy bitch![74]

McCUE: Whew!

MURPHY: You guys want to play some more poker?

ENDICOTT: What's the use? *I* can't win a pot.

MURPHY: I'm the big loser.

WILSON: Me too. I must be out three dollars, anyhow.

(*Plays and Players*, XIX, No. 11, Issue 227 [August 1972], 35–36. Compare Hildy Johnson's evaluation of his profession on p. 86.)

[70]*Chauncey Olcott.* A ballad singer, songwriter, and actor in musical comedy who specialized in Irish material. He was born in 1857 or 1858 and died in 1932.

[71]In the acting edition, "bastards" is replaced by "bums."

[72]In the acting edition, "crap" becomes "bunk."

[73]*God damn your greasy souls!* For the British censor's specific objections to this phrase, see the introduction.

[74]This line is replaced in the acting edition with "The nerve of that streetwalker."

ENDICOTT: It's goddamn funny who's got it.

SCHWARTZ: Don't look at me. I started in with five bucks, and I got two-eighty left.

McCUE: *(Who has taken up the phone again.)* Michigan eight thousand. *(SHERIFF HARTMAN[75] enters, briskly, bitter words forming on his lips. He is a diabetic and overwrought little fellow, an incompetent fussbudget. He has come to raise hell, but an ovation checks him. "Ah, Sheriff!" "Hello, Pinky!" "How's the old statesman?" BENSINGER puts down his book; MCCUE abandons his telephoning.)*

ENDICOTT: Any news, Sheriff?

SHERIFF: *(Briefly.)* Hello fellas. *(In another tone.)* Now, who dumped that bucket of water out the window?

KRUGER: What bucket of water?

SHERIFF: Who threw it out the window is what I asked, and I want to know!

MURPHY: Judge Pam[76] threw it out.

SHERIFF: I suppose Judge Pam threw that bottle!

ENDICOTT: Yeah. That was Judge Pam, too.

MURPHY: He was in here with his robes on, playing fireman.

---

[75]*Sheriff Peter B. Hartman.* Peter M. Hoffman, sheriff of Cook County from 1922 to 1926. Hoffman had entered politics as a member of the Cook County Board of Commissioners in 1898 and served as coroner from 1904 to 1922. A lifelong resident of Des Plaines in northwestern Cook County, he was widely looked upon in the western suburbs as a tool of the John Torrio mob, predecessor of the Capone organization. Because Hoffman was not a physician, his qualifications for the office of coroner were suspect. (See the editorial, "Retire Coroner Hoffman," *Oak Leaves* [Oak Park, IL], May 29, 1920, p. 8.)

As sheriff, Hoffman had the unusual experience of being himself imprisoned. In 1925 Hoffman and Warden Wesley Westbrook were accused of providing illicit privileges, including unauthorized leaves from the Cook County jail, to two leading figures in the Torrio-Capone mob, Terry Druggan and Frankie Lane. Judge James H. Wilkerson found both officials in contempt of court for allowing the leaves in violation of the judge's incarceration order, sentencing Hoffman to thirty days in jail plus a fine of $2,500 and Westbrook to four months without a fine. Mercifully, Wilkerson ordered Hoffman to the DuPage County jail in Wheaton, sparing the sheriff the embarrassment of being incarcerated in his own jail. He served his full term from June 12 to July 12, 1926. Westbrook was sent to the DeKalb County jail in Sycamore. Particularly because the episode appeared to verify the popular image of Hoffman as a toady of the Capone mob, not even with the moral standards being demonstrated in the play could Hoffman have survived in office. He had protested his in-

SHERIFF: Come on now, fellas, I know who it was. *(Wheedling.)* It was Hildy Johnson, wasn't it? Where is he?

McCUE: Out with a lady.

ENDICOTT: Hildy's quit, Sheriff. Didn't you hear?

SHERIFF: Well, I'm glad of it. It's good riddance! Now personally, I don't give a goddamn, but how do you suppose it looks to have a lot of hoodlums yelling and throwing things out of windows? *(In a subdued voice.)* Besides there's somebody *in* that death house. How do you suppose he feels, listening to all this re-*vel*-ery?

MURPHY: A hell of a lot you care how he feels!

SCHWARTZ: Keep your shirt on, Pinky.

SHERIFF: Wait a minute, you! I don't want to hear any more of that Pinky stuff. I got a name, see, Peter B. Hartman.

MURPHY: What's the matter with Pinky?

McCUE: *(Taking the cue.)* He's all right.

THE REPORTERS: *(Lustily.)* Who's all right?

SHERIFF: *(Desperate.)* Now stop! *(Whining.)* Honest, boys, what's the idea of hanging a name like that on me? Pinky Hartman! How's that look to the voters? Like I had sore eyes or something.

---

nocence of wrongdoing throughout, but he resigned as sheriff on December 27, 1926, citing the impossibility of enforcing the Prohibition laws locally. Hoffman was replaced by Charles E. Graydon, who was supported by the Democrats and Deneen Republicans. (See the *Chicago Daily News*, December 27, 1926, p. 1.)

The nickname of "Pinky" that the Sheriff finds so offensive in the play is thought to derive from Hoffman's practice of wearing a ring on his little finger. Hoffman died in St. Francis Hospital in Evanston on July 30, 1948, at age eighty-five. (Obituary in the *Chicago Tribune*, July 31, 1948, p. 4.) A short biographical sketch dating from early in his career is in *Notable Men of Chicago and Their City* [Chicago: Chicago Daily Journal, 1910], p. 159.)

[76]*Judge Pam.* Hugo Pam, judge of the Cook County Superior Court. Pam was born in Chicago on January 20, 1870, and educated in Chicago schools. He graduated from the University of Michigan in 1892 and prepared himself for the bar. He was elected to the Superior Court as a Republican in 1911 and remained in office until his death. A lifelong bachelor of independent income, Pam devoted himself to a wide variety of efforts at improvement of procedures in criminal law, better administration of pardons and paroles, and care of the mentally ill both in legal actions and in penology. He was chairman of the planning committee for the criminal court-jail complex of 1929.

Pam died in New York on May 29, 1930, on his way home to Chicago from Palm Beach, Florida, where in declining health he had spent the winter. (On Pam, see

MURPHY: You never heard of Bathhouse John[77] kicking, did you?

WILSON: Or Hinky Dink?[78]

ENDICOTT: It's made you famous!

SHERIFF: I swear I don't know what to do about you fellows. You abuse every privilege you get. I got a damn good notion to take this pressroom away from you.

MURPHY: That would be a break.

ENDICOTT: Yeah. The place is so full of cockroaches you can't walk.

BENSINGER: *(Rising.)* Wait a minute, fellows. Now listen, Pete, this is the last favor I'm ever going to ask you, and it ain't me that's asking it. Get me? *You* know who's asking it—a certain party is asking it.[79] Once and for all, how about hanging this guy at five o'clock instead of seven? It ain't going to hurt you and we can make the City Edition.

SHERIFF: *(Sincerely.)* Aw, now, Roy, that's kind of raw. You can't hang a fella in his sleep, just to please a newspaper.

MURPHY: No, but you can reprieve him twice so the hanging'll come three days before election! So you can run on a law and order ticket! You can do that all right!

SHERIFF: I had nothing whatsoever to do with those reprieves. That was entirely up to the Governor.

ENDICOTT: And who told the Governor what to do?

SCHWARTZ: How do we know there won't be another reprieve tonight? For all I know I'm hanging around here for nothing! When I've got a sick wife!

Hyman L. Meites, *History of the Jews of Chicago* [Chicago: Jewish Historical Society, 1990; reprint of original of 1924], p. 331; obituary in the *Chicago Tribune*, May 30, 1930, p. 3.)

[77] *Bathhouse John.* Alderman John Coughlin (1860–1938) of the first ward. The sobriquet had its origin in Coughlin's early employment as a masseur in public bathhouses, but was later identified with his toleration of prostitution in bathhouses and elsewhere in his ward. (See Robert K. King, "The Legend of Bathhouse John," *The Prohibition Era Times* 6, no. 4 [August–September], 1995, p. 6.)

[78] *Hinky Dink.* Alderman Michael Kenna (1858–1946), also of the First Ward. Coughlin and Kenna were closely identified with corruption, especially with toleration of prostitution in their ward, notably in the vicinity of 22nd and Clark Streets.

[79] *a certain party.* Probably, but not assuredly, Colonel Robert R. McCormick (1880–1955), publisher of the *Tribune* from 1911 to his death. On McCormick, see Richard Norton Smith, *The Colonel: The Life and Legend of Robert R. McCormick* (Boston: Houghton Mifflin, 1997).

WILSON: Yeah, with another alienist getting called in!

MURPHY: This wop gooser![80]

SCHWARTZ: Sure—what's all that about? Suppose he finds he's insane or something?

SHERIFF: He *won't* find he's insane. Because he isn't. This ruse of reading the Declaration of Independence day and night is pure fake. But I've got to let this doctor see him, on account of his being sent by these Personal Liberty people, or whatever they call themselves. You and I know they're nothing but a bunch of Bolsheviks, but a hanging is a serious business. At a time like this you want to please everybody.

ENDICOTT: Everybody that can vote, anyhow.

SHERIFF: Now he's going to look him over in my office in a couple of minutes, and then you'll know all about it. Besides, there's nothing he *can* find out. Williams is as sane as I am.

SCHWARTZ: Saner!

SHERIFF: The hanging's going to come off exactly per schedule. And when I say "per schedule" that means seven o'clock and not a minute earlier. There's such a thing as being humane, you know.

BENSINGER: Just wait till *you* want a favor.

SHERIFF: *(To change the subject.)* Now here are the tickets. Two for each paper.

McCUE: What do you *mean,* two for each paper?

SHERIFF: *(Stung.)* What do you want to do—take your family?

SCHWARTZ: Now listen, Pete. I promised a pair to Ernie Byfield.[81] He's never seen a hanging.

---

[80] The acting edition replaces "This wop gooser" with "This wop or whatever he is."

[81] *Ernie Byfield.* Ernest L. Beifeld, owner-manager of the Sherman Hotel, and one of the most conspicuous Chicagoans of the first half of the twentieth century. The family under the name of Beifeld immigrated from Hungary and anglicized the name in the wave of anti-German feeling in World War I. As host of the Sherman's night club, the College Inn, Byfield was among the first to direct a large facility to a youthful crowd for the dating relation. A public-spirited man, he used the hotel for various benevolent purposes. He was later to be proprietor of the two Hotels Ambassador on the near North Side, including the Ambassador East's Pump Room, the traditional dining place of celebrities when changing trains in Chicago. Byfield died at age sixty on February 10, 1950. (See his obituary, "Ernest Byfield Death Mourned Coast to Coast," *Chicago Tribune,* February 11, 1950, sec. 2, p. 7. On his operations, mainly at the Ambassador East, see Alva Johnston, "Chicago's Gaudy Innkeeper," *Saturday Evening Post,* October 17, 1947, p. 15 ff.; October 25, 1947, p. 39 ff.; November 1, 1947, p. 24 ff.)

WILSON: The boss wants a couple for the advertising department.

SHERIFF: *(Passing out tickets.)* This ain't the "Follies," you know. I'm tired of your editors using these tickets to get advertising accounts.

ENDICOTT: You got a lot of nerve! Everybody knows what *you* use 'em for— to get in socially.

MURPHY: He had the whole Union League Club[82] over here last time.

ENDICOTT: Trying to suck in with Chatfield-Taylor.[83] I suppose you'll wear a monocle tomorrow morning.

SHERIFF: *(Melting.)* Now that ain't no way to talk, boys. If any of you want a couple of extra tickets, why I'll be more than glad to take care of you. Only don't *kill* it.

SCHWARTZ: Now you're talking!

WILSON: That's more like it.

SHERIFF: Only you fellas got to lend a hand with us once in a while. We got a big job on our hands, smashing this Red menace —

ENDICOTT: We gave you four columns yesterday. What do you want?

SHERIFF: *(Always the boy for a speech.)* That ain't it. The newspapers got to put their shoulders to the wheel. They've got to forcibly impress on the Bolsheviks that the death warrant for Earl Williams is a death warrant for every bomb-throwing un-American Red in this town. This hanging means more to the people of Chicago today— *(To MURPHY, who is reading a comic supplement.)* This is a *statement,* Jimmie. What's the matter with you?

MURPHY: Aw, go home.

SHERIFF: All right, you'll just get scooped. Now we're going to reform these Reds with a rope. That's our slogan. Quote me if you want to: "Sheriff Hartman pledges that he is going to reform the Reds with a rope."

---

[82]*Union League Club.* The leading downtown club of suburban-dwelling executives in the Loop, a citadel of Republican political sympathies. At Jackson Boulevard and Federal Street, it is still in existence.

[83]*Chatfield-Taylor.* Hobart Chatfield Chatfield-Taylor (1865–1945), a Chicago author of independent means, who wrote novels for an upper-class market. He was the sort of writer for whom the reporters could only have contempt, but he did write well-reviewed biographies of Molière and the Italian comic dramatist Carlo Goldoni. (See his *Molière: A Biography* [New York: Duffield & Co., 1906]; *Goldoni: A Biography* [New York: Duffield & Co., 1913]. For a favorable evaluation of his lifework, see Jessica Calhoun Schwartz, "Hobart Chatfield-Taylor's Place in History," *Townsfolk* 38, no. 3 [June, 1948], pp. 16, 24.)

ENDICOTT: Oh, for Christ's sake, Pinky! We've been printing that chestnut for weeks! *(He goes into the can.)*

SHERIFF: Well, print it once more, as a favor to me.

WILSON: You don't have to worry about the election. You're as good as in now, with the nigger vote coming around.

SHERIFF: *(Lafayette, at least.)* I was never prejudiced against the Negro race in any shape, manner, or form.

MURPHY: Are *you* still talking?

SHERIFF: *(Suddenly querulous.)* During the race riots[84] I just had to do my duty, that's all. And of course I was misunderstood.

KRUGER: Go on! You're a southern gentleman, and you know it. *(Phone rings.)*

SHERIFF: Now, boys!

MURPHY: Shoah! *(In bogus Negro dialect.)* Massa Hartman, of the Vahginia Hartmans. *(Phone on small table rings. MCCUE heads for it.)*

ENDICOTT: *(In the can, his voice rising above the plumbing.)* I hear you used to own slaves.

SCHWARTZ: *(Answering phone.)* Pressroom! *(Into phone.)* Who? Yeah, he's here. . . . For you, Sheriff.

SHERIFF: Me? *(Into phone—very businesslike.)* Sheriff Hartman talking. . . . *(An eagle falling out of the clouds.)* Oh, hello, dear.

KRUGER: Sounds like the ball and chain.

SHERIFF: Why, no, I didn't figure on coming home at all. . . . Well, you see on account of the hanging being so early—

MURPHY: Tell her she's getting a break when you don't go home.

SHERIFF: *(Winningly.)* But you see this is business, dear. You don't think a hanging's any fun for me!

ENDICOTT: Music for this, Ernie!

SHERIFF: *(Agitatedly motions for silence.)* But I have a whole lot to do first— getting things ready.

MURPHY: Why don't you take him out to your house and hang him?

SHERIFF: *(Fish hooks in his pants.)* I'll call you up later, Irma[85]—I'm not in

---

[84]The reference is to the Chicago race riots of July 28–30, 1919. The passage is an anachronism, for Hoffman was still coroner at the time.

[85]*Irma.* Hoffman's wife, whom he had married about 1889, was named Emma May. (See the account of Mrs. Hoffman's visit to the sheriff while he was incarcerated in the *Chicago Tribune*, June 16, 1924, p. 4.) This is the first of two appearances in the play of the name "Irma," which the authors seem to have considered particularly suitable for comic uses.

my own office, now. Besides, I've got to meet an alienist. . . . No—alienist. No. Not for me. For Williams.

(HILDY reenters, bringing back Jennie's mop.)

HILDY: *(Throwing the mop across the room.)* Boy, we cleaned up!

SHERIFF: *(Hurriedly.)* I'll call you later, dear. *(He hangs up; turns on HILDY.)* Now Johnson, what the hell do you mean? Throwing things out of windows. Who do you think you are?

(During the quieter moments of the remainder of this act, HILDY is opening his parcels and putting the contents into his suitcase.)

HILDY: Who wants to know?

SHERIFF: You think you and Walter Burns are running this town! Well, I'm going to send a bill to the *Examiner* tomorrow for all the wreckage that's been committed around here in the past year! How do you like that?

HILDY: I think that's swell! You know what else you can do!

SHERIFF: *(Belligerently.)* What?

HILDY: Guess.

SHERIFF: You stick your nose in this building tomorrow and I'll have you arrested!

HILDY: It's damn near worth staying for!

SHERIFF: And I'll tell you another thing, and you can pass it on to Walter Burns! The *Examiner* don't get any tickets for this hanging after the lies they been printing! You can make up your story like you do everything else—out of whole cloth.

HILDY: Listen, you big pail of lard! If I wanted to go to your goddamn hanging I'd go! See? And sit in a box!

SHERIFF: The hell you would!

HILDY: And I'd only have to tell *half* of what I know, at that!

SHERIFF: You don't know *any*thing.

HILDY: No? Tell me, Mr. Hartman, where'd you spend the night before that last hanging! At the Planter's Hotel with that librarian. Room six hundred and two. And I got two bellboys and a night manager to prove it!

SHERIFF: If I didn't have to go and see that alienist, I'd tell *you* a few things. *(Exits.)*

HILDY: *(Calling after him.)* And if I were you I'd get two tickets for the hanging over to Walter Burns pretty fast, or he's liable to come over here and stick a firecracker in your pants![86]

---

[86]Following up the previous joke, the acting edition adds a line here, "That Planters crack doubled him up."

WILSON: Hey! Hildy! Your girl called up.

HILDY: *(Stricken.)* My girl? When? *(Starts for the telephone.)*

WILSON: Just after you went out. And if you take my advice, you'll call her back.

HILDY: Jesus! Why didn't you tell a fellow! *(WOODENSHOES re-enters with sandwiches and a bottle of ketchup.)*

McCUE: *Yea!* Sandwiches!

HILDY: *(At phone.)* Edgewater two-one-six-four. *(To the rest.)* Was she mad at me?

McCUE: Did you bring the ketchup? *(They are crowding about WOODEN-SHOES.)*

BENSINGER: How about my plain lettuce?

ENDICOTT: A hamburger for me!

SCHWARTZ: I ordered one, didn't I!

KRUGER: You did not! This way, Woodenshoes! *(They are taking their sandwiches from WOODENSHOES—ENDICOTT tosses one at KRUGER.)*

HILDY: *(Into phone.)* Hello, Peggy? . . . Hello. . . . *(His voice becomes romantic.)*

McCUE: Attaboy! God, I'm starved.

HILDY: *(Into phone.)* Why, darling, what's the matter?

BENSINGER: For God's sake, I said gluten bread.

HILDY: *(Into phone.)* But there isn't anything to cry about.

MURPHY: The service is getting terrible around here.

HILDY: *(Into phone.)* But listen, darling! I had business to attend to. I'll tell you all about it the minute I see you . . . Aw, darling, I just dropped in here for one second. . . . Because I *had* to. I couldn't go away without saying good-bye to the fellows. *(To the others.)* Will you guys talk or something? *(Back to phone.)* But listen! Sweetheart! . . . Yes, I . . . Of *course* I handed in my resignation . . . Yes, I've got a taxi waiting . . . Right outside.

WOODENSHOES: *(Uneasily.)* Go easy on that ketchup. I'm responsible for that.

HILDY: *(Into phone.)* I've got them right in my pocket, honey . . . Three on the eleven-eighteen. I'm bringing 'em right out, mile a minute.

WOODENSHOES: She says you fellows have got to pay something soon.

HILDY: *(Into phone.)* Aw, darling, if you talk like that I'm going to go right out and jump in the lake. I swear I will, because I can't stand it. Listen! *(He looks around to see if it is safe to continue.)*

KRUGER: We're listening.

HILDY: *(Trying to lower his voice. With his mouth pasted to the mouthpiece, the following speeches are gargled into phone.)* Darling . . . I love you. *(Appropriate music by KRUGER.)* I said . . . I love you. *(Music again.)*

SCHWARTZ: Aw, give him a break, Ernie. *(KRUGER stops playing.)*

HILDY: *(Into phone.)* That's more like it.

WOODENSHOES: Are you finished with this? *(Reaching for ketchup.)*

McCUE: *(Operating the bottle.)* No.

HILDY: *(Into phone.)* Feel better now? . . . Well, smile. And say something . . . You know what I want to hear.

SCHWARTZ: *(A Cinderella.)* Give me a half a one, somebody!

ENDICOTT: Nothing doing.

HILDY: *(Into the phone.)* That's the stuff. That's better . . . Are you all packed? . . . Oh, swell . . . I'll be right there.

WOODENSHOES: You fellas ought to pay her a little something on account. *(Exits.)*

WILSON: *(Answering Examiner phone.)* What do you want?

HILDY: Listen, darling, will you wear that little blue straw hat?

WILSON: *(Into phone.)* Wait a minute—I'll see.

HILDY: *(Into phone.)* And are you all happy now? I bet you're not as happy as I am. Oh, I'll bet you anything you want . . . All right . . . All right . . . I'm on my way. . . Not more than fifteen minutes. *Really* this time . . . Bye. *(Hangs up.)*

WILSON: *(His hand over the mouthpiece.)* Jesus Christ, Hildy—here's Walter again! Tell him to give us a rest, will you?

HILDY: Oh, bollocks![87] *(Into phone.)* You're just making a goddamn nuisance of yourself! . . . What's the idea of calling up all the time! . . . *No!* I'm through with newspapers! I don't give a goddamn what you think of me! I'm leaving for New York tonight! Right now! This minute! *(Hangs up. Phone rings again. He tears it from the wall and throws it out the window.)*

KRUGER: *(Calmly.)* Wrong number.

McCUE: *(Nervous.)* For God's sake, Hildy.

SCHWARTZ: *(Putting out the lights.)* You'll get us in a hell of a jam!

BENSINGER: Haven't you got any sense?

HILDY: *(Yelling out the window.)* Tell Pinky to stick that among his souvenirs! *(To the rest.)* If that lunatic calls up again, tell him to put it in writing and mail it to Hildebrand Johnson, care of the Waterbury-Adams Corporation,[88] Seven Thirty-five Fifth Avenue, New York City. . . .

---

[87] *Oh, bollocks!* "Bollocks" was an archaic term for testicles, which survived on the level of an oath, and in some slang locutions.

[88] *Waterbury-Adams Corp.*, 735 Fifth Avenue, New York City. Apparently a fictional

MURPHY: Put it on the wall, Mike.

ENDICOTT: *(Going to the rear wall.)* Waterbury what?

McCUE: Adams.

HILDY: *(Opening a parcel and showing a pale pair of gloves.)* How do you like those onions? Marshall Field!

McCUE: Very individual.

HILDY: Where's my cane?

ENDICOTT: What cane?

HILDY: *(Suddenly desperate.)* Come now, fellas. That ain't funny, who's got my cane?

MURPHY: *(In a Central Office manner.)* Can you describe this cane?

HILDY: *(Frantic.)* Aw, for God's sake! Now listen, fellas—

KRUGER: *(Solicitous.)* Are you sure you had it with you when you came into the room?

WILSON: Was there any writing on it?

HILDY: *(Diving into BENSINGER's desk.)* Come on! Cut the clowning! Where is it?

BENSINGER: Keep out of my desk! Of all the goddamn kindergartens!

HILDY: Jesus! I only got fifteen minutes. Now, cut the kidding! My God, you fellows have got a sense of humor!

MURPHY: Aw, give him his fairy wand!

ENDICOTT: *(A Uranian[89] for the moment, he produces cane from trouser leg.)* Here it is, Gladys.[90]

HILDY: God! You had me worried. *(He picks up his suitcase. Bravura.)* Well,

---

enterprise. Neither Hilding Johnson nor Charles MacArthur left Chicago for an advertising agency in New York. The prototype for this may be Ernie Pratt, who did operate an advertising agency in New York in midcareer, after his early experiences as a reporter in Chicago, and before returning to the *Tribune* to end his career as copy editor.

[89]*Uranian.* A celestial, or a being from outer space. In the context, it may be a corruption of "uranist," an informal medical term for a male homosexual. See Richard A. Spears, *Slang and Euphemism* (Middle Village, NY: Jonathan David Publishers, Inc., 1981), p. 410.

[90]*Gladys.* Believed to be a reference to Gladys Ryan Wherity, telephone operator at the City News Bureau for forty-two years. She died in 1986 at age ninety-one. Her principal talent was an encyclopedic knowledge of the reporters' hangouts, so as to be able to locate any of them on short notice. Wherity's tenure apparently began about the time the play appeared, however. An alternative is Gladys A. Erickson, a state correctional officer who also wrote for the Hearst papers. Helen Hayes wrote

good-bye, you lousy wage slaves! When you're crawling up fire escapes, and getting kicked out of front doors, and eating Christmas dinner in a one-armed joint, don't forget your old pal, Hildy Johnson!

ENDICOTT: Good-bye, Yonson.

McCUE: So long, Hildy.

MURPHY: Send us a postcard, you big stewbum.

KRUGER: When'll we see you again, Hildy?

HILDY: The next time you see me I'll be riding in a Rolls-Royce, giving out interviews on success.

BENSINGER: Good-bye, Hildy.

WILSON: Good-bye.

SCHWARTZ: Take care of yourself.

HILDY: So long, fellows! *(He strikes a Sidney Carton[91] pose in the doorway; starts on a bit of verse.)* "And as the road beyond unfolds"[92] *(He is interrupted by a terrific fusillade of shots from the courtyard. A roar of voices comes up from the jail yard. For a tense second everyone is motionless.)*

VOICES: *(In the courtyard.)* Get the riot guns! Spread out, you guys! *(Another volley.)*

WILSON: There's a jail break!

MURPHY: *(At window, simultaneously.)* Carlson![93] Jacobi! What's the matter? What's happened?

VOICES: *(In the jail yard)* Watch the gate! He's probably trying the gate! *(A huge siren begins to wail.)*

SCHWARTZ: *(Out the window.)* Who got away? Who was it?

VOICES: *(Outside.)* Earl . . . Williams!!!

THE REPORTERS: Who? Who'd he say? Earl Williams! It was Earl Williams! He got away!

McCUE: Holy God! Gimme that telephone! *(He works hook frantically.)* Hurry!

Gladys Wherity a letter of congratulation for her retirement dinner on April 21, 1980, an act that would be difficult to explain if Mrs. Wherity were not the Gladys of the play.

[91]*Sidney Carton*. The noble and self-sacrificing character of Charles Dickens's *A Tale of Two Cities*.

[92]If this is a quotation, I have failed to identify it. See my query in *Notes and Queries*, vol. 241 [New Series, vol. 43], no. 2 (June, 1996), p. 194; Professor Ralph MacPhail placed a query on the Internet. Neither of these evoked an identification.

[93]In the summary of the play in *Theatre* magazine in August 1928, p. 26, the line reads "Carlson! Jacobi!" Carlson was dropped from the Covici-Friede version but survives as "Carl" in footnote 151, following.

Hurry up! Will you! This is important. *(Others are springing for the telephones as searchlights sweep the windows from the direction of the jail.)*

SCHWARTZ: Jeez, this is gonna make a bum out of the Sheriff! *(HILDY stands paralyzed, his suitcase in his hand. There is a second rifle volley. Two windowpanes crash within the room. Some plaster falls. Gongs sound above the siren.)*

McCUE: *(Screaming.)* Look out!

MURPHY: *(Out of the window.)* Where you shooting, you goddamn fools! For Christ's sake! *(Another pane goes.)* Look out where you're aiming, will you!

SCHWARTZ: There's some phones in the state's attorney's office!

KRUGER: Yeah! *(There is a general panic at the door. The reporters leave as if a bomb had broken in a trench. HILDY is left alone, still holding his suitcase. It falls. He moves back into the room, absently trailing a chair. Another shot.)*

HILDY: Ahh, Jesus Christ! *(He lets go of the chair and takes one of the telephones.)* Examiner? Gimme Walter Burns! Quick! *(Very calmly he sits on one of the long tables, his back against the wall. Then, quietly.)* Hello, Walter! Hildy Johnson! Forget that! Earl Williams just lammed out of the County Jail! Yep. . . yep. . . yep. . . don't worry! I'm on the job! *(There is a third volley. HILDY sails his hat and coat into a corner and is removing his overcoat as the curtain falls.)*

CURTAIN

ACT II

The Scene is the same as Act I. It is twenty minutes later. Searchlights play outside the windows. JENNIE, the scrubwoman, is on stage, sweeping up broken glass and doing a little miscellaneous cleaning. WOODENSHOES enters.

WOODENSHOES: Where are all the reporters? Out looking for him?

JENNIE: They broke all the windows. And pulled off a telephone. Aiiy, those newspaper fellows. They're worse'n anything.

WOODENSHOES: There wasn't any excuse for his escaping. This sort of thing couldn't ever happen if they listened to me.

JENNIE: Oooh, they'll catch him. Those big lights.

WOODENSHOES: What good will that do society? The time to catch 'em is while they're little kids. That's the whole basis of my crime prevention theory. It's all going to be written up in the papers soon.

JENNIE: Ooooh, what they print in the papers. I never seen anything like it. *(She is sweeping. ENDICOTT enters and makes for a phone. WOODENSHOES watches him.)*

WOODENSHOES: Has anything happened, Mr. Endicott?

ENDICOTT: *(Into phone.)* Endicott calling. Gimme a rewrite man.

WOODENSHOES: You know, this would be just the right time for you to print my theory of crime prevention that you said you were going to. *(Pulling out a sheaf of documents.)*

ENDICOTT: *(Into phone, waving him off as if he were a horsefly.)* Well, hurry it up.

WOODENSHOES: Now here I got the city split up in districts. I got them marked in red.

ENDICOTT: What? For God's sake, can't you see I'm— *(Into phone.)* Hello! Gill?[94]

WOODENSHOES: But you been promising me you'd—

ENDICOTT: *(Snatches papers.)* All right—I'll take it home and study it. Now for God's sake stop annoying me—I got to work! I can't sit around listening to you! Get out of here and stop bothering me! *(Back to phone.)* Ready, Gill? . . . Now, here's the situation so far.

---

[94]*Gill.* The context requires Gill to be a rewrite man on the *Post*, but the reference is probably to Richard S. Gill, assistant wire chief at Associated Press during Hecht's early years in Chicago.

WOODENSHOES: *(To JENNIE.)* He's going to take it home and study it. You'll see it in the paper before long. *(Exits.)*

ENDICOTT: *(Into phone.)* Right! . . . At ten minutes after nine Williams was taken to the Sheriff's private office to be examined by this Professor Eglehofer, and a few minutes later he shot his way out . . . No nobody knows where he got the gun. Or if they do they won't tell . . . Yeah . . . Yeah . . . He run up eight flights of stairs to the infirmary and got out through the skylight. He must have slid down the rain pipe to the street . . . Yeah . . . No, I tell you nobody knows where he got it. I got hold of Jacobi, but he won't talk. *(MURPHY enters.)*

MURPHY: *(Crossing to phone.)* Outside, Jennie! Outside!

ENDICOTT: They're throwing a dragnet around the whole North Side. Watching the railroads and Red headquarters. The Chief of Police[95] has ordered out every copper on the force and says they'll get Williams before morning.

MURPHY: *(Into phone.)* Hello, sweetheart. Give me the desk, will you?

ENDICOTT: *(Into phone, after a final look at his notes.)* The Crime Commission[96] has offered a reward of ten thousand dollars for his capture . . . Yeah. I'm going to try to get hold of Eglehofer. He knows what's happened, if I can find him. Call you back. *(Hangs up and exits swiftly.)*

MURPHY: For Chris' sake, Jennie! Every time we turn our backs you start that goddamn sweeping.

JENNIE: *(Picking up her traps.)* All right. Only it's dirty. I get scolded.

MURPHY: *(Into phone.)* Murphy talking . . . No clue yet as to Earl Williams's

---

[95]*The Chief of Police.* Probably Charles C. Fitzmorris, chief of police at the time of the O'Connor escape. Fitzmorris was a police reporter until appointed secretary to Mayor Carter Harrison in 1911. He continued in that office under William Hale Thompson until Thompson appointed him chief of police in November 1920. Fitzmorris resigned without assigning a reason in April 1923. Thompson appointed Fitzmorris Comptroller of the city in 1927, but he resigned in July 1928. Fitzmorris died in Chicago on August 19, 1948. (Obituary in the *New York Times*, August 20, 1948, p. 17.)

[96]*Crime Commission.* This body had its origin in joint private efforts of Chicago businessmen as early as 1903 to reduce crime in the city. The executive committee of the Chicago Association of Commerce in 1917 set up a committee of ten to investigate crime. This body on June 13, 1918, recommended establishment of a permanent commission of Chicago business leaders. As the Chicago Crime Commission it began to operate in January 1919. It is still in existence. (Bertram J. Cahn, *The Story of the Chicago Crime Commission* [Chicago: Chicago Crime Commission, circa 1940].)

whereabouts. Here's a little feature, though. . . . A tear bomb . . . *tear bomb . . . criminals cry for it . . . (SHERIFF HARTMAN appears in the doorway. He has been running around, shouting a million orders, nervous, bewitched, and sweating like a June bride. He is in his shirt sleeves, and his diamond-studded badge of office is visible.)*

MURPHY: *(Into phone.)* Yeah! Tear bomb.

SHERIFF: *(As he enters, speaking to someone in the corridor.)* To hell with the Mayor! If he wants me he knows where I am.

MURPHY: *(Into phone.)* A tear bomb went off unexpectedly in the hands of Sheriff Hartman's bombing squad.

SHERIFF: *(Stunned.)* What went off?

MURPHY: *(Into phone.)* The following deputy sheriffs were rushed to Passavant Hospital[97] . . .

SHERIFF: A fine fair-weather friend you are!

MURPHY: *(Remorselessly, into phone.)* Philip Lustgarten[98] . . .

SHERIFF: After all I've done for you!

MURPHY: *(Phoning.)* Herman Waldstein[99]. . .

SHERIFF: Putting stuff like that in the papers!

MURPHY: *(Phoning.)* Sidney Matsburg[100] . . .

---

[97]*Passavant Hospital.* Passavant Memorial Hospital, 149 W. Superior Street. It is still in existence.

[98]*Philip Lustgarten.* This and the five following characters are said to be deputy sheriffs. They were not. Rather, the names are chosen from actual Chicago residents for the realism they convey. Probably, Paul A. Lustgarten, a clerk at 115 S. Dearborn. Alternatively, this may be Harry Lustgarten of the firm of Lustgarten & Mendelson, manufacturers' agents, 209 S. State Street, or a member of his family.

[99]*Herman Waldstein.* Herman S. Waldstein, a lawyer with an office at 155 N. Clark Street.

[100]*Sidney Matsburg.* Because the other men in this set of alleged deputy sheriffs are identifiable, there is little question that this man is actual, also. The name "Matsburg" is a fabrication. Consistent with the authors' methods of altering identifications, the most likely name is "Stamberg." The only apparent prospect is Rudolph Stamberg, a lithographer. Stamberg was born in Sweden, but was brought to Waukegan, Illinois, at age five. He moved to Chicago in 1913 and died there at age sixty-five on May 3, 1929. (Obituary in the *Waukegan Daily News,* May 4, 1929, p. 2.) Alternatively, the name may possibly be adapted from Peter G. Drautzburg (1871–1953), a police reporter for the *American, Inter Ocean,* and *Tribune* around the turn of the century.

SHERIFF: That's gratitude for you! *(He exits.)*

MURPHY: *(Phoning.)* Henry Koo[101] . . .

JENNIE: *(Going toward door.)* Ain't that terrible? *(KRUGER enters and goes to a phone.)*

MURPHY: *(Phoning.)* Abe Lefkowitz[102]

JENNIE: All those fellows! *(Exits.)*

KRUGER: *(At his phone.)* Give me rewrite.

MURPHY: *(Phoning.)* And William Gilhooly.[103] Call you back. *(Hangs up and exits.)*

KRUGER: *(Into phone.)* Ready? . . . A man corresponding to Earl Williams's description was seen boarding a southbound Cottage Grove Avenue car at Austen Avenue[104] by Motorman Julius L. Roosevelt.[105] *(McCUE enters.)* Yeah—Roosevelt. I thought it would make a good feature on account of the name.

McCUE: *(Phoning.)* McCue talking. Give me the desk.

KRUGER: *(Phoning.)* All right, I'll go right after it. Call you back. *(Exits.)*

McCUE: *(Into phone.)* Hello. Is that you, Emil? Are you ready? . . . Sidelights on the man hunt . . . Mrs. Irma Schlogel,[106] fifty-five, scrublady, was shot

---

[101]*Henry Koo.* Henry Kuh of Kuh, Nathan & Fisher, wholesale clothiers. In the acting edition the surname is spelled Koogh.

[102]*Abe Lefkowitz.* Abraham Lefkovitz, a clothier whose shop was at 1228 S. Wabash Avenue.

[103]*William Gilhooly.* William Gilhooley, a clerk resident at 344 W. 14th Street at the time of Hecht's arrival in Chicago in 1910.

[104]*Austen Avenue.* Austen Avenue is probably a typographical error for Austin Avenue, the street on which the Criminal Court Building was located during the period of the play. This spelling appears in all five printings of the Covici-Friede book and in the British edition, which was printed from the same plates. The name was changed from Michigan Street in 1914, and then again changed to Hubbard Street in 1937 to avoid confusion with Austin Boulevard, a major north-south thoroughfare on the far West Side. The two Cottage Grove Avenue car lines did not cross Austin Avenue per se, but rather ran south from a loop off Wabash Avenue adjacent to the Chicago Public Library between Washington and Randolph Streets. The passage may be an effort to present yet another example of the disdain of the reporters for the truth. More probably, Kruger refers to the Number 1 car line, which ran from Broadway and Howard Street at the city's north limits to a loop at 56th Street and Lake Park Avenue, using Cottage Grove for most of its mileage on the South Side.

[105]*Julius L. Roosevelt.* The name is adapted from Julius Rosenwald (1862–1932), president of Sears Roebuck & Co. and Chicago's leading public benefactor of the time.

[106]*Mrs. Irma Schlogel, fifty-five, scrublady.* The name identifies the woman as a

in the left leg while at work scrubbing the eighth floor of the Wrigley Building[107] by one of Sheriff Hartman's special deputies. *(There is a fusillade of shots in the distance. HILDY JOHNSON enters.)*

HILDY: There goes another scrublady. *(Goes to phone but starts arranging notes.)*

McCUE: *(Phoning.)* No, just a flesh wound. They took her to Passavant Hospital. *(Hangs up. To HILDY.)* Any dope on how he got out!

HILDY: From all I can get they were playing leapfrog.[108]

McCUE: How about Jacobi! Did he say anything to you?

HILDY: Not a word. *(McCUE goes. HILDY quickly picks up his receiver.)* Gimme Walter Burns. *(He gets up and closes the door carefully; comes back to his phone.)* Walter? Say, listen. I got the whole story from Jacobi and I got it exclusive . . . That's right, and it's a pip. Only listen. It cost me two hundred and sixty bucks, see? . . . Just a minute—I'll *give* you the story. I'm telling you first I had to give him all the money I had on me and it wasn't exactly mine. Two hundred and sixty bucks, and I want it back. *(Yells.)* Well, did you hear what I said about the money? . . . All right, then here's your story. It's the jailbreak of your dreams . . . Dr. Max J. Eglehofer, a profound thinker from Vienna, was giving Williams a final sanity test in the Sheriff's office you know, sticking a lot of pins in him

---

member of the Schlogl family, proprietors of Schlogl's Restaurant, 37 N. Wells Street, the principal gathering place of the literati of the so-called Chicago Renaissance of the first two decades of the twentieth century. The restaurant was established by Joseph Schlogl in 1879 and in the 1920s operated by his son, Edward H. Schlogl. The women of the family were Joseph's wife, Rosa, and her daughter, Flora Schlogl Mullin. Edward Schlogl never married. Possibly because this is the second use of the name "Irma," in the acting edition of 1950 the character becomes "Henrietta Schlogel." (See the obituary of Edward H. Schlogl, *Chicago Tribune*, April 10, 1934, p. 18.)

[107]*Wrigley Building*. The headquarters of the William Wrigley, Jr. Corporation, the chewing gum firm, designed by the architectural firm of Graham, Anderson, Probst and White as one of the principal elements in the North Michigan Avenue development of the immediate post–World War I era. The cornerstone of the original structure, now known as the South Section, was laid on November 11, 1920, and the building was completed in April 1921. An annex, the North Section, was added across a narrow plaza in 1924. The design of the original structure was based on the Giralda Tower of the Seville Cathedral, but the architectural ornamentation of both buildings is an adaptation of a French Renaissance style. Along with Tribune Tower of 1925, diagonally opposite, the Wrigley Building represents one of the twin introductions to the North Michigan Avenue shopping area to people crossing the Chicago River from the Loop area on the south. As such, the two buildings have come to pro-

to get his reflexes. Then he decided to reenact the crime exactly as it had taken place, so as to study Williams's powers of coordination. . . . Well, I'm coming to it, goddamn it. Will you shut up? . . . Of course he had to have a gun to reenact with. And who do you suppose supplied it? . . . Peter B. Hartman . . . B for brains. . . . I tell you, I'm *not* kidding. Hartman gave his gun to the professor, the professor gave it to Earl, and Earl shot the professor right in the belly. . . Ain't it perfect! If the Sheriff had unrolled a red carpet like at a Polish wedding and loaned Williams an umbrella, it couldn't have been more ideal . . . Eglehofer? No, not bad. They spirited him away to Passavant Hospital. . . No, we got it exclusive. Now listen, Walter. It cost me two hundred and sixty bucks for this story, and I want it back . . . I had to give it to Jacobi before he'd cough up his guts. Two hundred and sixty dollars—the money I'm going to get married on . . . Never mind about fine work—I want the money . . . No, I tell you, I'm not going to cover anything else—I'm going away. *(PEGGY[109] appears in the doorway. She is a pretty girl of twenty. HILDY has his back to the door.)* Listen, you lousy stiff. I just did this as a personal favor. Now I'm leaving town and I gave Jacobi every cent I got, and I want it back right away! . . . *When* will you send it over? . . . Well, see

---

vide a visual symbol of Chicago as Tower Bridge does of London. To pursue the analogy, the three structures provide this function so perfectly that they render architectural criticism irrelevant.

[108]In the acting edition, "leapfrog" becomes "stoop tag."

[109]*Peggy Grant.* This character is best looked upon as fictional. The name is adapted from Peggy Chalfont, the heroine of the play, *Petticoat Influence*, Neil forbes Grant (1882–1970), the Scottish journalist and playwright. The play opened in London on March 2, 1930. At the time *The Front Page* was written, Helen Hayes was apparently reading the play and considering acting in the American production; she opened as Peggy Chalfont on Broadway on December 15, 1930. (See the *New York Times*, December 16, 1930, p. 34.)

Because of MacArthur's marital involvements at the time *The Front Page* opened, it was impractical to modify the name of the actual person involved by altering spelling or other methods the authors used. As stated in the introduction, the plot revolves in part around MacArthur's effort to leave for New York with Carol Frink, a colleague on the *Herald and Examiner*, to marry her in August 1920. They were divorced on June 26, 1926, and the play was produced in New York only three days before MacArthur married Helen Hayes on August 17, 1928. By that time MacArthur's relations with the former Ms. Frink were thoroughly hostile; he reportedly avoided the desk at which she worked as motion picture critic of the *Herald and Examiner* on his visits back to the newspaper. She endeavored to prevent the divorce decree

that you do or I can't get married! . . . All right, and tell him to run. I'll be waiting right here in the Press— *(He hangs up and sees PEGGY. With a guilty start.)* Hello, Peggy.

PEGGY: What was that, over the telephone?

HILDY: Nothing. I was just telling Walter Burns I was all through, that's all. Hello, darling.

(PEGGY, despite her youth and simplicity, seems overwhelmingly mature in comparison to HILDY. As a matter of fact, PEGGY belongs to that division of womanhood that dedicates itself to suppressing in its lovers or husbands the spirit of D'Artagnan, Roland, Captain Kidd, Cyrano, Don Quixote, King Arthur, or any other type of the male innocent and rampant. In her unconscious and highly noble efforts to make what the female world calls "a man" out of HILDY, PEGGY has neither the sympathy nor acclaim of the authors, yet regarded superficially, she is a very sweet and satisfying heroine.)

PEGGY: You haven't done something foolish with that money? Our money!

HILDY: No. No!

PEGGY: You still *have* got the rest of it?

HILDY: Of course. Gee, darling, you don't think for a minute —

PEGGY: I think I'd better take care of it from now on!

HILDY: Now listen, honey, I can look after a couple of hundred dollars all right. . . .

PEGGY: Hildy, if you've still got that money I want you to give it to me.

HILDY: Now, sweetheart, it's going to be perfectly all right. . . .

PEGGY: *(She divines, alas, her lover's failing.)* Then you haven't got it.

---

from becoming final and, failing that, sought in 1929 to have the divorce annulled, thereby voiding MacArthur's marriage to Helen Hayes. When that effort also failed, she sued Helen Hayes for alienation of affections in 1932. Accordingly, it is unlikely MacArthur would have included a generally favorable treatment of her in the play. In addition, James MacArthur observes it would be very inconsistent for Carol Frink, who was herself a newspaperwoman, to urge someone to leave journalism, as Peggy Grant does in the play (letter of James MacArthur to George W. Hilton, January 26, 1994).

It was also impractical to use a character who could be identified as Helen Hayes, for she was by 1928 already an actress of considerable fame. On the complexities of the marital relations involved, see Jhan Robbins, *Front Page Marriage* (New York: G. P. Putnam's Sons, 1982).

Similarly, there was nothing in Hilding Johnson's life to provide a prototype for the role. By the time of the play, Johnson was married to his wife Marjorie; their son Louis was then five years old.

HILDY: Not—this minute, but I—

PEGGY: You *did* do something with it!

HILDY: No, no. He's sending it right over, Walter, I mean. It'll be here any minute.

PEGGY: *(Her vocabulary is reduced to a coal of fire.)* Oh, Hildy!

HILDY: *(A preposterous fellow.)* Listen, darling, I wouldn't have had this happen for the world. But it's going to be all right. Now here's what happened: I was just starting out to the house to get you when this guy Williams broke out of jail. You know, the fellow they were going to hang in the morning.

PEGGY: *(Intolerant of the antics of the Cyrano sex.)* Yes, I know.

HILDY: Ah now, listen, sweetheart, I *had* to do what I did. And—and the same thing when it came to the money— *(She turns away.)* Peggy! Now listen. I shouldn't tell you this, but I haven't got any secrets from you. Do you know how this guy escaped? He was down in the Sheriff's office when Hartman—that's the Sheriff—and Eglehofer—that's this fellow from Vienna—

PEGGY: Hildy!

HILDY: Aw, now I can't tell you if you won't listen. I *had* to give him the money so he wouldn't give the story to anybody else. Jacobi, I mean. That's the assistant warden. I got the story exclusive—the biggest scoop in years, I'll bet.

PEGGY: Do you know how long mother and I waited, out at that house?

HILDY: Aw, Peggy, listen. You ain't going to be mad at me for this. I couldn't help it. You'd have done the same thing yourself. I mean, the biggest story in the world busting, and nobody on the job.

PEGGY: I might have known it would happen again.

HILDY: Aw, listen—

PEGGY: Every time I've ever wanted you for something—on my birthday, and New Year's Eve, when I waited till five in the morning—

HILDY: But a big story broke; don't you remember.

PEGGY: It's always a big story—the biggest story in the world, and the next day everybody's forgotten it, even you!

HILDY: What do you mean forgotten? That was the Clara Hamon murder[110]—on your birthday. Now for God's sake, Peggy, it won't hurt to wait five more minutes. The boy's on his way with the money now.

---

[110]*The Clara Hamon murder.* Jacob L. Hamon, a Republican national committeeman who had become wealthy in the oil and railroad industries, was shot in a hotel room

PEGGY: Mother's sitting downstairs waiting in a taxicab. I'm just ashamed to face her, the way you've been acting. If she knew about that money— it's all we've got in the world, Hildy. We haven't even got a place to sleep in, except the train, and—

HILDY: Aw, gee, I wouldn't do anything in the world to hurt you, Peggy. You make me feel like a criminal.

PEGGY: It's all that Walter Burns. Oh, I'll be so glad when I get you away from him.—You simply can't resist him.

HILDY: For God's sake, Peggy, I've told you what I think of him. I wouldn't raise a finger if he was dying. Honest to God.

PEGGY: Then why did you loan him the money?

HILDY: I didn't! You see, you won't listen to me, or you'd know I didn't. Now, listen. I had to give the money to Jacobi, the assistant— *(WOODEN- SHOES ushers in MRS. GRANT.[111] MRS. GRANT is a confused little widow who has tried her best to adjust her mind to HILDY as a son-in-law.)*

WOODENSHOES: Here they are, Ma'am. *(Exits immediately.)*

HILDY: Oh, hello, Mrs. Grant—Mother. I was just explaining to Peggy—

PEGGY: Mother, I thought you were going to wait in the cab.

MRS. GRANT: *(A querulous yet practical soul.)* Well, I just came up to tell you the meter's gone to two dollars.

HILDY: Yeah, sure. But that's all right. . . .

MRS. GRANT: *(With the wandering egoism of age.)* I had a terrible time find- ing you. First I went into a room where a lot of policemen were playing cards.

---

in Ardmore, Oklahoma, on November 21, 1920. He died on November 26. His mis- tress and former secretary, Clara Smith Hamon, whom he had caused to be mar- ried to his nephew to legitimize her position, was indicted for the murder. Walter Howey, apparently sensing an opportunity to embarrass a Republican politician— Hamon had been widely expected to become secretary of the interior in the Hard- ing administration—ordered Sam Blair of the *Herald and Examiner*'s staff to go to Oklahoma to investigate. The Hearst papers strongly supported Clara Hamon, even paying her legal fees. She was found not guilty on March 17, 1921. (See the *Chicago Herald and Examiner,* March 18, 1921, p. 1.) By calling the crime "the Clara Hamon murder" instead of "the Jacob Hamon murder," Hildy seems to be questioning the verdict, and thus the Hearst papers' support of the accused.

[111]*Mrs. Amelia Grant.* Based on Helen Hayes's mother, Mrs. Catherine Estell Hayes Brown. (See Helen Hayes with Katherine Hatch, *My Life in Three Acts* [New York: Har- court Brace Jovanovich, 1990], p. 60.) Mrs. Brown died while dining with friends at the Croydon Hotel in New York on July 1, 1953.

HILDY: Yeah—that was—now, I'll—tell you what we'll do.

MRS. GRANT: Then I met that policeman and I asked him where Mr. Johnson's office was, and he brought me here.

PEGGY: Now, listen Mother, I think you'd better go down stairs and we'll come as soon as we can.

MRS. GRANT: *(Inspecting.)* You've got a big room, haven't you? Where do you sit?

HILDY: Now, I tell you what you do. You and Peggy go on over to the station and get the baggage checked . . . now here's the tickets.

PEGGY: Now, Hildy.

HILDY: I'll be along in fifteen minutes—maybe sooner.

MRS. GRANT: How do you mean—that you aren't going?

HILDY: Of course I am. Now, I'll meet you at the Information Booth—

PEGGY: Come, Mother. Hildy has to wait here a few minutes. It's something to do with the office—he's getting some money.

MRS. GRANT: *(On familiar ground.)* Money?

HILDY: Yeah—they're sending over—it's my salary. They're sending over my salary.

MRS. GRANT: *(The voice of womankind.)* Your salary? At this hour?

HILDY: They were awful busy, and I couldn't disturb them very well.

MRS. GRANT: The trouble is you're too easy with people—letting them wait till this hour before paying you your salary. How do you know they'll give it to you at all?[112]

PEGGY: Mother, we'll go on over. Hildy'll be along.

MRS. GRANT: Do you know what I'm beginning to think?

HILDY: *(Apprehensive.)* What?

MRS. GRANT: I think you must be a sort of irresponsible type or you wouldn't do things this way. It's just occurred to me you didn't do one blessed thing to help our getting away.

PEGGY: Now you stop picking on my Hildy, Mother.

MRS. GRANT: Why, I had to sublet the apartment and pack all the wedding presents— *(McCUE enters. Goes to phone, with side glances at the others.)* —why, that's work a man ought to do. You weren't even there to put things in the taxi—I had to give the man fifty cents. And now here you are standing here with the train leaving any minute—

---

[112]This entire speech of Mrs. Grant and the following speech of Peggy are eliminated from the acting edition.

HILDY: Now, mother, I never missed a train in my life. You run along with Peggy—

McCUE: *(Into phone.)* Hello. McCue talking.

PEGGY: Come on, Mother. We're disturbing people.

HILDY: This is my girl, Mac, and her mother. Mr. McCue.

McCUE: *(Tipping his hat.)* Pleased to meet you. *(Into phone.)* Here's a hell of a swell feature on the manhunt. *(To the ladies.)* Excuse my French! *(Into phone.)* Mrs. Phoebe De Wolfe,[113] eight-sixty one and a half South State Street, colored, gave birth to a pickaninny in a patrol wagon, with Sheriff Hartman's special Rifle Squad[114] acting as midwives.

MRS. GRANT: Mercy!

McCUE: *(Pleased at having interested her.)* You oughta have seen 'em, ma'am.

PEGGY: Come on, Mother.

HILDY: Listen, Mother, you better run along. I'll put my suitcase in the cab.

McCUE: *(Phoning.)* Well Phoebe was walking along the street when all of a sudden she began having labor pains. No! Labor pains! Didn't you ever have labor pains? Righto! She was hollering for her husband, who's been missing for five months, when the police seen her. And Deputy Henry Shereson,[115] who's a married man, saw what her condition was. So he

---

[113]*Phoebe De Wolfe.* The name is probably adapted from John C. De Wolfe, a prominent lawyer in the Loop, in practice from about 1910 to his retirement in 1959. He died at age eighty on July 5, 1963. (See his obituary in the *Chicago Tribune*, July 7, 1963, sec. IA, p. 10.) Mr. De Wolfe's wife was named Gertrude, and Phoebe is presumably a construction of the authors.

[114]*Sheriff Hartman's special Rifle Squad.* The sheriff's department did not literally have a rifle squad. The reference is probably to the rifle squad of the Detective Bureau of the Chicago Police Department, which was replaced by a shotgun squad in January 1921. (See "Shotguns Replace Police Rifles," *Chicago Tribune*, January 30, 1921, p. 2) Alternatively, Richard C. Lindberg believes this is a reference to the Cook County Highway Police, established in the sheriff's department in April 1922, mainly to provide policing of the roads in rural areas of Cook County. The escape of Tommy O'Connor, with which the play is so basically concerned, was thought to have been into Wisconsin through the north or northwest suburban area. This was interpreted as demonstrating the weakness of policing in what were then lightly populated reaches of the county. Roadhouses and speakeasies were proliferating in the area. The force was later known as the Cook County Sheriff's Police. (See Richard C. Lindberg, *To Serve and Collect: Chicago Politics and Police Corruption from the Lager Beer Riots to the Summerdale Scandal* [New York: Prager Publishers, 1991], p. 225.)

[115]*Henry Shereson.* Possibly Samuel L. Shereson, an accountant who resided at 3825

coaxed her into the patrol wagon, and they started a race with the stork for Passavant Hospital.

HILDY: *(To McCUE, as he goes out.)* If a boy comes here for me hold him. I'll be right back! *(They are gone.)*

McCUE: *(Into phone.)* Listen—when the pickaninny was born the Rifle Squad examined him carefully to see if it was Earl Williams, who they knew was hiding somewhere. *(Laughs at his own joke.)* They named him Peter Hartman De Wolfe in honor of the Sheriff, and they all chipped in a dollar a piece on account of it being the first baby ever born in a manhunt. *(The MAYOR[116] enters.)* Wait a minute here's the Mayor himself. Maybe there's a statement. *(Under ordinary circumstances the MAYOR is a bland, unruffled soul, full of ease and confidence; a bit stupid, walking as if he were on snowshoes and carrying an unlighted cigar with which he gestures as if it were a wand. The events of the last hour have unhinged him. He is eager for news—even the worst.)*

MAYOR: Don't pester me now, please. I got a lot on my mind.

McCUE: *(Into phone.)* The Mayor won't say anything. *(He hangs up.)*

MAYOR: Have you seen Sheriff Hartman?

McCUE: Been in and out all night, your Honor . . . *(MURPHY and ENDICOTT enter.)*

MURPHY: Now listen, your Honor. We've got to have a statement . . .

ENDICOTT: We go to press in twenty minutes.

MAYOR: I can't help that boys. I have nothing to say—not at this time.

MURPHY: What do you mean—"not at this time"? Who do you think you are, Abraham Lincoln?

ENDICOTT: Come on, cut the statesman stuff! What do you know about the escape? How'd he get out?

MURPHY: Where'd he get the gun?

MAYOR: Wait a minute, boys . . . Not so fast!

ENDICOTT: Well, give us a statement on the election, then.

MURPHY: What effect's all this going to have on the colored voters?

W. Jackson Boulevard, or a member of his family. The name does not accord with any known deputy sheriff of the period.

[116]*The Mayor.* William Hale Thompson, Republican mayor of Chicago from 1915 to 1923 and 1927 to 1931. The anglophobic reference to King George in the play (see page 122) would unambiguously identify the Mayor as Thompson to an audience of the time. The references to him as Fred are probably a use of the name Mayor Fred A. Busse.

MAYOR: Not an iota. In what way can an unavoidable misfortune of this sort influence the duty of every citizen, colored or otherwise?

MURPHY: Bologny . . .

ENDICOTT: Listen here, Mayor. *Is* there a Red Menace or ain't there? And how did he get out of that rubber jail of yours?

McCUE: Are you going to stand the gaff, Mayor? Or have you picked out somebody that's responsible?

MURPHY: *(Innocently.)* Any truth in the report that you're on Trotsky's[117] payroll?

ENDICOTT: Yeah—the Senator[118] claims you sleep in red underwear.

MAYOR: Never mind the jokes. Don't forget that I'm Mayor of this town and that the dignity of my office . . . *(HARTMAN enters—the MAYOR turns abruptly on him.)* Hartman! I've been looking for you. . . .

ENDICOTT: *(Leaping at the SHERIFF.)* What's the dope, Pinky? How did he get out?

McCUE: What was he doing in your office?

MURPHY: What's this about somebody gettin' shot?

ENDICOTT: Where did he get the gun?

SHERIFF: *(Jotting notes on a piece of paper with the hope that he will seem busy.)* Just a minute, fellas.

MURPHY: For God's sake, cut the stallin'! Who engineered the getaway?

ENDICOTT: Was it the Reds?

SHERIFF: Just a minute, I tell you. We've got him located!

---

[117]*Trotsky.* In the acting edition of 1950 the reference is updated to "Stalin."

[118]*the Senator.* J. Hamilton Lewis, Democratic Senator from Illinois, 1912 to 1918 and 1930 to 1939. Although Lewis was out of office during nearly all the datable events of the play, he was an important figure in Democratic politics thoughout the period. Immediately following the election of November 7, 1922, which sent a slate of mainly anti-Thompson candidates to office, Lewis cabled from Switzerland where he was finishing some business that he was delighted with the outcome, but he declined to state whether he was considering running for mayor in 1923. (See the *Chicago Tribune*, November 11, 1922, p. 2.) He was to decide against running. As a Democratic paper, the *Herald and Examiner* considered itself allied with Lewis, about as closely as the *Tribune* was with Charles Deneen, who was appointed to the Senate on February 25, 1925. The implication of the dialogue in later passages is that the projected embarrassment of the Mayor will so weaken the Cook County Republican machine as to make Lewis the dominant politician in the state—an emminently reasonable presumption. While still in office, Lewis suffered a coronary thrombosis on a train from Chicago to Washington and died on arrival on April 9, 1939.

MURPHY: Who? Williams!

ENDICOTT: Where?!

McCUE: Where is he?

SHERIFF: Out to the place where he used to live . . . on Clark Street . . . Just got the tip.

ENDICOTT: Holy God!

McCUE: Why didn't you say so?

SHERIFF: The Rifle Squad is just going out.

ENDICOTT: Where are they?

SHERIFF: Downstairs. All the boys are with them.

MURPHY: For the love of God! *(MURPHY, ENDICOTT, and McCUE rush out.)*

ENDICOTT: *(In the hall.)* Hey, there, Charlie![119]

SHERIFF: *(Calling into the corridor.)* Report to me, Charlie, the minute you get there! I'll be in the building!

MAYOR: Pete, I want to talk to you!

SHERIFF: I ain't got time, Fred—honest. I'll see you after.

MAYOR: Pete, there's one thing I've got to know. Did you yourself actually give Williams that gun?

SHERIFF: *(Wailing.)* The Professor asked me for it. I didn't know what he wanted it for. I thought it was something scientific.

MAYOR: Now listen, Fred— *(KRUGER enters, whistling. Both statesmen become silent and self-conscious.)*

KRUGER: *(Heading for phone.)* Hello, your Honor. Any statement on the Red uprising tomorrow?

MAYOR: What Red uprising?

SHERIFF: There'll be no Red uprising!

KRUGER: The Senator claims the situation calls for the militia.

MAYOR: You can quote me as saying that anything the Senator says is a tissue of lies.

KRUGER: *(At phone.)* Kruger calling.

SHERIFF: Why aren't you with the Rifle Squad? They've just gone out.

KRUGER: We've got a man with them. *(Into phone.)* Here's a red-hot statement from the Senator. Ready? . . . He says the City Hall is another Augean stables[120]. . . Augean! . . . Oh, for God's sake! *(Turns.)* He don't know what Augean means.

---

[119]*Charlie.* Probably Charles E. Singer, a deputy sheriff in 1923.

[120]*Augean stables.* The reference is to the Greek myth of Augeas, King of Elis, who housed 3,000 oxen in his stables without cleaning the structures for thirty years.

MAYOR: The Senator don't know either.

KRUGER: Well, take the rest, anyhow. *(Into phone.)* The Senator claims that the Mayor and the Sheriff have shown themselves to be a couple of eight-year-olds playing with fire. Then this is a quote: "It is a lucky thing for the city that next Tuesday is Election Day, as the citizens will thus be saved the expense of impeaching the Mayor and the Sheriff." That's all—call you back. *(Hangs up.)* How are you, Mayor? *(Exits, whistling.)*

MAYOR: *(Closing the door.)* I've got a mighty unpleasant task to perform, Pete—

SHERIFF: *(Beside himself.)* Now listen, Fred, you're just gonna get me rattled.

MAYOR: *(Inexorably.)* Two years ago we almost lost the colored vote on account of that coon story you told at the Dixie Marching Club . . . Mandy and the traveling salesman . . . .

SHERIFF: Why harp on that *now?* . . .

MAYOR: Now you come along with another one of your moron blunders. . . . The worst of your whole career.

SHERIFF: *(Frantic.)* Listen, Fred. Stop worrying, will you? Just do me a favor and stop worrying! I'm doing everything on God's green earth! I've just sworn in four hundred deputies!

MAYOR: Four hundred! Do you want to bankrupt this administration?

SHERIFF: *(Pleadingly.)* I'm getting them for twelve dollars a night.

MAYOR: Twelve dollars —! For those goddamn uncles of yours? What do you think this is—Christmas Eve?

Hercules, confronted with the task of cleaning them, diverted the river Alpheus through them, cleansing them in a day.

[121]*fake tag days*. Tag days are charitable drives in which the donor is given a cardboard tag to wear to demonstrate that he or she has contributed. They are particularly characteristic of Chicago.

[122]*Czernecki*. Anthony Czarnecki, a man who had a remarkably varied career in journalism and public service. He was born in Poland and came to the United States as a young man and became a member of the Polish community on Chicago's Northwest Side—an identification he retained all his life. He entered journalism in 1896 with the *Chicago Daily News*, translating Polish in connection with a riot on Milwaukee Avenue. He was mainly identified with the *Daily News* but is reported also to have worked for the *Record, Chronicle,* and *American*. During and after World War I, Czarnecki made two trips to Europe, one in Army intelligence and the other as a reporter for the *Daily News*. In Poland he met Ambrogio Damiano Achille Ratti, an apostolic visitor, reportedly playing pool with him in an effort to improve the

SHERIFF: *(With dignity.)* If you are talking about my brother-in-law, he's worked for the city fifteen years.

MAYOR *(Bitterly.)* I know. Getting up fake tag days![121] . . . Pete, you're through!

SHERIFF: *(Stunned.)* What do you mean—through?

MAYOR: I mean I'm scratching your name off the ticket Tuesday and running Czernecki[122] in your place. It's nothing personal. . . . And Pete—it's the only way out. It's a sacrifice we all ought to be glad to make.

SHERIFF: *(David to Jonathan.)*[123] Fred!

MAYOR: Now, Pete! Please don't appeal to my sentimental side. . . .

SHERIFF: Fred, I don't know what to say. A thing like this almost destroys a man's faith in human nature. . . .

MAYOR: I wish you wouldn't talk like that, Pete. . . .

SHERIFF: Our families, Fred. My God, I've always looked on Bessie[124] as my own sister.

MAYOR *(Wavering and desperate.)* If there was any way out . . .

SHERIFF: *(As a phone rings.)* There is a way out. I've got this Williams surrounded, haven't I? What more do you want? Now if you just give me a couple of hours *(Into phone.)* Hello. . . . Yes. . . . Hello! *(Wildly.)* Four

---

clergyman's game by knowledge gained in Milwaukee Avenue pool halls. Ratti, as Pope Pius XI, recognizing Czarnecki as a prominent Catholic layman, made him a member of the Papal Order of St. Gregory. Poland awarded him the Order of Poland Restituta, and Italy gave him the Cavalier Crown for his wartime services.

Czarnecki simultaneously pursued a second career in local politics. He became the leading Republican in a Polish community that was mainly Democratic and by the time of the play was, in fact, a plausible alternative to the sheriff on a Republican ticket. Czarnecki became a member of the Board of Election Commissioners in 1910 and of the Board of Education in 1917. President Calvin Coolidge appointed him collector of customs for Chicago in 1926. He served in that office to 1935, but thereafter devoted himself to his journalism, finally reporting mainly on religious subjects for the *Daily News*. He was actively writing for the paper less than a week before he died on May 4, 1952, at age seventy-four. (See obituaries in the *Chicago Daily News*, May 5, 1952, p. 27; the *Chicago Tribune*, May 5, 1952, p. 6; and the *New York Times*, May 6, 1952, p. 29.)

[123]*David to Jonathan.* The reference is to the Biblical tale of Jonathan, who protects David from the murderous intentions of Jonathan's father, Saul. It bespeaks a close, protective relation between persons without a family connection. See 1 Samuel 18:1: "And it came to pass, when he had made an end of speaking unto Saul, that the soul of Jonathan was knit with the soul of David, and Jonathan loved him as his own soul."

hundred suppers! Nothing doing! This is a manhunt—not a banquet! . . .
The twelve dollars includes everything! . . . Well, the hell with them! Earl
Williams ain't eating, is he?! *(He hangs up.)* That gives you an idea of what
I'm up against!

MAYOR *(Hotly.)* We're up against a lot more than that with that nutty slogan you invented. "Reform the Reds with a rope." *(SHERIFF winces.)*
There ain't any goddamn Reds and you know it!

SHERIFF: Yeah, but why go into that now, Fred?

MAYOR: The slogan I had was all we needed to win—"Keep King George
Out of Chicago!"[125]

SHERIFF: My God, I ain't had a bite to eat since this thing happened.

MAYOR: Pete, two hundred thousand colored votes are at stake! And we've
got to hang Earl Williams to get them.

SHERIFF: But we're *going* to hang him, Fred. He can't get away. *(A knock on
the door.)*

MAYOR: What do you mean he can't get away! He *got* away, didn't he? Now
look here, Pete— *(Knocking louder.)* Who's out there? . . .

VOICE: *(Outside.)* Is Sheriff Hartman in there!

SHERIFF: *(Starts for door, relieved.)* Ah! It's for me! *(Opens the door. A small
man named PINCUS[126] stands there.)* I'm Sheriff Hartman. Do you want me?

PINCUS: *(A very colorless and ineffectual person.)* Yes, sir. I've been looking all
over for you, Sheriff. You're certainly a hard fellow to find.

MAYOR: *(Annoyed.)* What do you want!

PINCUS: *(Taking a document from his pocket and proffering it to the SHER-
IFF. He smiles in a comradely fashion.)* From the Governor.

MAYOR: What's from the Governor!

SHERIFF: Huh?

PINCUS: The reprieve for Earl Williams.

SHERIFF: *(Stunned.)* For *who?*

---

[124]*Bessie.* The name is a fabrication. Thompson's wife, from whom he was estranged
for most of his career, was the former Mary Walker Wyse.

[125]*"Keep King George Out of Chicago."* As noted in the introduction, the maximum
displeasure of the British censor was directed to this passage, which at once brought
a reference to the British monarch onto the stage and identified the mayor as an
actual person, William Hale Thompson. For the controversy on this line, and its resolution in the first British performance, see the introduction, pages 17–19.

[126]*Irving Pincus.* Samuel E. Pincus, assistant attorney general of Illinois. See
pp. 47–49.

PINCUS: *(Amiably.)* Earl Williams. The reprieve. *(A ghastly pause.)* I thought I'd never find you. First I had a helluva time getting a taxi—

MAYOR: Wait—a minute. *(Getting his bearings.)* Is this a joke or something?

PINCUS: Huh?

SHERIFF: *(Bursting out.)* It's a mistake— There must be a mistake! The Governor gave me his word of honor he wouldn't interfere! Two days ago!

MAYOR: And you fell for it! Holy God, Pete! It frightens me what I'd like to do to you! Wait a minute! Come here you! Who else knows about this?

PINCUS: They were all standing around when he wrote it. It was after they got back from fishing.

MAYOR: Get the Governor on the phone, Hartman.

PINCUS: They ain't got a phone. They're duck shooting now.

MAYOR: A lot of goddamn nimrods.

SHERIFF: *(Who has been reading the reprieve.)* Can you beat that? Read it! *(Thrusts the paper into MAYOR's hands.)* Insane, he says! *(Striding over to the messenger.)* He knows goddamn well that Earl Williams ain't insane!

PINCUS: Yeah! But I—

SHERIFF: This reprieve is pure politics and you know it! It's an attempt to ruin us!

MAYOR: *(Reading.)* Dementia praecox![127] My God! If this goes through the Republican Party is finished in this state.[128]

SHERIFF: We got to think fast before those lying reporters get hold of this. What'll we tell 'em?

MAYOR: What'll you tell 'em? I'll tell you what you can tell 'em! You can tell 'em your damn relatives were out there shooting everybody they see, for the hell of it!

SHERIFF: Now Fred, you're just excited. *(Phone rings; SHERIFF starts for the phone, talking as he goes.)* We aren't going to get any place, rowing like this.

---

[127] *dementia praecox*. The term is an archaic one for schizophrenia. William J. Hickson, Chicago city alienist, examined Tommy O'Connor in August 1919 and reported him as a high-grade sociopath with psychopathic tendencies, a chronic alcoholic, and a probable dementia praecox case. (*Chicago Daily News*, December 14, 1921, p. 1.) Thus, the ground for the reprieve is consistent with the clinical evaluation of O'Connor.

[128] This line, which appears in excerpts from the script in *Theatre* magazine of August 1928, was dropped from the Covici-Friede edition, probably as redundant given the Mayor's subsequent lines at the top of page 124.

MAYOR: And you can tell 'em the Republican Party is through in this state on account of you.

SHERIFF: *(Into phone.)* Hello! This is Hartman.

MAYOR: *(Apoplectic.)* And you can add as an afterthought that I want your resignation now.

SHERIFF: *(From the phone.)* Sssh. Wait, Fred. *(Excitedly, into phone.)* What? Where? . . . Where? My God!

MAYOR: What is it?

SHERIFF: They got him! *(Back to phone.)* Wait a minute—hold the wire. *(To the MAYOR.)* They got Earl Williams surrounded . . . the Rifle Squad has . . . in his house.

MAYOR: Tell 'em to hold the wire.

SHERIFF: I did. *(Into phone.)* Hold the wire.

MAYOR: Cover up that transmitter! *(SHERIFF does so. MAYOR faces PINCUS.)* Now listen! You never arrived here with this—whatever it is. Get that?

PINCUS: *(Blinking.)* Yes, I did.

MAYOR: How much do you make a week?

PINCUS: Huh?

---

[129]*City Sealer.* An actual municipal officer of the City of Chicago, with duties as stated in the text, certifying the accuracy of scales. The office was established in 1887; at the time of the play the holder and his staff occupied rooms in the basement of City Hall. The last city sealer was Nicholas J. Melas, who was kind enough to write for me a description of the position on the basis of his experience:

> The correct title of the office was Commissioner of The Department of Weights and Measures. The term "City Sealer" was more commonly used in referring to the individual. Within the City Administration, the Heads or Commissioners of each Department, e.g., Streets and Sanitation; Public Works; Law, etc., constituted the Mayor's cabinet. As such, the Commissioner of Weights and Measures or City Sealer, carried the prestige of being a member of the Mayor's cabinet. The Department had a number of employees among whose duties was included the certification of scales, in all commercial establishments within the City. These would be tested annually and, upon approval, a seal would be affixed thereon. It is from this function that the term "City Sealer" was derived. The duties of the department also included checking the honesty with which city merchants were weighing their merchandise. The department employed a number of investigators who inspected various commercial establishments. These investigators had the authority, upon finding items that were being "short weighted," to issue summons and bring the offenders into court where the Corporation Council would prosecute. (Letter of Nicholas J. Melas to George W. Hilton, June 9, 1994.)

MAYOR: *(Impatiently.)* How much do you make a week? What's your salary?

PINCUS: *(Reluctantly.)* Forty dollars.

SHERIFF: *(Into phone.)* No—don't cut me off.

MAYOR: How would you like to have a job for three hundred and fifty dollars a month? That's almost a hundred dollars a week!

PINCUS: Who! Me?

MAYOR: Who the hell do you think? *(PINCUS is a little startled; the MAYOR hastens to adopt a milder manner.)* Now, listen. There's a fine opening for a fellow like you in the City Sealer's office.[129]

PINCUS: The what!

MAYOR: The City Sealer's office!

PINCUS: You mean here in Chicago?

MAYOR: *(Foaming.)* Yes, yes.

SHERIFF: *(At phone.)* Well, wait a minute, will you? I'm in conference.

PINCUS: *(A very deliberative intellect.)* No, I couldn't do that.

MAYOR. Why not?

PINCUS: I couldn't work in Chicago. You see, I've got my family in Springfield.

Mr. Melas held the office from his appointment in January 1962 until he resigned on December 6, 1962. The position then lay unfilled until 1966, when the name of the office was changed to the Department of Scales, Weights and Measures. This department was, in turn, merged into a Department of Consumer Services on January 1, 1979.

The text is realistic in showing Thompson with jobs to offer on impulse. The city in 1923 had about 18,000 employees, with approximately 14,000 in civil service and about 3,900 that could be allocated arbitrarily. It will be no surprise that Thompson used his authority to convert the innocuous office of the city sealer into a sinkhole of patronage, graft, and malfeasance. George Murray stated that the office of the city sealer was the political payoff point on the city level, parallel to the sheriff for the county and the auditor for the state government. (George Murray, *The Legacy of Al Capone: Portraits and Annals of Chicago's Public Enemies* [New York: G. P. Putnam's Sons, 1975], p. 65.) In particular, the support, financial and otherwise, of Al Capone in the 1927 election left Thompson politically indebted to the Capone organization. Thompson appointed a reputed Capone lieutenant, State Senator Daniel A. Serritella, as city sealer and Harry Hochstein as chief deputy sealer. Hochstein was the brother-in-law of Maxie Eisen, a Capone syndicate member, West Side labor racketeer, and head of the Chicago Fish Dealers Union. State's Attorney John A. Swanson, a week before the election of 1931 that finally unseated Thompson, raided the offices of the city sealer and also the headquarters of Eisen's

MAYOR: *(Desperate.)* But you could bring 'em to Chicago! We'll pay all your expenses.

PINCUS: *(With vast thought.)* No, I don't think so.

MAYOR: For God's sake, why not?

PINCUS: I got two kids going to high school there, and if I changed them from one town to another, they'd probably lose a grade.

MAYOR: No, they wouldn't—they'd gain one! They could go into any class they want to. And I guarantee that they'll graduate with highest honors!

PINCUS: *(Lured.)* Yeah?

MAYOR: And the Chicago school system is the best in the world.[130] *(To SHERIFF.)* Isn't it?

SHERIFF: Far and away! *(Into phone.)* Hold your horses—will you, Mittelbaum.[131] Hurry up, Fred!

MAYOR: Now what do you say?

PINCUS: What did you say this job was?

MAYOR: In the City Sealer's office!

PINCUS: What's he do!

MAYOR: *(Jumping.)* Oh, for God's sake!

SHERIFF: He has charge of all the important documents. He puts the City seals on them.

MAYOR: That's about on a par with the rest of your knowledge! The City Sealer's duty, my friend, is to see that the people of Chicago are not mulcted by unscrupulous butchers and grocers.

SHERIFF: That's what I meant.

---

union. Swanson alleged that Serritella had run "an organized system of cheating and short-weighting" of some four hundred merchants. Honest merchants were threatened with prosecution for short-weighting if they did not participate. Hochstein was accused of using the threat of actions for short-weighting to force fish dealers into Eisen's union, effectively cartelizing fish retailing in the city. Harold M. Steel, deputy state's attorney, estimated the losses to consumers in 1930 at nearly $54.5 million. There were additional allegations of short-weighting of coal, up to 2,500 pounds in ten-ton lots. (See the *Chicago Tribune*, April 2, 3, 4, 5, 10; July 11, 1931.)

The treatment of the city sealer in the play implies that the authors were aware of Thompson's misuse of the office for his own purposes well before the Chicago press broke the story.

[130]The exchange between the Mayor and the Sheriff praising the Chicago school system is dropped from the acting edition.

[131]*Mittelbaum.* Probably P. G. Mittleburger, a salesman at 121 N. State Street. On the

MAYOR: It's his duty to go around and test their scales.

PINCUS: Yeah?

MAYOR: But only twice a year.

PINCUS: This puts me in a hell of a hole.

MAYOR: No it doesn't. . . . *(Hands him the reprieve.)* Now remember. You never delivered this, whatever it is. You got caught in the traffic or something. . . . Here, Pincus, get out of here; have a drink while you are about it. Why don't you see a movie or something? There's a Greta Garbo film at the Tivoli.[132]

PINCUS: But how do I know. . . .

MAYOR: Come in and see me in my office tomorrow. What's your name!

PINCUS: Pincus.

MAYOR: All right, Mr. Pincus, all you've got to do is lay low and keep your mouth shut. Here! *(He hands him a card.)* Go to this address. It's a nice homey little place, and you can get anything you want. *(He sees PINCUS through the door.)* Just tell 'em Fred sent you. *(PINCUS goes.)*

SHERIFF: *(Into phone, desperately.)* Will you wait, for God's sake? I'll tell you in a minute! *(He turns to the MAYOR with a gesture of appeal.)*

MAYOR *(Huskily.)* All right. Tell 'em to shoot to kill.

SHERIFF: What?

MAYOR: Shoot to kill, I said.

SHERIFF: I don't know, Fred. There's that reprieve if they ever find out.

MAYOR: Nobody reprieved that policeman he murdered. Now do as I tell you.

---

basis of the excerpts from the play in *Theatre* magazine, the authors originally spelled the name "Mittlebaum."

[132] The lines inserted here, taken from the excerpts from the play in *Theatre* magazine, were superseded in the Covici-Friede edition by "Now get out of here and don't let anybody see you," and presumably also by the invitation to stop at a speakeasy in the Mayor's second speech, below.

The Tivoli Theatre was opened on February 16, 1921, the first of the "merely colossal" motion picture palaces of the Balaban and Katz chain in Chicago designed by the architectural firm of C. W. and George L. Rapp. The Tivoli was planned as the premier house of the chain for the South Side. At 63rd Street and Cottage Grove Avenue, it was about nine miles south of the Criminal Court Building, as close as the Mayor cared for Pincus to be. On the theater, see Terry Helgesen, "Tivoli Theatre," *The Console*, April 1967, the entire issue of sixteen pages. As noted in the introduction, Greta Garbo's first film to play the Tivoli, *The Temptress*, opened there on January 3, 1927.

SHERIFF: *(Into phone.)* Hello, Mittelbaum . . . Listen. *(His voice is weak.)* Shoot to kill. . . . That's the orders—pass the word along. . . . No! We don't want him! And listen, Mittelbaum—five hundred bucks for the guy that does the job. . . . Yes, I'll be right out there. *(Hangs up.)* Well, I hope that's the right thing to do. *(There is a great kicking on the door.)*

HILDY: *(Outside.)* Hey! Who's in there? Open that door!

MAYOR: *(En route to the door.)* For God's sake take that guilty look off your face. And stop trembling like a horse. *(The SHERIFF starts whistling, "Ach, du Lieber Augustine" in what he imagines is a care-free manner. The MAYOR opens the door; HILDY enters.)*

HILDY: Oh, it's you two! Well, what's the idea of locking the door! Playing post office? *(Going to phone.)*

SHERIFF: *(With elaborate unconcern, as he walks toward the door.)* Oh, hello, Hildy.

MAYOR: Come on, Hartman.

HILDY: *(Into the phone.)* Gimme Walter Burns. *(To the others.)* Was there a fellow in here asking for me?

SHERIFF: Did you hear we've got Williams surrounded?

HILDY: Yeah. I heard you only let him out so he could vote for you on Tuesday.

MAYOR: Hartman! *(He pulls SHERIFF out of the room.)*

HILDY: *(Into phone.)* Hello, Duffy[133] . . . this is Hildy. Listen, where's Walter? Well, where did he go? Goddamn it, Duffy, I'm waitin' here for the boy to bring over my money . . . the two hundred and sixty dollars he

---

This passage may have been dropped in favor of the Mayor's directing Pincus to a speakeasy, immediately below, because the authors believed they had found a preferable means of establishing why Pincus should arrive drunk in Act III. Alternatively, the passage may have been excised because the effect depends in part on a particularly close acquaintance with Chicago geography. Eliminating the Tivoli removes, however, a piece of humor highly consistent with the rest of the play.

Note that, with the line intact, the Mayor uses Pincus's name although he has not yet heard it. When the passage was dropped, the text must have been rewritten to introduce the name immediately following.

[133]*Duffy.* Roscoe Conkling "Duffy" Cornell, city editor of the *Herald and Examiner,* and the obvious man for one of the paper's reporters to call. A native of Goshen, Indiana, Cornell had gone to work for the *Examiner* in 1909 and served variously as reporter, sports editor, news editor, and circulation director. Hardly less a career Hearst editor than Howey, Cornell transferred to Hearst's *Los Angeles Examiner* in 1930, rising to Sunday editor. He later served as editor of the *Daily Variety* in

owes me. . . . Yeah . . . in the pressroom. He told me the boy was on his way. . . . What the hell are you laughin' about? . . . Listen, Duffy, has that maniac started the money over or not! . . . No, I ain't got time to come over to the office. I'll miss the train. . . . Oh, for God's sake! . . . That doublecrossing louse! *(He hangs up. WOODENSHOES enters.)*

WOODENSHOES: The trouble is, nobody's using the right psychology. Now you take this aspect of the situation: you got a man named Earl Williams who has escaped . . .

HILDY: *(Seizing at a straw.)* Have you got two hundred and sixty dollars on you?

WOODENSHOES: What?

HILDY: Have you got two hundred and sixty dollars?

WOODENSHOES: No, but I got a way of making it, and more. I know how we can get ten thousand dollars, if you'll just listen. *(Pointing his finger at HILDY in the manner of a man letting the cat out of the bag.)* Serchay la femme!

HILDY. What?

WOODENSHOES: *(Inexorably—for him.)* Who is it that's been defendin' this feller Williams right along? Who is it that was hangin' around his room just before the escape happened?

HILDY: Oh, for God's sake! I ain't got time, Woodenshoes. I got to get two hundred and sixty dollars in the next five minutes!

WOODENSHOES: It's gonna take longer than five minutes. I know where Earl Williams is!

HILDY: He's out at Clark and Fullerton, getting his head blown off. But that don't get me any money.

WOODENSHOES: Earl Williams is with that girl, Mollie Malloy! *That's* where he is!

HILDY: *(Despairing.)* Can you imagine—this time tomorrow I'd have been a gentleman. *(DIAMOND LOUIE enters. HILDY leaps for him.)* Thank God! Have you got the dough?

LOUIE: Huh?

Hollywood and adviser to the *Los Angeles Times* in establishing of its short-lived evening paper, the *Los Angeles Mirror*. Finally, he spent fifteen years as public relations director for the Agua Caliente race track in Tijuana, Baja California, until retiring in 1964. He died at age eighty-three in Los Angeles on April 28, 1967. His obituary in the *Los Angeles Herald-Examiner* (April 30, 1967, p. D-11) is explicit that Cornell is the "Duffy" of the play. As noted below (see footnote 173), the acting edition of 1950 makes clear that the authors referred to Duffy Cornell.

WOODENSHOES: She sent him a lot of roses, didn't she?

HILDY: Goddamn it—the hell with your roses. Gimme the dough. I'm in a hell of a hurry, Louie.

LOUIE: What are you talkin' about?

WOODENSHOES: I'll betcha I'm right. *(Exits.)*

HILDY: Listen, Louie! Do you mean to say Walter didn't give you the dough he owes me!

LOUIE: Walter's pretty sore. You better come over and see him.

HILDY: But that's all settled! Walter and I are like this! *(He illustrates with two twined fingers.)* I just did a swell favor for him—scooped the whole town! We're pals again! I'm telling you.[134]

LOUIE: He just told me be sure and get you, you known what I mean?

HILDY: *(Frantically.)* I tell you that's fixed! By God, Louie, do you think I'd try to put something over on you?

LOUIE: What do you mean fixed? He wants to talk to you. I been looking all over—

HILDY: But I did talk to him! Everything's all right! I swear to you!

LOUIE: *(Weakening.)* Jesus, Hildy, I don't know.

HILDY: Certainly! My God, he *wants* me to go! Now listen, Louie—you've always got a lot of money—will you help me out? This two hundred and sixty bucks —Walter's sending a boy with it, but I can't wait! I gotta catch a train, see? Now—

LOUIE: What two hundred and sixty bucks!

HILDY: The money I spent on the story! He's sending it over, but I want *you* to take *that* and give *me* the money now!

LOUIE: Oh! You want two hundred and sixty dollars—now.

HILDY: *YES!*

LOUIE: Well, that's a lot of money, you know what I mean?

HILDY: You can get it from Walter. I'll give you my I.O.U.

LOUIE: Lis'en, Hildy, I'd like to help you out. But I've been stung on so many I.O.U's lately that I made myself a promise.

HILDY: But this ain't an I.O.U. . . . . It's money comin' to me from the paper!

LOUIE: What have you got to show for it?

HILDY: Louie, listen! My whole future is dependent on this. My girl's waitin' at the train. I've just got fifteen minutes to get there. If you'll help me out, I swear . . . Honest to God. . . .

---

[134]In the acting edition, this entire speech of Hildy is replaced with "But that's all settled, Louie. Everything's all right."

LOUIE: *(Interrupting.)* Two hundred and sixty dollars . . . that's a big gamble!

HILDY: It's no gamble at all. I'll write out a note to Walter sayin' for him to give you the money he owes me.

LOUIE: Well, I'll tell you what I'll do with you. I'll take a chance.

HILDY: *(As he writes out note.)* That's the stuff. You're a white man, Louie, you're a real white man. God—I knew I could depend on you.

LOUIE: I tell you what I'll do. I'll give you hundred and fifty dollars for the debt. *(HILDY stares at him.)*

HILDY: That's just takin' advantage, Louie.

LOUIE: That's the best I can do.

HILDY: Well, Christ! I lose almost a hundred bucks by that.

LOUIE: All right. *(Puts money back in his pocket.)* Have it your own way.

HILDY: Make it two hundred.

LOUIE: One hundred and fifty!

HILDY: All right, give me the dough. *(DIAMOND LOUIE takes the paper that HILDY has written out and reads it very carefully, folds it, puts it in his pocket, and then proceeds to count out the money, as HILDY is looking for his hat and coat.)*

LOUIE: Here you are. *(HILDY grabs the money and begins to count it.)* Well, good-bye and good luck. I'll look you up in New York—if there's anything wrong with this. *(LOUIE exits.)*

HILDY: *(Counting the money.)* Ten, twenty, thirty, thirty-five, forty-five— *(Gets confused; starts again.)* Ten, twenty, thirty, forty, forty-five, fifty-five— *(In trouble again; he gives up.)* The hell with it. Anyway, I get out of this lousy place. They can take their story now and *(HILDY pockets the money and starts hurriedly to pick up his parcels, including his old felt hat in a paper bag. As he starts for the door, he is arrested by a sound at the window. The sound is caused by EARL WILLIAMS[135] falling through the window into*

---

[135]*Earl Williams.* The plot is based on the escape of Tommy O'Connor on Sunday, December 11, 1921. O'Connor was an Irish immigrant under sentence to be hanged on December 15 for the murder of a police sergeant who was leading a party to arrest him. He escaped cleanly, however, and was never recaptured. For details of the crime and the escape, see pp. 49–51. The description of a "harmless looking man with a moustache" is that of O'Connor. The use of a gun that had been smuggled into the jail is also true to the actual event. Hecht had used the O'Connor escape as central to the plot of his first film, *Underworld,* written for Joseph von Mankewicz, and released in 1927.

If O'Connor had been reapprehended and the court order remained unchanged, his execution would have had to be by hanging, carried out on the site of the

the room. WILLIAMS is a little harmless-looking man with a moustache.
He is coatless and is shod with death-house sneakers. He carries a large gun.
He is on the verge of collapse and holds on to a chair for support. He talks in
an exhausted voice. HILDY at the sight of him drops his packages and stands
riveted.)

EARL: They're after me with searchlights. . . .

HILDY: Put—put down that gun!

EARL: *(Supporting himself.)* It ain't loaded. I fired all the bullets already.

HILDY: Holy God Almighty! . . .

EARL: *(Weakly—handing HILDY the gun.)* I surrender. . . . I couldn't hang
off that roof any longer.

HILDY: Holy God!—Get away from that window. *(EARL obeys. HILDY strides*
to the door and locks it. He comes back and stands staring at EARL and
scratches his head.) Well, for God's sake . . .

EARL: I'm not afraid to die. I was tellin' the fella that when he handed me
the gun.

HILDY: Shut up a second! *(He locks the door.[136])*

EARL: *(Babbling on.)* Wakin' me up in the middle of the night . . . talking
to me about things they don't understand. Callin' me a Bolshevik. I ain't
a Bolshevik. I'm an anarchist. *(HILDY is pulling down the blinds and put-*
ting out the lights.) It's got nothin' to do with bombs. It's the one philos-
ophy that guarantees every man freedom. *(Weakly.)* All those poor people
being crushed by the System. And the boys that were killed in the war.
And in the slums—all those slaves to a crust of bread—I can hear 'em
cryin'—

---

former jail, neither by electrocution nor by hanging in the replacement building
opened in 1929. The gallows built for his execution was kept in the basement of the
old Criminal Court Building and not destroyed until 1977. (On the gallows, see the
Chicago Tribune, October 21, 1974, sec. II, p. 1.)

The name given the character is that of Earle R. Williams, a prominent actor in
silent films of the second decade of the century. As noted in footnote 115, "Earle
Williams" was the spelling used in the Atlantic City tryout and also in the stillborn
Philadelphia run. The choice is an odd one, for Earle R. Williams was born in Sacra-
mento, began his career in a stock company in New Orleans, did his first work in
motion pictures with Vitagraph in Brooklyn about 1912, progressed to Hollywood,
and had no known associations with Chicago. He retired in 1922 and died of pneumonia in Los Angeles at age forty-seven on April 25, 1927, as the play was being
undertaken. (See his obituary in the *New York Times*, April 26, 1927, p. 27.)

[136]*He locks the door.* The stage direction is redundant. Hildy has already locked the
door in the directions for his previous speech.

HILDY: Be quiet! The hell with that. Shut up! . . . will you? *(He is hunting for a hiding place.)*

EARL: Go on . . . take me back and hang me . . . I done my best. . . . *(He crumples and falls to the floor. HILDY stands for a second, desperate. His eye falls on the toilet door. He considers, picks up WILLIAMS, and hurriedly dumps him inside the toilet. He closes the door and springs for the telephone.)*

HILDY: *(Into phone.)* Hello . . . . Gimme Walter Burns, quick! *(Second phone rings. HILDY hesitates, then answers it, propping first receiver between ear and shoulder.)* Hello! . . . Hello! . . . Oh, hello, Peggy. . . . Listen, for God's sake have a heart, will you? Something terrific has happened! *(Into first phone.)* Walter? Hildy . . . No, the hell with that. Listen—come right over here. . . . Come over here *right away.* . . . Wait a minute. *(Into second phone.)* For God's sake, Peggy, quit bawling me out, will you? I'm in a hell of a jam! *(Back to Walter.)* Walter! Get this—I only want to say it once. . . . I got Earl Williams. . . . Yes!. . . Here in the pressroom! . . . Honest to God! . . . For God's sake, hurry! I need you. . . . I will *(Hangs up Into Peggy's phone again.)* Listen, darling, this is the biggest thing that ever happened. . . . Now, wait! Don't cry. Wait till I tell you. *(Lowers his voice.)* I just captured Earl Williams! *(In an intense whisper.)* Earl Williams . . . the murderer! I got him. . . . For God's sake, don't tell anybody. . . . Aw, Peggy . . . Peggy . . . I can't. . . . I can't now! . . . Good Lord! Don't you realize . . . *I know,* but Peggy . . . *(She has hung up.)* Hello, Peggy . . . Peggy! *(HILDY hangs up the phone dejectedly. During the last few speeches, there has been a knocking on the door. Hildy glares apprehensively and holds himself ready for a fight. He moves to the door, and as he approaches it, cries.)* Who is it! *(There is no answer. HILDY opens the door cautiously. MOLLIE bounds in like a wildcat. He seizes her and wrestles with her.)* Wait a minute! What the hell do *you* want?

MOLLIE: *(Wildly.)* Where they gone? You know where they are.

HILDY: Get outa here, Mollie!

MOLLIE: They got him surrounded. They're gonna shoot him—like a dog.

HILDY: Listen! They're lookin' for you, too! If you're smart, you'll get outa here.

MOLLIE: For God's sake, tell me where they've gone. I ain't afraid of them, the yella murderers . . .

HILDY: I'll tell you where they are. They're out at Clark Street! That's where they are! Clark and Fullerton!

MOLLIE: Where? Where? . . . *(The toilet door opens and EARL WILLIAMS appears, dazed and blinking. MOLLIE sees him.)* Oh! *(A knock on the outer door is heard.)*

HILDY: *(With a desperate look at the door.)* Oh, for Christ's —! . . . Sh—! *(With a desperate gesture for silence, and tiptoeing toward door.)* Who is it?

WOODENSHOES *(Outside.)* It's me.

HILDY: What do you want, Woodenshoes?

WOODENSHOES: *(Outside.)* I got some important information for you . . . a clue . . .

HILDY: I'll be right with you. I'm making a personal call. . . . *(Turning to the two, tensely.)* Get back in there! *(Indicating toilet.)*

MOLLIE: What's this . . . a double cross?

HILDY: Damn it! I'm trying to save him. . . .

WOODENSHOES: *(Outside.)* This is very important.

MOLLIE: *(To EARL.)* What are *you* doing here?

HILDY: *(To MOLLIE.)* Keep him *quiet!* It's a cop! *(On his way to the door.)* I'll get rid of him . . . *(He opens the door cautiously and steps quickly into the hall, leaving his arm behind him, his hand on the inside knob of the door. Loud and friendly.)* Hello, Woodenshoes! What's on your mind? *(During the ensuing scene a hardly audible conversation takes place between HILDY and WOODENSHOES. HILDY's shoulder is visible in the door.)*

EARL: Thank you for those roses. . . .

MOLLIE: How did you get here? Does anybody know!

EARL: I came down the rain pipe. I didn't mean to shoot him. I don't know what happened.

MOLLIE: But what are you going to do? You can't stay here! They'll get you!

EARL: I don't care any more.

MOLLIE: You've got to hide! You've got to hide somewhere! The rats![137]

EARL: No. Don't do anything. I'm ready to go. I don't care. It's better to die for a cause than the way most people die—for no reason.

MOLLIE: You won't die. They'll never get you.

EARL: I ain't important. It's humanity that's important, like I told you. Humanity is a wonderful thing, Mollie.

MOLLIE: No, it ain't. They're just dirty murderers. Look what they done to you . . . and to me . . .

EARL: That's because they don't know any better.

MOLLIE: You're too good for 'em . . . that's why.

EARL: You're good, too.

---

[137] In the acting edition, "The rats!" is dropped.

MOLLIE: *(With wonder.)* Me?

EARL: Yeah, I think you're wonderful. . . . I wrote out a statement today and left it with Mr. Jacobi, so that when I was dead people would understand what I meant. There was a lot about you in it. I said you were the most beautiful character I ever met.

MOLLIE: *(Blinking and dazed.)* Yeah?

HILDY: *(Entering, indicating toilet.)* Get back in there! The fellows are coming down the hall now! *(He locks the door.)*

MOLLIE: They'll find him there!

HILDY: Well, there isn't any place else. *(He looks helplessly around the room; at that moment someone tries the doorknob.)*

MOLLIE: There's somebody!

HILDY: Sssh!

ENDICOTT: *(Outside.)* Who locked the door!

HILDY: Coming right away, Mike. *(Whispers to MOLLIE.)* He's got to go in there!

ENDICOTT: *(Outside.)* Well, for God's sake, hurry.

MOLLIE: Oh, my God!

HILDY: Wait a minute! I got an idea! *(Springs and opens the desk.)* Can you get in this desk?

WILSON: *(Outside.)* What the hell's going on in there! *(Starts to pound on door.)*

EARL: What good'll it do?

HILDY: We'll get you out in ten minutes.

WILSON: *(Outside.)* Open up there, will you?

HILDY: All right, all right. God damn it!

EARL: Please, don't talk like that in front of her.[138]

MOLLIE: *(To EARL.)* Go on! Please! Please!

EARL: They'll find me, anyhow. *(More pounding.)*

HILDY: All right, I'm coming! *(To EARL.)* Keep dead quiet. Don't even breathe.

MOLLIE: I'll be right here. I won't leave you.

ENDICOTT: *(Outside, shouting.)* Hey, what the goddamn hell.

HILDY: Keep your shirt on! *(He opens the door.)* What are you trying to do! Kick down the building? *(ENDICOTT and WILSON enter. Head for phones at back.)*

ENDICOTT: Kind of exclusive, ain't you? *(Sees MOLLIE.)* Oh! *(Elaborately.)* I beg your pardon.

WILSON: City Desk, please! What's the idea of locking the door?

---

[138]This line is deleted from the acting edition.

HILDY: I was interviewing her.

ENDICOTT: *(At phone.)* Gimme the city desk. . . What was he doing to her?

WILSON: With the blinds down. *(MURPHY enters.)*

MURPHY: Where the hell you been, Hildy? There's the damnedest Halloween going on—the whole police force standing on its ear. *(At phone.)* Murphy talking. Gimme the desk.

WILSON: *(Into phone.)* Wilson speaking. No luck yet on Williams. Call you back! *(KRUGER enters.)*

KRUGER: God, I never was so tired in my life.

HILDY: Any news?

MURPHY: *(Into phone.)* This is Murphy. . . . Well, they surrounded the house, only Williams wasn't there.

KRUGER: Gimme a rewrite man. *(McCUE enters.)*

McCUE: *(Entering.)* Jesus, what a chase!

MURPHY: *(Into phone.)* Wait a minute. They shot somebody, anyhow. Here you are! Ready? Herman Schulte,[139] the Sheriff's brother-in-law. He was leading the squad through the house and was looking under a bed when Deputy John F. Watson[140] came in the room and mistook him for Earl. Shot him right in the pants. Yeah. A bull's-eye. Right. *(Hangs up.)*

HILDY: *(On edge.)* He always had lead in his pants.

McCUE: *(At his phone.)* McCue talking. Gimme the desk.

KRUGER: *(Phoning.)* This is Kruger, out with Hartman's deputies. . . . Yeah. . . . I'm in the drugstore, at Clark and Fullerton. Well, call me back if you don't believe me. *(Hangs up.)*

McCUE: *(Into phone.)* That so! I'll check on it. *(Hangs up.)* There's something

---

[139]*Herman Schulte.* Herman W. Schulte, a travel agent at 236 W. Jackson Boulevard.

[140]*John F. Watson.* Sir Arthur Conan Doyle chose the name John H. Watson for Sherlock Holmes's colleague because John Watson is a very common name, without being obvious as such, as in the instances of John Smith or John Brown. Inevitably, there are many possible John Watsons. If the name was used without alteration, the person is John F. Watson, a chief clerk at 29 E. Madison Street. Other candidates are John Watson, a bartender; John A. Watson, a lawyer at 127 N. Dearborn Street; John A. Watson, a salesman at 243 S. Dearborn; and John M. Watson, a copywriter at 104 S. Michigan. Because the next reference is to Sherlock Holmes, the possibility that this is a reference to Dr. John H. Watson should not be ignored.

It has been suggested that this may refer to Victor Watson, a career editor and troubleshooter for the Hearst papers. He was mainly identified with the *New York American,* and it is doubtful that he had enough associations with Chicago to be mentioned.

doing at Harrison Street Station. *(Into phone.)* Gimme Harrison twenty-five hundred. Hurry it, will you please?

KRUGER: *(To MOLLIE, who is in the swivel chair in front of the desk.)* What's the idea, Mollie? Can't you flop somewhere else?

MURPHY: Yeah, parking her fanny in here like it was a cathouse.[141] *(Takes a sniff of the air.)* Fleur de Floozie, she's got on.

KRUGER: *(Neighing like a horse.)* Makes me passionate!

MURPHY: Go on, Mollie, put it somewhere else. Go out and stink up Clark Street.

MOLLIE: *(Nervous and twitching.)* You lay off me!

McCUE: Look out—she'll start bawling again. *(Into phone.)* I'll hold the wire. Only don't forget me.

HILDY: Let her alone, fellas. She's not doing anything.

MURPHY: *(To HILDY.)* What the hell are you two so chummy about?

ENDICOTT: Yeah, they were locked in here together when we come along.

WILSON: Wouldn't open the door.

McCUE: You'll be out of training for your honeymoon—playing pinochle with this baby.

MURPHY: I thought you were going to catch a train.

KRUGER: He was running around here ten minutes ago with his pants on fire about going to New York.

ENDICOTT: Told us he was interviewing her.

MURPHY: What are you trying to do! Scoop us?

HILDY: I'm waiting here for Walter. He's coming over with some dough.

McCUE: *(Phoning.)* Hello, Sarge. McCue. I hear you got a tip on Williams.

WILSON: Look, she's got the shakes. What the hell you making faces about?

ENDICOTT: *(Singing childishly.)* She's jealous because Hildy's going to be married.

HILDY: Go on—show 'em you can smile through your tears. Relax.

MOLLIE: You let me alone—all of you. *(SCHWARTZ enters.)*

McCUE: *(Into phone.)* Yeah! What's the address!

SCHWARTZ: Hello, fellas. What the hell, Hildy? You still here?

ENDICOTT: Yeah, and trying to hang something on us, if you ask me. What's the lowdown Hildy?

SCHWARTZ: Who the hell pulled these shades down!

McCUE: *(Turning from phone.)* Hey! This looks good. An old lady just called up the detective bureau and claims Williams is hiding under her piazza.

---

[141]In the acting edition, "a cathouse" is replaced with "her house."

ENDICOTT: Tell her to stand up.

MURPHY: Who you got there?

McCUE: The Captain.[142]

MURPHY: Let me talk to him. *(Taking the phone.)* Hello, Turkey. . . . How's your gussie Mollie? . . . I hear this guy Williams is hiding in your mustache. . . . Yeah? Well, get your nose out of the way. *(Hangs up. Points to MOLLIE's crossed and highly visible legs.)* Oooh! Lookit! Pike's Peak!

McCUE: Listen, fellows, that sounds like a pretty good tip. What do you say?

HILDY: If you boys want to get out, I'll cover this end for you.

ENDICOTT: Aw, the hell with chasing around any more. I spent a dollar forty on taxis already.

KRUGER: *(Flat on his back.)* Don't let's do any more going out.

SCHWARTZ: *(Who has gone to the window.)* If you ask me, I got a hunch Williams ain't anywhere they been looking for him.

WILSON: How do you mean?

SCHWARTZ: Well, I just been talking to Jacobi about that roof he's supposed to have jumped off of. Look! Now there's that skylight he got out of.

ENDICOTT: Where?

McCUE: *(Looking out.)* Jesus, how could he get from there to the ground?

SCHWARTZ: That's just the point. Jacobi's gone up there with a couple of cops to look over the whole roof.

McCUE *(Leaning out.)* I tell you what he could have done, though. Look! He could have jumped over to this roof. That's only about four feet.

ENDICOTT: Yeah, he could have done that, all right.

KRUGER: *(Wearily.)* I'm pretending there ain't no Earl Williams.

SCHWARTZ: And that's why I'm telling you guys that I don't think this guy Williams is anywhere they been looking for him. I got a stinking hunch he's right in this building.

HILDY: *(Derisive.)* Hanging around like a duck in a shootin' gallery, I suppose! You're a lot of bright guys —

McCUE: *(Still looking.)* It'd be easy, once he got on this roof. . . .

HILDY: *(With nervous hilarity.)* Hey—Sherlock Holmes,[143] what correspondence school did you graduate from?

---

[142]*The Captain.* Not identifiable.

[143]*Sherlock Holmes.* The well-known consulting detective, in active practice in London from about 1877 to 1903, with individual cases both earlier and later. Holmes's date of birth has never been firmly established, but on the basis of internal evidence in the accounts of his professional activity, it was likely about 1854. We have it on the authority of his biographer, the late Vincent Starrett, that he will never

SCHWARTZ: What's the matter with that? He could come down the rain pipe and crawl into any one of those windows on this side. . . .

KRUGER: Well if the story's going to walk right in the window —!

HILDY: The masterminds at work! Why don't you guys go home—he'll probably *call* on you. . . . *(BENSINGER enters and approaches his desk. MOLLIE, sitting in his chair, is hidden from him at the moment by one or two of the reporters.)*

BENSINGER: Hello, Hildy. Thought you were going to New York. *(HILDY has sprung into action with BENSINGER's entrance. BENSINGER sees MOLLIE.)* For God's sake, what's she doing in my chair? *(MOLLIE springs up.)* Is that the only place you can sit? That's my property and I don't want anybody using it!

HILDY: *(Leaning against the closed desk.)* Nobody's using it, Roy. Everything's all right.

BENSINGER: *(Anxiously.)* Any of you fellows got some aspirin?

ENDICOTT: No, sweetheart, but I got some nice cyanide.

BENSINGER: *(Sitting down.)* Cut the kidding, fellows. I tell you I'm sick.

SCHWARTZ: How about a good truss? I'll sell it to you cheap.

HILDY: What's the matter, Roy? Off your feed?

BENSINGER: If I haven't got a good case of grippe coming, I miss my guess. *(Reaching for desk cover.)* Get out of the way, will you?

HILDY: *(Not moving.)* I hope you didn't get it off me.

BENSINGER: I got it off somebody. Everybody using my phone all the time— it's a wonder I ain't caught anything worse. *(Pushing HILDY slightly.)* Look out, I got to get my cup.

HILDY: *(Doubling up as if with a violent cramp.)* Wait a minute, will you?

BENSINGER: *(Frightened.)* What's the matter?

HILDY: *(Faintly.)* I don't know, oh—

BENSINGER: Don't you feel all right?

HILDY: No. *(Coughs violently in BENSINGER's face.)*

BENSINGER: Don't do that!

HILDY: *(Weakly.)* Do what?

BENSINGER: Cough on a guy! Jesus!

HILDY: Well, I don't know what's the matter. I suddenly got a pain right— *(Vaguely indicates his throat.)* —and a kind of rash on my chest. *(Opening his shirt.)*

---

die, however. See Vincent Starrett, *The Private Life of Sherlock Holmes*, 2d ed. (Chicago: University of Chicago Press, 1960), especially chapter 8, "Ave Sherlock Morituri et cetera," pp. 93–101.

BENSINGER: *(Recoiling.)* What?! You've probably got some disease!

MURPHY: Sure! He's got the pazooza![144]

HILDY: *(Advancing on BENSINGER, tries to take his hand.)* Feel! Ain't that fever?

BENSINGER: *(Retreating from the desk.)* Hey, cut it out! It may be diphtheria!

HILDY: I woke up this morning, and had yellow spots all over my stomach. . . .

BENSINGER: That ain't funny!

KRUGER: For God's sake, Roy, can't you see he's kidding you. *(HILDY, following BENSINGER, seizes him.)*

BENSINGER: Let go of me! You may have something contagious! If you're sick go to a hospital! *(HILDY coughs in his face.)* For the love of God!

MURPHY: It's no worse than a bad cold, Roy.

HILDY: *(Opening his mouth.)* Can you see anything in there? Aaah!

BENSINGER: Listen, fellows! You ain't got any sense, letting him hang around here. We'll all catch it, whatever it is! *(They all laugh.)* All right, laugh! But I'm going to get this place fumigated![145]

MURPHY: The hell you are!

BENSINGER: *(Furiously.)* The hell I ain't! We got to breathe this air. I'm gonna get Doc Springer[146] and clean this whole place up! You goddamn maniacs. *(Exits. HILDY leans weakly up against the desk and laughs hysterically.)*

ENDICOTT: What's the idea, Hildy? Now he'll be burning sulphur for a week like last time. . . .

---

[144]*the pazooza.* On the basis of the standard dictionaries of unconventional American English, this is not a slang term for a disease but was probably coined by the authors for the play.

[145]The threat to get the place fumigated is dropped from the acting edition.

[146]*Doc Springer.* Joseph Springer, M.D., the most prominent physician on the coroner's staff. Springer took his medical degree from the Illinois College of Physicians and Surgeons in 1895. He was appointed by coroner George Berz in 1897 and served under Berz and his successors, John E. Traeger, Peter M. Hoffman, and Oscar Wolff. Springer retired abruptly on June 1, 1923, stating that at age fifty-five he no longer felt able to serve in a position that required him to be on call twenty-four hours a day. He returned later in the year to the extent of participating in murder investigations. (See the *Chicago Tribune*, June 2, 1923, p. 9; August 13, 1923, p. 7.) He had long since established himself as one of the leading figures in forensic medicine in the United States. In 1927 he became chief criminologist of the Chicago Police Department, but he retired in 1929. He died on November 3, 1936, at age sixty-nine. (See his obituary in the *Chicago Tribune*, November 4, 1936, p. 34.)

McCUE: Yeah, you're leavin', but we gotta work here, with all them stink pots. . . . What a sense of humor you got.

SCHWARTZ: Now look here. What about Williams? Let's get the cops and search the building. What do you say!

ENDICOTT: I could use that reward. . . .

MURPHY: What the hell could you do with ten grand!

ENDICOTT: You could have a girl in every room at the Sherman Hotel[147] for that. . . .

MURPHY: You'd never get past the basement.

McCUE: It would be funny if we found him right here in the building.

SCHWARTZ: What do you say? Should we get the cops?

MURPHY: Call up Lieutenant Callahan,[148] Mac. Tell him we got a hot tip.

HILDY: Wait! What do you want to call the cops for? Suppose he *is* in the building. They'll grab all the reward and you guys won't get a smell.

SCHWARTZ: Huh?

WILSON: That's right.

HILDY: Listen! Each of us take a floor and whoever finds him—we split it up. What do you say?

WILSON: That's not a bad idea.

KRUGER: I'll stay here.

HILDY: Two grand apiece! Why we could retire for life! You could pay off all those loan sharks, Jimmie, and have enough left to stay stinko forever![149]

McCUE: I don't know, getting my can blown off.

---

[147]*the Sherman Hotel.* One of the city's traditional major commercial hotels, located at Clark and Randolph Streets. Hotels on the site dated from the City Hotel of Francis C. Sherman in 1837. The structure of the post–Chicago Fire era was bought by Joseph Beifeld in 1902. His son Ernest built the Sherman Hotel to which the text refers in 1910 and greatly expanded it in 1925. Because the Sherman of 1910 had 757 rooms and as expanded had 1,400, in either case Endicott was dreaming of considerable sexual excess. (See "Hotel Sherman of Chicago," *The Hotel Monthly* 19, no. 216 [March, 1911], 34–53.) The hotel closed on January 24, 1973, and was razed in the spring of 1980.

[148]*Lieutenant Callahan.* Charles Callahan, a career member of the Chicago Police Department since 1906, who was promoted from sergeant to lieutenant on January 4, 1924. He resigned from the force on July 1, 1926. (Manuscript personnel records of the Chicago Police Department, searched by Ed Griffin of the Department, 1994.)

[149]This entire speech is dropped from the acting edition and the text otherwise shortened in this exchange.

HILDY: What else is it good for? . . . Besides, he can't hurt anybody. . . . What do you say? Do you want to try it?

MRS. GRANT: *(Enters, in a very righteous mood.)* Well!

HILDY *(Stricken.)* Now—now, listen, Mother—

MRS. GRANT: Don't you mother me! If you've got anything to say for yourself you come downstairs and say it to Peggy.

HILDY: Listen, Mother, tell Peggy I'll be downstairs in five minutes, will you? Will you go down and tell her that?

MRS. GRANT: No, sir—I don't move out of here without you.

HILDY: Listen, Mother, you don't understand. Now I told Peggy—

MRS. GRANT: I know what you told her! A lot of gibberish about a murderer!

HILDY: No—no!

MRS. GRANT: I don't care if you *did* catch him, you come with me this minute!

THE REPORTERS: I knew something stunk around here. Who says he caught him? What's going on. What do you mean caught a murderer? *(Etc.) (In the midst of this babel, WOODENSHOES enters; stands listening.)*

HILDY: No, no! I don't know what she's talking about! I didn't tell her any such thing.

MRS. GRANT: Yes, you did!

MOLLIE: He never told her that!

HILDY: I said I was *trying* to catch one, that's all! You got it balled up, mother!

MURPHY: *(To MOLLIE.)* What do *you* know about it? How do you know he didn't?

MOLLIE: Let go of my arm!

ENDICOTT: Hildy and that tart were in here together!

WOODENSHOES: Yah! Yah! She's the one that knows! Ask *her!*

MURPHY: *(Wheeling on him.)* What do you mean she knows?

WOODENSHOES: Serchay la femme! *(To MOLLIE.)* Where's Earl Williams?

MOLLIE: How the hell should I know?

WOODENSHOES: Where have you got him hid?

MURPHY: *(Viciously.)* Who you holding out on, Hildy? Come clean, or goddamn it, we'll knock it out of you! *(The reporters surround HILDY menacingly.)*

McCUE: Yeah. What the hell! Sock him, Jimmie!

ENDICOTT: You dirty double-crosser!

MOLLIE: *(Wildly.)* Wait! You goddamn stool pigeons! He don't know where Earl Williams is. I'm the one that knows.

ENDICOTT: What do you mean you know? *(The reporters turn on MOLLIE.)*
WOODENSHOES: Where is he!
MOLLIE: Go find out, you lousy heels. You don't think I'm gonna tell!
WOODENSHOES: You'll tell all right! We'll make you . . .
MOLLIE: *(Slowly backing toward the door.)* Yeah? . . . Yeah . . . the hell I will.
HILDY: *(Who has remained riveted to the desk.)* Let her alone . . . she's goofy!
(MOLLIE lunges suddenly for the door.)
THE REPORTERS: Look out! . . . Close that door . . . For Christ' sake! Don't
let her get away. *(She is headed off at the door.)*
McCUE: You ain't gettin' out o' here, Mollie.
ENDICOTT: Now where is he? In the building?
McCUE: Where you hidin' him?
MOLLIE: I ain't gonna squcal! I ain't gonna squcal!
MURPHY: *(Approaching her slowly.)* Come on, you lousy tart! Before we kick
your teeth out!
ENDICOTT: D'ye want us to call the cops and give you the boots?
MURPHY: Go on, Woodenshoes. Slap it out of her!
WOODENSHOES: *(Reaching for her.)* Come on now. Where is he before I
hurt you!
MOLLIE: *(Tearing away from him, wild and blubbering.)* Take your hands off
me, you goddamn kidney foot! *(She snatches at a chair and swings it at
the slowly advancing circle of men.)* Let me alone or I'll knock your god-
damn heads off. . . .
ENDICOTT: Put down that chair!
SCHWARTZ: Get around—get on the side of her.
MOLLIE: *(Backing away, swinging her chair.)* No you don't! You bastards! Keep
away from me!
KRUGER: Grab her.
MOLLIE: *(With a last wild look at the circling foe.)* You'll never get it out of
me. . . . *(She hurls the chair at their heads and screams.)* I'll never tell! Never!
(She leaps for the open window and disappears.[150] *Her scream of terror and*

---

[150]*She leaps for the open window and disappears.* The drop would not have been to
the ground, but to the roof of the jail about a floor below. It was, as the text indicates, a fall that one could survive. In the acting edition, Murphy estimates the
drop at twenty feet (p. 100). In that edition, the entire text concerning Mollie's leap
is extensively rewritten.

The British critic St. John Ervine in the course of his unfavorable review of the
play was particularly hostile to the reporters' callous treatment of Mollie, whom
he considered a sympathetic figure. He took especial offense at their apathetic

exultation is heard as she drops through the darkness to the ground. The re-
porters stand riveted for an instant, powerless before the tragedy. Then they
rush forward. An assortment of awed and astonished oaths rise from them.
They lean out of the window. WOODENSHOES the Theorist, stands sick
at heart. His body is doubled up with pain for a moment. Through the bab-
ble of cries his voice comes thickly.)

WOODENSHOES: Oh! I never thought she'd do that! That's terrible. . . .

MRS. GRANT: *(Coming out of a trance.)* Take me out of here! Take me out
of here! Oh my God! *(She collapses in a chair.)*

THE REPORTERS: *(At the window.)* She ain't killed. . . . No. . . . She's moving. . . . Get the cops, Woodenshoes. . . . Come on fellas. . . .

HILDY: Holy God—the poor kid . . . the poor kid. *(Voices come from the jail*
yard—"Hey Carl[151] *. . . . Get a doctor! What the hell! Who is it? What hap-*
pened?" etc. The reporters rush out to get to MOLLIE. HILDY stands dazed,
looking out of the window. MRS. GRANT moans through her hands. As the
vibrations subside, a newcomer is standing in the door. This is MR. WAL-
TER BURNS,[152] *the Managing Editor. Beneath a dapper and very citizen*
like exterior lurks a hobgoblin, perhaps the Devil himself. But if Mr. Burns
is the Devil he is a very naif one. He is a Devil with neither point nor pur-
pose to him—an undignified Devil hatched for a bourgeois Halloween. In
less hyperbolic language, Mr. Burns is that product of thoughtless, pointless,
nerve-drumming unmorality that is the Boss Journalist—the licensed eaves-

---

reaction to her plunge from the window. (*The Saturday Review of Literature* 5, no.
31 [February 23, 1929], pp. 706–7.) Harry C. Read in his article on the accuracy of
the play at the time of the first Chicago production in the *American* observed that
the plunge is unnecessary; Mollie could have slid down the same rain pipe that Earl
used to reach the pressroom. (*Chicago American*, November 26, 1928, p. 2.)

For the first New York performance, a hole of about six feet diameter was cut in
the stage and a mattress placed in the basement below it to catch the actress. In
the dress rehearsal, Dorothy Stickney slightly fractured her right elbow in the fall.
Taken up in the excitement of the play's opening, she did not immediately notice
the break, but had medical treatment three days later. She acted Mollie for about
three weeks with a cast and sling, colored black so as to be unobtrusive against
her costume. (See Dorothy Stickney, *Openings and Closings* [Garden City, NY:
Doubleday & Co., 1979], pp. 82–88.)

[151]*Carl.* Carl J. Carlson, Deputy Sheriff. See footnote 93.

[152]*Walter Burns*, editor of the *Herald and Examiner* and other Hearst papers. See
p. 52.

dropper, troublemaker, bombinator,[153] and Town Snitch, misnamed The Press. At this moment Mr. Burns, in the discharge of his high calling, stands in the door, nerveless and meditative as a child, his mind open to such troubles as he can find or create.)

HILDY: *(Seeing him.)* Walter! My God—did you see that?

WALTER: *(Quietly.)* Yes. Where is he?

HILDY: She jumped out of the window.

WALTER: I know. . . . Where is he, I said?

HILDY: *(Looking out of the window.)* She's moving! Thank God she ain't killed herself!

WALTER: Come to, Hildy! Where have you got Williams?

HILDY: *(Still absorbed in the Mollie matter.)* Huh? He's—he's in the desk. *(As WALTER goes to desk.)* Thank God she ain't dead. *(WALTER opens desk a crack.)*

EARL: *(Muffled.)* Let me out, I can't stand it!

WALTER: Keep quiet! You're sitting pretty.

MRS. GRANT: *(Staring at the Editor.)* What's the matter?

WALTER: *(He wheels.)* Who the hell is that?

HILDY: It's my girl's mother.

MRS. GRANT: What are you doing? Oh, my God!

WALTER: Shut up!

MRS. GRANT: I won't shut up! That girl killed herself. Oh! You're doing something wrong. What's in there? *(DIAMOND LOUIE appears in the doorway.)*

HILDY: Now, Mother, please!

WALTER: Take her out of here, will you?

MRS. GRANT: What did you say?

HILDY: Now look here, Walter—

WALTER: Louie, take this lady over to Polack Mike's and lock her up. See that she don't talk to anyone on the way![154]

MRS. GRANT: What's that? What's that?

HILDY: *(Startled.)* Aw, now, Walter, you can't do that!

LOUIE: *(Calls.)* Hey, Tony![155]

MRS. GRANT: Don't you touch me!

WALTER: Tell 'em it's a case of delirium tremens.

---

[153]*bombinator.* One who makes a buzzing or droning sound. Note that this obscure noun recurs in the epilogue.

[154]In the acting edition the second sentence of this speech is replaced by "Tell 'em it's a case of delirium tremens," replacing Walter's next line.

[155]*Tony.* Not identifiable.

LOUIE: Tony, give me a hand with this lady.

HILDY: *(Helplessly.)* Listen, Walter, this'll get me in a hell of a jam. . . . *(To MRS. GRANT who, a hand over her mouth, is being dragged off, her heels trailing.)* Now don't worry, mother, this is only temporary. . . . Honest to God, Walter . . .

MRS. GRANT: *(Vaguely heard.)* Peggy, Peggy! Oh, my God! *(Exit TONY, LOUIE, and MRS. GRANT. HILDY starts out.)*

WALTER: *(Grabs his arm.)* Where the hell do you think you're going!

HILDY: Let go of me! I gotta get my girl! She's downstairs in a cab all alone.

WALTER: Your girl! Good God, what are you? Some puking college boy! Why, in time of war you could be shot for what you're doing—for less than you're doing!

HILDY: To hell with you—there's your story locked up in that desk! Smear it all over the front page—Earl Williams caught by the *Examiner*—and take all the credit. . . . I covered your story and I covered it goddamn right. . . . Now I'm gettin' out. . . .

WALTER: You drooling saphead . . . What do you mean—a story? You've got the whole city by the seat of the pants!

HILDY: I know all about that, but . . .

WALTER: You know hell—You got the brains of a pancake. . . . Listen Hildy, if I didn't have your interests at heart, would I be wastin' time now arguin' with you! You've done somethin' big—you've stepped into a new class . . .

HILDY: *(D'Artagnan never gave Richelieu an ear more startled or more innocent.)* Huh?

WALTER: Listen, we'll make such monkeys out of these ward heelers that *nobody* will vote for them—not even their *wives.*

HILDY: Expose 'em, huh . . .

WALTER: Expose 'em! Crucify 'em! We're gonna keep Williams under cover till morning so's the *Examiner* can break the story exclusive . . . Then we'll let the Senator in on the capture—share the glory with him.

HILDY: I see—I see! *(Blinking and warming up.)*

WALTER: You've kicked over the whole City Hall like an applecart. You've got the Mayor and Hartman backed against a wall. You've put one administration out and another in. . . . This ain't a newspaper story—it's a career. And you standin' there bellyachin' about some girl. . . .[156]

---

[156]The final sentence of this speech is deleted from the acting edition.

HILDY: Jesus, I—I wasn't figuring it that way, I guess. We'll be the white-haired boys, won't we?

WALTER: Why, they'll be naming streets after you. Johnson Street! You and I and the Senator are going to *run* this town. . . . Do you understand that?

HILDY: Yeah . . . Yeah! But—wait a minute we can't leave Williams here . . . One of those reporters'll . . .

WALTER: We're going to take him over to my private office right away. . . . Where's the *Examiner* phone?

HILDY: That one. The red one. How the hell you gonna do it? They'll see him!

WALTER: Not if he's inside the desk. . . . We'll carry the desk over. *(Into phone.)* Hello! *Examiner.* Give me Duffy[157]. . . . I'd have had him there now if you hadn't give me such an argument.

HILDY: You can't take that out. It's crawling with cops outside.

WALTER: We'll lower it out of the window with pulleys. Quit stallin'. *(To HILDY.)* Hildy! Get that machine and start pounding out a lead, will you. . . . Come on—snap into it. . . .

HILDY: How much you want on it? . . .

WALTER: All the words you got. . . .

HILDY: Where the hell is there some paper?

WALTER *(Into phone.)* Hello. . . . Hello!

HILDY *(Moving for BENSINGER's desk.)* Can I call the Mayor an animal at bay?

WALTER: Call him a nigger if you want to! Come on! Come on!

HILDY: How about that time he had his house painted by the fire department.

WALTER: Give him the works. . . . *(Into phone.)* Hello Duffy. Get set! We got the biggest story in the world. Earl Williams caught by the *Examiner* . . . exclusive. . . . *(HILDY has opened the drawers of BENSINGER's desk and in a frantic search for paper is tossing play manuscripts, syringes, patent medicines, and old socks in the air.)*

WALTER: *(Continuing into phone.)* Duffy! Send down word to Butch McGuirk[158] I want ten huskies from the circulation department to lam right over here—pressroom criminal courts building. That's what I said—Butch McGuirk. *(To HILDY.)* He'll get that desk out—nothin' ever stopped those boys yet.[159]

---

[157]In the acting edition of 1950, this reads "Duffy Cornell."

[158]*Butch McGuirk.* John McGuirk, an inspector with the *Journal* at the time of Hecht's arrival in Chicago.

[159]The last sentence and Hildy's response are eliminated in the acting edition.

HILDY *(Has unearthed a full package of BENSINGER's personal stationery. He now picks up the typewriter.)* What if they start shootin'?

WALTER: Fine! *(Into phone.)* Now listen, Duffy. I want you to tear out the whole front page. . . . That's what I said—the whole front page . . . out . . . *(Into phone.)* Johnson's writing the lead. . . . *(PEGGY enters—a desperate and strident antagonist.)*

PEGGY: Hildy!

WALTER: What the hell do you want!

PEGGY: Hildy!

HILDY: *(Holding the typewriter in his arms. Dazed.)* What!

WALTER: Listen, Miss, you can't come in here! *(Into phone.)* To hell with the Chinese earthquake! . . .[160] What's that?

HILDY: Listen, darling —

PEGGY: Where's Mother?

WALTER *(Into phone.)* I don't care if there's a *million* dead.

HILDY: Peggy, I got to ask you to do something! A big favor!

PEGGY: You're not coming!

WALTER *(Into phone.)* What? I don't hear you.

HILDY: Now don't get sore and fly off the handle, darling. What happened was—

PEGGY: You're *not! Are* you? Tell me, Hildy! Tell me the truth!

WALTER: *(Into phone.)* Take all those Miss America pictures off page 6. Wait a minute, Duffy. *(Turns.)* Now look here, little girl—

PEGGY *(Wheels on WALTER.)* You're doing this to him! He was going and you stopped him!

HILDY: Something terrific's happened, Peggy! Wait till I tell you! I couldn't—

WALTER: You'll tell her nothing! She's a woman, you damn fool!

PEGGY: Well, I'm not going to let you do it! You're coming right now! With me!

WALTER: Holy God!

HILDY: But it's the biggest chance of my life. Now listen, darling—

---

[160]*the Chinese earthquake.* There were, inevitably, several earthquakes in China in the period, but the most catastrophic, and the one to which the reference is most likely, was reported as the play was being written: on May 23, 1927, an earthquake ravaged Kansu province in western China, killing what was initially estimated at 100,000 people. Because of destruction of local communications facilities, reports did not reach the outside world until summer. (See the *New York Times*, July 29, 1927, p. 1.) Given the magnitude of the disaster, Walter's ejaculation here is a fine demonstration of how seriously he took the story of the escape.

WALTER: *(Frenzied.)* Shut up, will you!

PEGGY: You don't *want* to marry me! That's all!

HILDY: *(Putting down the typewriter.)* That ain't true! Just because you won't listen, you're saying I don't love you when you know I'd cut off my hands for you! I'd do anything in the world for you! Anything!

WALTER: *(Into phone.)* Hello, Duffy! What? . . . What's that? . . . To hell with the League of Nations![161] Spike it!

PEGGY: You never intended to be decent and live like a human being! You were lying all the time!

HILDY: Peggy, don't keep saying that!

WALTER: *(Into phone.)* What's that? What?

PEGGY: Lying! That's what you were! Just lying!

HILDY: *(His tortured male spirit takes refuge in hysteria.)* All right! If that's what you think!

WALTER: *(Shouting at the lovers.)* H. Sebastian God! I'm trying to concentrate!

PEGGY: I see what you are now! You're just a bum! Like him— *(Indicates WALTER.)* and all the rest!

HILDY: Sure! That's what I am!

WALTER: *(Into phone.)* No! Leave the rooster story alone—that's human interest!

PEGGY: You're just a heartless selfish animal without any feelings! *(To WALTER.)* And you're worse! It's all your fault and if you think I'm going to put up with it—

WALTER: Shut up, will you? *(Into phone.)* Duffy, let me talk to Butch—

HILDY: Shut up, will you? Yeah! That's what I am! A bum! Without any feelings! And that's all I want to be!

WALTER: *(Into phone.)* Get a hold o' Butch as fast as you can.

PEGGY: You never did love me or you couldn't talk to me like that! *(The desk top opens slowly and EARL WILLIAMS sticks his head out.)*

WALTER: *(Screaming across the room.)* Get back in there—you goddamn turtle[162] . . . *(The desk top falls, the fugitive disappears within, and PEGGY, her heartbreak audible in her sobs, moves blindly toward the door.)*

---

[161]*League of Nations.* There is probably no single action of the League of Nations that can be fitted to this passage. At the time the Kansu Province earthquake was reported in the West, the League was not in session. When it resumed, it was mainly occupied with disarmament proposals and a specific Polish resolution to outlaw war, any of which might reasonably be on the front page of a major daily.

[162]This speech in the acting edition is reassigned from Walter to Hildy.

HILDY: *(Sitting before his typewriter calls after her, his voice tormented but his egoism intact.)* If you want me you'll have to take me as I am instead of trying to turn me into some lah de dah with a cane! I'm no stuffed shirt writing peanut ads. . . . Goddamn it—I'm a newspaper man. . . . *(PEGGY exits, her sobs filling the room and corridor.)*

WALTER: Shut up! *(Into phone as the curtain is falling.)* Hello Duffy! The edition gone in yet? . . . Well don't. . . . Never mind the mail trains. . . . You ain't working for the advertising department. . . . The hell with Marshall Field's!! Stick on this wire![163]

HILDY: *(Has started typing. The click of the keys stops suddenly and he rips the piece of copy paper from the machine. He is not quite himself—he has made an error in his lead.)* . . . Goddamn it—[164]

CURTAIN

---

[163]The excerpts from an earlier draft in *Theatre* show that this speech was directed to Butch McGuirk, not to Duffy: "Hello, Butch? The edition gone in yet? . . . Well don't! . . . The hell with the mail trains! Hold the presses till you hear from me!"

[164]Heywood Broun in his review in the *New York Telegram*, although generally favorable to the play, considered Lee Tracy not credible as a reporter, mainly because Broun thought Tracy's performance on the typewriter here not convincing. (See "'The Front Page' Proves First Good Newspaper Play: Authors Founded Farce on Tale Worthy of Belief," reprint from *New York Telegram*, no date, no page, in a set of reprints in standard format furnished to Jed Harris by Richard Maney, papers of Jed Harris, Theatre Collection, University of Memphis, box 13, folder 21. The review is apparently not in the edition microfilmed.)

Hildy's final speech in Act II is dropped from the acting edition; the text ends with Walter's final speech.

ACT III

The same Scene, five minutes later. HILDY is typing furiously. WALTER is pacing up and down. He finally picks up the receiver, which has been standing on the table. Into phone, with moderate excitement:

WALTER: Duffy. . . . Duffy! *(To HILDY.)* Goddamn it! I told him to stay on that phone. If I had a few people who did what they were told I could get something accomplished. . . . I bet he never told 'em to take taxis. . . . Butch and the gang are probably *walking* over here. . . . *(Looking out of the window.)* Oh, for Chris' sake. . . Now the *moon's* out! *(HILDY types on. WALTER skitters to the desk and taps three times. EARL taps back three times from within.)* Fine! Three taps is me! Don't forget! . . . You're sitting pretty now. Got enough air? *(He raises the rolltop an inch or two and fans air in with his hand.)* Is that better? *(Closing the desk and going to phone.)* I am into 'em, Hildy! Below the belt! Every punch! *(Into phone, with great sarcasm.)* Hello! . . . Duffy! Where the hell you been? Well, the hell with your diabetes! You stick on this phone! Listen, did you impress it on Butch to take a taxi—that every minute counts? Who's he bringing with him? What do you mean, you don't know! But you told Butch it was life and death, huh? All right, stick on the wire! *(Putting down receiver.)* Duffy's getting old. . . .[165] Well, Butch is on the way, Hildy. All we got to do is hold out for fifteen minutes. . . .

HILDY: *(Over his typing.)* The boys'll be back. They'll be coming in to phone.

WALTER: I'll handle them. It's that three-toed Sheriff I'm worrying about. If he starts sticking his snoot into this . . . *(Cudgeling his brain.)* I wonder if we could arrest him for anything? *(HILDY has never ceased his typing.)* Did you ever get the dope on that stenographer he seduced?

HILDY: *(Over his shoulder.)* That was the coroner.[166]

---

[165]*Duffy's getting old.* Although the identification of "Duffy" as "Duffy Cornell" appears indisputable, this reference to him is difficult to explain. Cornell, born in 1884, would have been only thirty-seven at the time of the O'Connor escape and forty-four when the play appeared. This raises the question whether the authors here shifted to Sherman Reilly Duffy, a journalist with whom Hecht was associated during his early years in Chicago. Note that on page 155, the character is referred to as "Mr. Duffy." Sherman Reilly Duffy, who was born in 1873, would have been fifty-five in 1928, still not old enough for the suggestion of senility in the passage.

[166]*Coroner.* The coroner of Cook County at the time of the O'Connor escape in 1921 was still Peter M. Hoffman. The text reads as if Johnson believed that Sheriff Peter

151

WALTER: Haven't we got anything on him besides graft?

HILDY: *(Thoughtfully.)* He's got an idiot kid in the asylum.[167]

WALTER: *(Depressed.)* I don't see how we can use that against him. *(Brightening.)* Wait a minute! Idiot kid. Idiot kid. . . . *(He meditates, then sighs.)* No, that's impractical. . . *(Approaching HILDY.)* What's your lead?

HILDY: *(With authorly pride.)* "While hundreds of Sheriff Hartman's paid gunmen stalked through Chicago shooting innocent bystanders, spreading their reign of terror, Earl Williams was lurking less than twenty yards from the Sheriff's office where . . .

WALTER: That's *lousy!* Aren't you going to mention the *Examiner?* Don't we take *any* credit?

HILDY: I'm putting that in the second paragraph. . . .

WALTER: Who the hell's going to read the second paragraph? Ten years I've been telling you how to write a newspaper story—My God, have I got to do everything? Get the story? Write the story? . . .[168]

HILDY: Listen, you bastard! I can blow better newspaper stories out of my nose than you can write!

WALTER: *(Cackling.)* "While hundreds of paid gunmen are out taking a walk . . ." God, that stinks! You ought to go back to chasing pictures!

HILDY: Yeah?

WALTER: You were *good* at that!

HILDY: You ungrateful bastard! Who wrote the Fitzgerald confession?[169] Who

---

Hoffman and the coroner of that name were different men of the same name, whereas they were, of course, the same person. Hoffman's successor as coroner was Oscar Wolff, a Republican of the Deneen faction, appointed to succeed Hoffman in 1922 and elected to the office in November 1923. He proved eclectic in his affiliation, running unsuccessfully as the Thompson-Lundin faction's candidate for city treasurer in 1927. He remained coroner until defeated by Dr. Herman N. Bundesen in 1928. Wolff died on April 5, 1934, at his home in South Chicago. (Obituary in the *Chicago Tribune*, April 6, 1934, p. 24.)

[167]*an idiot kid in the asylum.* This appears to be fictional. There is no evidence that Hoffman had such a child.

[168]*Ten years I've been telling you how to write a newspaper story.* The didactic style evident here was actually characteristic of Walter Howey. See Starrett, *Born in a Bookshop,* p. 76.

[169]*Fitzgerald confession.* The confession was of Thomas Richard Fitzgerald for murder of a child, Janet Wilkinson, on July 22, 1919. Fitzgerald, a janitor at the Virginia Hotel at Rush and Ohio Streets, was suspected as a child-molester because of his practice of carrying candy to give to children. The police were unable to bring him to confess to the crime, but on July 27 Harry J. Romanoff, a crime reporter for

wrote Ruth Randall's diary?[170] How about the Dayton flood?[171] Even the telegraph operator was crying!

WALTER: All right, make me cry now! *(Into phone.)* Duffy! Listen, Duffy. What's the name of that religious editor of ours? The fellow with the dirty collar? Sipper what? Well, tell the Reverend Sipperly.[172] I want to see him right away! . . . *(To HILDY.)* Do you know what I'm gonna do?

HILDY: Shut up, or I'll throw this typewriter at your head!

WALTER: *(Happily.)* I'm going to get the Reverend Sipperly to make up a prayer for the City of Chicago—right across the top of the paper! . . . "Our Father Who Art in Heaven—There were four hundred and twenty-one murders in Chicago last year!" All in religious lingo, see! Eight columns Old English Boldface! The goddamnedest prayer you ever heard. . . . *(Awed at his own resourcefulness).* Christ, what an idea!

HILDY: You better pray that this desk will float out of the window over to the paper.

WALTER: Wait a minute, Hildy. . . . *(The Pentecostal fire upon him.)* Wait, wait!. . . I got an inspiration! Now take this down, just as I say it! *(He yanks a page from the typewriter.)*

---

the *Herald and Examiner*, by showing Fitzgerald a newly purchased doll, which he said was the child's, and by stating that the child's mother was near death, brought Fitzgerald to confess. Fitzgerald stated he brought the girl to his apartment simply to stroke her hair, but when she became frightened, he strangled her and buried the body under a coal pile. He pleaded guilty and was hanged on October 17, 1919. (See Edward Baumann, *May God Have Mercy on Your Soul: The Story of the Rope and the Thunderbolt* [Chicago: Bonus Books, 1993], pp. 167–69.)

The confessions published in the *Herald and Examiner* on July 28, 1919, were the transcript of the interrogation of Fitzgerald in the office of state's attorney Maclay Hoyne and a short formal statement, witnessed by Romanoff, also made in the office of the state's attorney. If Hilding Johnson had anything to do with the confession, it was probably phoning in the unsigned story on the confession that the paper ran on page 1 of that issue. Howey, needless to say, gave great prominence to the story and treated the entire episode as one of the *Herald and Examiner*'s greatest coups. (See the accounts of the hanging in the *Herald and Examiner*, October 16, 1919, p. 3; October 17, p. 1; October 18, p. 4.)

Hecht in *A Child of the Century* (p. 152) stated that this case provided the basis for Theodore Dreiser's play, *The Hand of the Potter*. Although the plot does concern the smothering of a young girl, the play was published in 1918, a year before the crime.

[170]*Ruth Randall's diary.* The reference is to a murder-suicide early in 1920. Captain Clifford M. Bleyer, head of a prominent advertising agency and a member of the

HILDY: *(Leaping.)* Some day you're going to do that, Walter, and I'm gonna belt you in the jaw . . . ! You goddamn know-it-all!

WALTER *(Chanting.)* Here's your lead: "The *Chicago Examiner* again rode to the rescue of the city last night in the darkest hour of her history! *(Lowering his voice.)* Earl Williams—Earl Williams, the Bolshevik Tiger, who leaped snarling from the gallows upon the flanks of the city, was captured . . .

HILDY: I got you! I got you! . . .

WALTER: Go on from *there! (HILDY is hurriedly putting another sheet into the machine as the doorknob is rattled. A pause.)*

HILDY: What do you want to do?

BENSINGER'S VOICE: *(Outside.)* What's the idea of locking that door?

HILDY: That's Bensinger. That's his desk.

WALTER: What's his name again? *(The doorknob is rattled violently.)*

HILDY: Bensinger. Reporter for the *Tribune.* . . . Covers the building.

BENSINGER'S VOICE: Open this door, will you? Who's in there?

WALTER: I'll handle him! The *Tribune*, eh? Watch me. *(He opens the door. BENSINGER appears.)*

BENSINGER: *(Entering.)* Ain't you got any more sense than to . . . *(Sees WAL-*

Union League Club, late in 1917 had assisted Ruth Vale Randall to secure a divorce from an abusive husband. Although Bleyer had a wife and two children, he rented an apartment at 3607 Lake Park Avenue and began to cohabit with Randall about October 1, 1919. On March 8, 1920, the police found Bleyer, who was then thirty-six, and Randall, who was twenty-seven, both dead in the apartment. From the positions of the bodies, the police concluded that Randall shot Bleyer in the head while he was asleep and then turned the pistol on herself. The police found a manuscript diary, begun in 1911, which, if valid, demonstrated that as early as October 12, 1919, Randall had been considering the murder-suicide in approximately the form it took but had doubted that she had the fortitude to go through with it. City editor Frank Carson in a fashion unstated secured the diary from police custody, copyrighted it, and ran it serially in the *Herald and Examiner* between March 10 and March 18, 1920. At the inquest on March 16, Randall's mother, Jennie Vale, verified the handwriting in the diary as her daughter's, and Peter M. Hoffman, who was then coroner, officially accepted the police's findings as correct. (See the *Chicago Tribune*, March 17, 1920, p. 17). Thus, the diary does appear to have been valid, not the fabrication that the text implies.

Howey's directives in cases concerning attractive women were, first, to get the story, second, to find a photograph, and third, to produce a diary. (See William Randolph Hearst, Jr., *The Hearsts Father and Son* [Niwot, CO: Roberts Rinehart Publishing Co., 1991], p. 202.) Securing the photograph, referred to immediately above,

TER. Is overcome at this visitation.) Oh, hello, Mr. Burns. . . . Why, quite an honor, having you come over here.

WALTER: *(Casually.)* Hello, Bensinger.

BENSINGER: Excuse me. I just want to— *(Starts for the desk.)*

WALTER: *(Blocking his path.)* Quite a coincidence, my running into you tonight. . . . Isn't it, Hildy?

HILDY: Yeah.

BENSINGER: How do you mean?

WALTER: I was having a little chat about you just this afternoon—with Mr. Duffy.[173]

BENSINGER: Is that so? *(Essaying a pleasantry.)* Nothing detrimental, I hope.

WALTER: I should say not! That was one swell story you had in the paper this morning.

BENSINGER: *(Deeply moved.)* Well, I'm glad you think so, Mr. Burns. Did you care for the poem?

WALTER: The poem? . . . The poem was great! I got a big kick out of that.

BENSINGER *(Blinking at these sweet words.)* Did you like the ending? *(He recites.)*

> And all is well, outside his cell
> But in his heart he hears
> The hangman calling and the gallows falling
> And his white-haired mother's tears . . .

---

typically entailed theft, and Hildy's implication is that the morality of bringing forth the text of the diary was no better.

Randall's name is changed to Randolph in the acting edition of 1950.

[171]*the Dayton flood.* A flood of March 24, 1913, that seriously afflicted much of the Midwest, but which wrought its maximum havoc on Dayton, Ohio. The reference is an anachronism, for Hilding Johnson went to work for the *Examiner* in 1916, three years later. Alternatively, Charles MacArthur was active in Chicago journalism only from 1915. Hecht was sent to Dayton to cover the flood for the *Journal*, however. (See Hecht, *A Child of the Century*, p. 192.)

[172]*Reverend Sipperly.* The religion editor of the *Herald and Examiner* in this period was Irwin St. John Tucker, a popular figure among the reporters, who called him "Friar Tuck." According to George Murray, Rev. Sipperly was the editor and publisher of a religious newsletter, rather the precursor of the televangelists of more recent times, but I have been unable to identify him.

[173]*Mr. Duffy.* Because "Duffy" has been identified as Cornell, this reference necessarily becomes "Duffy Cornell" in the acting edition.

WALTER: *(Overcome.)* Heartbreaking! Isn't it, Hildy? Bensinger, how would you like to work for me![174]

BENSINGER: What!

WALTER: I mean it. We need somebody like you. All we got now is a lot of lowbrows and legmen. Like Johnson, here. *(Pushing BENSINGER farther from the desk.)* I tell you what you do. Go over and talk to Duffy now. I just had him on the phone. You'll catch him if you hurry.

BENSINGER: You mean seriously, Mr. Burns?

WALTER: I'll show you how serious I am. . . . *(Clinging to BENSINGER's pants, he takes him to the phone. Into phone.)* Duffy! I'm sending Bensinger over to see you. *(To BENSINGER.)* Marvin, isn't it!

BENSINGER: No. Roy. Roy V.

WALTER: Funny I should forget that! *(Into phone.)* Roy Bensinger, the poet. Put him right on the staff!

BENSINGER: Right away, you mean?

WALTER: *(Into phone.)* Never mind what doing . . . He'll tell you. No, I'll talk salary with him right here. *(To ROY.)* How much you getting on the *Tribune,* Roy?

BENSINGER: Seventy-five.

WALTER: Bensinger, I'll give you a hundred and a byline.[175] *(Into phone.)* He's to get a hundred and a byline, Duffy. Tell the cashier. Let him have everything he wants. He can use the big desk in the corner. *(To BENSINGER, dropping receiver.)* Now hustle right over to the office and tell Duffy I've—I've assigned you to write the human interest side of the manhunt. I want it from the point of view of the escaped man. *(Acting it out.)* He hides, cowering . . . afraid of every light, of every sound . . . hears footsteps . . . his heart going like that . . . And all the time they're closing in . . . get the sense of an animal at bay!

BENSINGER: Sort of a Jack London[176] style?

---

[174]*Bensinger, how would you like to work for me?* Ad hoc hirings of reporters by editors of this sort were quite common, usually in casual meetings in bars.

[175]*a byline.* The anonymity of the reporters' status as legmen was a chronic sore point. As the passage indicates, rising to a level at which they would get bylines was a fairly universal ambition. They may have gotten bylines in exceptional circumstances, but I was never able to find a single byline of any of the reporters who appear in the play. Al Baenziger is known to have been one of the principal reporters covering the Loeb-Leopold murder of 1924, but the *American* did not provide him a byline.

[176]*Jack London.* The well-known novelist and short story writer (1876–1913). It hardly

WALTER: Exactly. Now you ain't got a minute to lose. Hop right over to the office.

BENSINGER: Well, I don't know about quitting the *Tribune* that way, Mr. Burns. It's not quite ethical. . . .

WALTER: What did they ever do for you? . . . They've never considered your interests—that is, from what I hear. . . .

BENSINGER: Well, between you and me they have given me a pretty rotten deal. The way they handle my copy's a shame—just butcher it.

WALTER: Your copy will be sacred on the *Examiner.* I guarantee that personally. . . . *(He edges BENSINGER toward the door.)*

BENSINGER: *(The artist.)* You can't lop off the end of a story and get the same effect. The whole *feeling* goes . . .

WALTER: Of course. Now I want a real Bensinger story tomorrow morning, with a crackerjack poem on the side. *(He has him nearly to the door.)*

BENSINGER: *(Indicating his desk.)* I got my rhyming dictionary in . . .

WALTER: It don't have to rhyme! Now duck!

BENSINGER: Gee, I'm terribly grateful, Mr. Burns. *(Pausing in the doorway.)* Do you suppose there might be an opening some time as foreign correspondent? I parlay a little French, you know.

WALTER: *(Shaking hands with him and pushing him out.)* That'll all depend on your self. I'll keep you in mind.

BENSINGER: *(On his way to Garcia.)* Well, au revoir, mon capitaine!

WALTER: *(Never at a loss in any language.)* Bon jour! *(WALTER closes the door and skips to the phone. Into phone.)* Duffy! Listen. Now get this! A goddamn *Tribune* sneak is coming over to get a job. Yeah, Bensinger, the fellow I told you about. Now listen, handle him with kid gloves and tell him to get busy writing poetry. No . . . no! We don't want him. But wait till he gets through. Then tell him his poetry stinks and kick him down the stairs. . . . *(Lays receiver down. To HILDY.)* His white-haired mother's tears! *(Picks up HILDY's copy.)* Come on, Hildy, tear into it! Don't sit there like a frozen robin!

HILDY: *(Coming out of the ether.)* You've just bitched up my whole life![177] That's what you've done!

WALTER: *(Oblivious to this mood.)* Listen, Hildy. We ought to have our plans all set when Butch gets here. All we can look for out of that guy is pure,

---

need be added that London's delineations of the lives of seamen and outdoorsmen were about as different from Bensinger's poem as could be imagined.

[177] In the acting edition "bitched up" is replaced by "messed up."

peasant strength . . . A mental blank. *(Sentimentally.)* But he'd go through hell for me!

HILDY: What a fine horse's bustle I turned out to be!

WALTER: *(As before.)* The window's *out.* . . . We'll have him pick it up and walk right out of the building with it. With ten guys it'll be a cinch.

HILDY: She was the most wonderful girl I'll ever know. . . *(WALTER looks at him in horror and disgust.)* She had spirit, brains, looks . . . everything!

WALTER: Who the hell you talking about?

HILDY: My girl! Goddamn it! Who do you think?

WALTER: What are you going to do? Start mumbling about your girl now? You got a story to write!

HILDY: I practically told her to go to hell—like she was some waitress!

WALTER: You acted like a man for the first time in your life! Now, don't start crawling now!

HILDY: I'll never love anybody else again! They don't come like that twice in a man's life.

WALTER: You'll sleep it off. Now, listen, Hildy. I got enough on my mind!

HILDY: When she was sick in the hospital and you sent me on that wild goose chase all over Kentucky for three weeks, she never even complained. . . .

WALTER: Ha, ha. Sick in the hospital!

HILDY: Damn it, she was! She nearly died!

WALTER: I see. She didn't complain, but she just nearly died! That's all!

HILDY: *(Almost to himself.)* I would have been on the train now . . . I would have been . . .

WALTER: *(Confidentially.)* Listen, Hildy. *I* was in love once—with my third wife.[178] I treated her white—let her have a maid and everything! I was sweet to her!

HILDY: Who cares about your goddamned wife?[179]

WALTER: I trusted her. Then I let her meet a certain party on the *Tribune* and what happened? One night I came home unexpectedly—I let myself in through the bathroom window—and there they were! In bed.

HILDY: I don't want to hear about your troubles. I got enough. . . .

WALTER: *(Interrupting ecstatically.)* The very next morning, what do I find

---

[178] *my third wife.* Howey married Elizabeth Board in 1900—his first marriage—and at the time of the play remained married to her. He remarried only after her death in 1935. He had no third wife. See Robert L. Gale, "Walter Crawford Howey," *American National Biography* XI (1999), 360–61.

[179] In the acting edition this line is truncated to "Who cares?"

in the *Tribune*, all over the front page? *My traction story,*[180] I'd been sav-
ing for two months!

HILDY: You know a lot about women! You and your goddamn stable of tarts!
You never met a decent woman! You wouldn't know what to *do* with a
pure girl! . . .

WALTER: *(Owlishly.)* Oh, yes I would!

HILDY: You take that back!

WALTER: *(Deciding to reason with his young friend.)* What do you think
women are? Flowers? Take that dame that shot the dentist![181] And Mrs.
Vermilya![182] Husband comes home all worn out, hungry, takes a spoon-
ful of soup and falls dead! Arsenic! And Mrs. Petras![183] Burning her husband up in a furnace! When you've been in this business as long as I have
you'll know what women are! Murderers! Borgias!

HILDY: My God, I'm a sap! Falling for your line of crap . . . ! Naming streets
after me!

WALTER: Now, listen, Hildy. You've had a good rest. Get back on the story.
That's all you got to do. . . . *(Hands him a pocket flask.)* Here. You're just
nervous. . . .

---

[180]*My traction story,* i.e., a story about electric railways.

[181]*that dame that shot the dentist.* Not identifiable. The line does not provide time,
place, or names such that the incident could be identified. It may refer to a widely
publicized case of 1908 in which a dentist, Dr. James W. Simpson, was indicted for
the murder of his father-in-law, Bartley T. Horner. Simpson was acquitted, but
Horner's widow, Ella S. Horner, shot and killed him on a street in Northport, Long
Island, on July 13, 1908. (See the *New York Times*, July 14, 1908, p. 1.)

[182]*Mrs. Vermilya.* Louise Vermilya, proprietor of a boardinghouse in her apartment
at 415 E. 29th Street, Chicago. The sudden death on October 26, 1911, of policeman Arthur F. Bisonette, twenty-six, one of her boarders, from apparent arsenic
poisoning, resulted in a quick revelation of a series of similar deaths of people connected with Mrs. Vermilya, dating from 1904. She was identified in the press with
at least nine possible arsenic-related deaths: Bisonette, who may have been her
fiancé; Fred Brinkamp, sixty-three, her first husband; Frank Brinkamp, son of her
first husband; Florence Brinkamp, four, and Cora Brinkamp, eight, daughters of her
first husband; Charles Vermilya, fifty-nine, her second husband; Harry G. Vermilya,
thirty-five, her son by her second marriage; Lillian Vermilya, twenty-one, grand-
daughter of her second husband; and Richard T. Smith, a conductor on the Illinois
Central Railroad, another resident of her boardinghouse, also said to be her fiancé.
Charles C. Boysen, a local undertaker, reported symptoms of arsenic poisoning from
food prepared by Vermilya and refused to take any more of it. She claimed that

HILDY: *I'll* take that! . . . *(Goes to the watercooler. Pouring.)* I'll get stewed
tonight, and I'm gonna stay stewed for the rest of my life! Yeah, I'll be a
newspaperman! Right in your class! *(The doorknob is tried.)*
WALTER: *(Whispering.)* Shut up!
HILDY: On my pratt in a monkey cage!
WALTER: Shut up, you *fathead!* *(HILDY drinks. The knocking continues. WAL-
TER approaches the door.)* If that's Bensinger again, we'll crown him and
throw him in the can for keeps! *(To the door.)* Who is it?
DIAMOND LOUIE: *(Outside.)* Hello, Boss. . . .
WALTER: It's Louie. . . . *(He opens the door. DIAMOND LOUIE appears, bear-
ing some evidence of a mishap. His hat is crushed, face bruised, clothes torn.
WALTER sees this with alarm.)* My God, what's the matter!
HILDY: *(Frantically.)* Where's the old lady?
WALTER: What did you do with her?
HILDY: What the hell happened?
WALTER: You been in a fight?
LOUIE: *(Still out of breath.)* Down Wentworth Avenue. We were going sixty-
five miles an hour, you know what I mean?

Boysen, too, was her fiancé. When the police arrived to interrogate Vermilya, she
attempted suicide by swallowing arsenic from an open pepper box in her pantry.
The Cook County coroner found that Bisonette had died of poisoning from arsenic
administered by Vermilya and recommended that she be bound over to the grand
jury. Vermilya maintained her innocence uniformly. She had been limited to a wheel-
chair by a partial paralysis from her suicide attempt and by an abscess of the spine.
The evidence against her, though abundant, was almost all circumstantial. The
state's attorney, believing that evidence of an overt act was strongest for the death
of Smith, chose to prosecute Vermilya for his murder. After a trial of sixteen days,
the jury deadlocked, voting 7 to 5 for conviction on April 6, 1912. It was immediately announced that she would be retried, but she was released from custody on
bail on June 27, and no second trial was held. (*Chicago Tribune*, October 31,
1911–June 28, 1912, passim.)

[183]*Mrs. Petras.* Ameta Matthews Petras of Aurora, Illinois. Hecht in a series of arti-
cles on his early journalistic experiences that he ran in his *Chicago Literary Times*
stated that as a reporter for the *Journal* he covered the trial in Geneva, Illinois, of
Tony Petras for the murder of Theresa Hollander. (*Chicago Literary Times* vol. I, no.
19 [December 1, 1923], p. 8.) Hollander was beaten to death shortly after 10 P.M.
on February 17, 1914, in the St. Nicholas Cemetery in Aurora with a four-foot scant-
ling used in the cemetery to hold a casket over an open grave during the ceremony
immediately preceding interment. Anthony Petras was arrested for the murder, having been seen with her on a streetcar immediately earlier. Petras was an Austrian

WALTER: Take the mush out of your mouth!

HILDY: Where's the old lady!

LOUIE: I'm *telling* you! We run smack into a police patrol. You know what I mean? We broke it in half!

HILDY: My God! Was she hurt?

WALTER: Where is she? Tell me! . . .

HILDY: For God's sake, Louie! . . .

LOUIE: I'm *telling* you. Can you imagine bumping into a load of cops! They come rolling out like oranges!

HILDY: *(Seizing him.)* What did you *do* with her, goddamn you!

WALTER: What became of her, I'm asking you!

LOUIE: Search me! When I come to I was running down Thirty-fifth Street! Get me?

HILDY: You were *with* her! You were in the *cab*, weren't you!

LOUIE: *(Exposing his bruised scalp.)* Was I! Tony got knocked cold!

WALTER: You goddamn butterfingers! I give you an old lady to take somewhere and you hand her over to the cops!

LOUIE: What do you mean, I hand her? The patrol wagon was on the wrong side of the street!

---

immigrant who had settled in Aurora around 1910 and became engaged to Hollander about a year later. The engagement was broken off in 1913, and Petras shortly married Ameta Matthews. In the last conversation the victim held with her father, Hollander was quoted as saying: "He said he didn't love this other woman. He married her to spite me. I was the only one he cared for." Hollander also said that Petras was endeavoring to interfere with her marrying Nicholas Fellner on her twentieth birthday, March 5, 1914. When arraigned, Petras denied his guilt of the murder. The prosecution stressed Petras's admissions of lack of affection for Matthews, even putting on the stand a former fellow-resident of Petras's boarding house, who testified that Petras about 1913 had told him of his intention of marrying Hollander, with an incidental reference to Matthews as "a bunch of bones."

In spite of the embarrassing situation in which the whole event had placed her, Mrs. Petras remained supportive of her husband. She was expected to provide Petras's alibi as to his whereabouts at the time of the murder and also to furnish the explanation of blood stains on his clothing, but she was prevented by Illinois law concerning testimony by wives. Petras's first trial resulted in a hung jury, but in the second trial on October 1, 1914, he was acquitted. Mrs. Petras upon hearing the verdict kissed and hugged the jurymen individually. (See *Aurora Beacon-News*, February 18–October 2, 1914, passim.) The marriage, which could hardly have been less promising, did not survive. Petras moved to Chicago, and Mrs. Petras on June 27, 1922, secured a divorce on the ground of desertion. The murder was by that time

WALTER: *(Bitterly.)* Oh, my God! She's probably squawking her head off in some police station! Now everything is *fine.*

LOUIE: *(Holding his head.)* I don't think she's talking much, you know what I mean! *(He winks reassuringly.)*

HILDY: My God! Was she killed?

WALTER: *(Hopefully.)* Was she? Did you notice?

LOUIE: Say, with that alky rap and the bank job and the big blow on my hip! I should stick around asking questions from a lot of cops!

HILDY: *(Overcome.)* Oh, my God! Dead! That finishes me! . . .

WALTER: Listen, Hildy. That's Fate. What will be, will be!

HILDY: *(Wildly.)* What am I going to say to Peggy, for God's sake! What'll I *tell* her? . . .

WALTER: You're never going to see her again. Snap out of it! Would you rather have the old dame dragging the whole police force in here? . . .

HILDY: I killed her! I did it! Oh, my God, what can I do *now?* How can I ever face her! . . .

WALTER: *(Becoming the entire Foreign Legion.)* Listen, Hildy, if it was my own mother, I'd carry on, you know I would!

HILDY: You goddamn murdering bastard!

WALTER: *(Crescendo.)* No matter how I felt! If my heart was breaking! I'd carry on! For the paper!

HILDY *(To LOUIE.)* Where was it? I'll go out!

WALTER: You stay here! I'll find out everything! *(Into phone.)* Duffy! . . . Just a minute. . . . *(To Louie.)* Where was it?

LOUIE: Wentworth and Thirty-fourth . . . near the corner . . .

WALTER: *(Into phone.)* Call up the Thirty-fifth Street station and ask Nick Gallagher[184] if he's got a report on any old lady that was in a smashup at Thirty-fourth and Wentworth. *(To HILDY.)* What's her name?

---

attributed to a "club murderer," a serial killer who had shortly killed two other women in similar fashion. (*Geneva Republican*, June 30, 1922, p. 1.) Mrs. Petras reverted to her maiden name, is shown in the city directory as a milliner in downtown Aurora until 1926, but then disappears from the historical record.

Lumping Mrs. Petras with Louise Vermilya as a murderess may have been an extreme attempt to delineate Walter's journalistic ethics, but even though the use of actual names strengthens the play overall, this particular use of an unaltered name seems a breach of taste for which the authors can hardly be forgiven.

[184]*Nick Gallagher.* The Chicago Police Department had a large number of officers named Gallagher, but none bore a name that could reasonably be contracted to "Nick." The reference may be to an officer of an entirely different first name. It is

HILDY: *(Brokenly.)* Mrs. Amelia Grant.

WALTER: *(Into phone.)* Millie Grant. About . . . fifty-seven? *(With an enquiring look at HILDY.)* Refined. White hair. Blue eyes. Black cotton stockings. She was wearing rubbers. *(To HILDY, pleased.)* How's that for noticing?

HILDY: *(Grabbing a phone.)* Gimme an outside wire.

WALTER: Never *mind.* We'll get the dope right here . . . in two minutes! *(Another phone rings.)*

HILDY: *(Into phone.)* Gimme Wentworth, Four, five, five, seven! . . .[185]

WALTER: *(Answering the other telephone in guarded tones.)* Hello. Hello. Who! *(Wildly.)* Hello, Butch! Where are you!!

HILDY: *(Into phone.)* Passavant Hospital? Gimme the receiving room, will you?

WALTER: Hotel? You mean *you're* in a hotel? What are you doing *there!* Ain't you even *started?!*

HILDY: *(Into phone.)* Hello, Eddie,[186] Hildy Johnson. Was there an old lady brought in from an auto smashup? . . .

WALTER: *(Panic.)* Oh, for. . . *(Screaming.)* H. Sebastian God! Butch! Listen, it's a matter of life and death, Butch! *Listen!*

HILDY: *(Into phone.)* Nobody? *(Jiggles hook.)* Archer three one two four. . . .

WALTER: *(Into phone.)* I can't hear you! You got who? Speak up! A what?!!! . . . Holy God, you can't stop for a dame *now!*

HILDY: *(Into phone.)* Is this the German Deaconess Hospital?[187]

WALTER: *(Howling.)* I don't care if you've been trying to make her for six *years!* Now, listen, Butch! Our whole lives are at stake! Are you going to let some blonde pushover ruin everything? . . . What do you mean—an hour? It'll be too late in an hour!

HILDY: *(Into phone.)* Hello, Max.[188] Hildy Johnson. Was there an old lady . . .

---

more likely that the reference is to Nicholas Gallagher, resident of 552 W. Ohio Street, immediately northwest of the Criminal Courts Building. He has no known associations with the police department.

The 35th Street Police Station was and is at 35th and Lowe, about a quarter mile west of Comiskey Park. The accident at 34th and Wentworth was a block east of Comiskey Park.

[185] *Wentworth 4557.* The context requires this call to be either to the 35th Street Police Station, the number of which was Douglas 6320, German Deaconess Hospital at Boulevard 1040, or to Passavant Hospital at Superior 1065. This tends to confirm the view expressed earlier that the phone numbers in the play are fictional.

[186] *Eddie.* Not identifiable.

[187] *German Deaconess Hospital.* German Deaconess Memorial Hospital, 959 W. 54th Place.

[188] *Max.* Not identifiable.

WALTER: *Butch!!* I'd put my arm in the fire for you up to here! *(Indicates up to where.)* I'd go through hell for you! Now you ain't gonna double-cross me. . . . She does? All right—put her on the wire. I'll talk to her. . . . *Hello!* . . . Oh, hello, Madam! Now listen here, you goddamn bum[189]. . . You can't keep Butch away from his duty!. . . What! *What!!!* . . . What kind of language is that! Hello, hello . . . *(Turning to LOUIE, hanging up the telephone.)* That tub of guts![190] Lousy whore-headed flannel mouth! *(Into phone.)* Duffy! *(To HILDY.)* I'll *kill* 'em—both of them! I'll butter this town with their brains! *(Into phone.)* Duffy! *(To the world.)* Mousing around with some big blond Annie! *That's* cooperation! *(Screaming into Examiner phone.)* Duffy! . . .

HILDY: *(To Walter.)* Shut up, will you? *(Into phone.)* You sure! Nobody?

WALTER: *(A howl.)* Duffy! *(Throwing the receiver to the desk.)* I ought to know better than hire anybody with a disease! *(To LOUIE, panting.)* Louie! It's up to you!

LOUIE: *(Loyally.)* Anything you want, boss.

WALTER: Beat it out and get me hold of some guys, will you?

LOUIE: Who do you want?

WALTER: *(Trembling.)* I want anybody with hair on their chests! Get them off the streets—anywhere! Offer them anything—only get them! *(Confidentially.)* Listen, Louie. We got to get this desk out of here!

LOUIE *(Surveys the desk calmly.)* Is it important?

---

[189]*you goddamn bum.* This phrase had probably replaced "You damned hound," the wording to which the British censor objected in the typescript submitted to the Lord Chamberlain for licensing in 1929. George S. Street's specific objection to the phrase was that it was "unpleasant" when addressed to a woman. See the passages on this in the introduction and in Notes on the Text.

[190]This line is eliminated in the acting edition.

[191]*some whisker at the Revere House.* "Whisker" was an archaic term for a prostitute, or more generally, for a woman who was wholly a sex object. The context implies the latter. See Spears, *Slang and Euphemism*, p. 421.

The Revere House was a hotel at 417 N. Clark Street at the southeast corner of Austin Avenue. This is to say that the hotel was diagonally across Austin Avenue from the Criminal Courts Building. In other words, Butch McGuirk was not highly inaccessible.

The hotel was built as the Mackin House in 1874, but shortly was given the name of the Revere House, one of the city's leading hostelries before the fire of 1871. The Revere House was initially a leading hotel, identified with theatrical people, but it declined along with North Clark Street. By the time of the play, it was iden-

WALTER: Is it important!!! Louie, you're the best friend I got. I'd go through hell for you and I know you won't fail me. Get me enough people to move it! Do you understand that! Now, beat it! And remember, I'm relying on you!

LOUIE: *(Departing.)* You know me. The shirt off my back.

WALTER: *(Yelling after him.)* Don't bump into anything! *(He locks the door.)*

HILDY: *(emotionally, into phone.)* Calumet two one hundred . . .

WALTER: That lousy immigrant'll flop on me! I know it. *(Bitterly.)* Can you imagine Butch laying up with some whisker at the Revere House![191] At a time like this! Listen Hildy . . . *(Confidentially.)* If Louie don't come back in five minutes, we'll get it out alone! There's millions of ways! We can start a fire and get the firemen to carry it out in the confusion! . . .

HILDY: Do anything you damn please! . . . *(Into phone.)* Ring that number, will you?

WALTER: *(Very excited.)* We don't even have to do that. We'll get the Chicago Historical Society[192] to claim it as an antique. We can move it out in a decent normal manner ourselves! Just the two of us!

HILDY: I don't give a goddamn what you do!

WALTER: Come on, Hildy! Come here and see if we can move it!

HILDY: *(Into phone.)* Hello! Hello! Is this the Lying-in Hospital![193] Did you have an auto accident in the last hour?

WALTER: Will you come here?

HILDY: *(Into phone.)* Oh, I see. I beg your pardon.

WALTER: Right when I'm surrounded, with my back against the wall, you ain't going to lie down on me!

---

tified with prostitution and assignations, as the text indicates. It was by that time a 200-room, six-story structure. It became the Hubbard Hotel in 1945 and was closed on May 23, 1947, for thirty-nine violations of the fire code. It reopened as the Capitol Hotel but was swept by fire on December 10, 1948. It was again restored to service and remained in operation until about 1976, when it was razed. (See *Land Owner* VII, no. 1 [January, 1875], p. 5; *Chicago Tribune*, May 24, 1947, p. 5; *Chicago Daily News*, December 10, 1948, p. 1.)

[192]*Chicago Historical Society.* This venerable institution, founded in 1856, was housed in a building that still stands at Dearborn and Ontario Streets, four blocks north of the Criminal Courts Building. The society moved into its present quarters at Clark Street and North Avenue in 1931.

[193]*Lying-in Hospital.* The maternity hospital of the University of Chicago. Hildy's following speech apparently reflects his being told this.

HILDY: *(Jiggling the phone hook.)* I'm going to lay down on you and spit in your eye, you murderer!

WALTER: Scared, huh? Yellow running out of your collar!

HILDY: I don't care what you think! I'm going to find my girl's mother! *(Madly jiggling the hook.)* Oh, for God's sake!

WALTER: Your girl! You and Butch McGuirk! Woman lovers!

HILDY *(Hangs up phone with a bang.)* Goddamn it! I'm going to go *out* and find her! *(Starts for door. At that instant there comes a loud knock.)*

WALTER: Who's that? Don't open that!

HILDY: The hell I won't! I'm going to the morgue! To . . . look! . . . *(He flings the door open. The SHERIFF, accompanied by two Deputies—CARL and FRANK[194]—surrounded by McCUE, KRUGER, and MURPHY, bar his exit.)*

THE REPORTERS: Oh, there he is! Say Hildy! Wait a second. *(Etc.)*

(HILDY is struggling past them. The SHERIFF grabs him.)

SHERIFF: Just a minute, Johnson!

HILDY: Let go of me! What the hell's the idea?

THE REPORTERS: What's your hurry? We want to see you! *(Etc.)*

HILDY: Take your goddamn paws off me!

SHERIFF: Hold him, boys!

WALTER: *(To the SHERIFF.)* Who the hell do you think you are, breaking in here like this?

SHERIFF: You can't bluff me, Burns! I don't care who you are or what paper you're editor of!

HILDY: Goddamn it! Let me go! *(Hysterically.)* Let me go, fellas! Something's happened to my girl's mother!

SHERIFF: Hang on to him!

THE REPORTERS: We know what you're up to! Going out to get Williams, probably! The door was locked! He and Mollie were talking! They know where he is! *(Etc.)*

HILDY: *(Retreating back into the room before HARTMAN and his deputies.)* Listen, guys! I don't know anything, I tell you! There's been an accident— I just been calling up the hospitals! I was just going out to the morgue to see if she was there! Now . . .

SHERIFF: Johnson, there's something very, very peculiar going on. . . .

---

[194]*Frank.* Not identifiable. The name does not accord with any known deputy sheriff of the period.

HILDY: Listen, Pinky! You can send somebody with me if you want to! If you don't believe me!

SHERIFF: I wasn't born yesterday, Johnson. Now the boys tell me you and Mollie . . .

HILDY: Nobody's trying to put anything over on you! Now, I'm getting out of here and you can't stop me!

MURPHY: You're not going anywhere! He's got the story sewed up, Pete! He and his goddamn boss. That's why he's here!

WALTER: *(Purring.)* If you've got any accusations to make, Hartman, make them in the proper manner! Otherwise I'll have to ask you to get out!

SHERIFF: *(Pop-eyed.)* You'll ask me to *what?*

WALTER: I'll ask you to get out.

SHERIFF: *(To his deputies.)* Close that door! Don't let anybody in or out!

MURPHY: Come on, Pinky! Give him a little third degree!

SHERIFF: Johnson, I'm going to the bottom of this! Now then, come clean! What do you know about Williams! Are you going to talk or aren't you!

HILDY: What the hell do *I* know about Williams?

SHERIFF: All right, boys! Take him along. I got ways of making him talk. *(HILDY struggles.)*

HILDY: Look out, you . . . !

McCUE: What's the use of fighting, Hildy? *(The reporters swarm around HILDY. Shouts of "I got him." "No, you don't!" "Hey, what you doing?" "Paste him!" "Aw, Hildy! What the hell!" etc. HILDY's voice rises out of the din.)*

HILDY: Say what the hell's the idea?

THE DEPUTIES: He's got a gun on him! Look out! He's got a gun! He's got a gun!

HILDY: No, you don't! Hey, Walter!

WALTER: What is it? Here!

SHERIFF: Gimme that! *(Takes the gun.)*

HILDY: *(Resisting.)* That's mine! . . .

MURPHY: Jesse James, huh! The drugstore cowboy!

McCUE: He's been going to the movies. Two-gun Johnson!

KRUGER: The terror of Wilson Avenue beach![195]

SHERIFF: *(Frozen, looking at the gun.)* Where did you get this?

HILDY: I got a right to carry a gun if I want to.

---

[195]*Wilson Avenue beach.* More accurately, the Montrose-Wilson Beach, part of the recreational development of the Chicago lakefront, serving the uptown area of the North Side.

SHERIFF: Not *this* gun!

WALTER: *(Easily.)* I can explain that, Hartman. He was having some trouble with the Durkin[196] story and I gave it to him . . . to defend himself!

SHERIFF: Oh, you *did!* . . . Well, that's very, *very* interesting! This *happens* to be the gun that Earl Williams shot his way out with!

THE REPORTERS: What? What's that? *(Etc.)*

WALTER: *(To HARTMAN.)* Are you trying to make me out a liar!

SHERIFF: *(wildly.)* I know my own gun,—don't I?

MURPHY: *(Bitterly to HILDY.)* Getting married, huh!

KRUGER: Maybe Williams was gonna be his best man.

SHERIFF: *(Trembling.)* Where is he? Where you got him?

WALTER: *(Sympathetically.)* You're barking up the wrong tree, Hartman . . .

SHERIFF: I'll give you three minutes to tell me where he is!

HILDY: He went over to the hospital to call on Professor Eglehofer!

SHERIFF: What!!!

HILDY: With a bag of marshmallows. *(The SHERIFF stands silent, a gypsy; then streaks wildly for the toilet and throws open the door.)*

WALTER: Take a magazine along.

---

[196]*Durkin.* Martin Durkin, who was convicted of having murdered Department of Justice agent Edward C. Shanahan in 1925. Durkin was, indeed, someone to make a rational reporter want to carry a pistol. Durkin was wanted on sixteen federal counts of violation of the Dyer Act, the prohibition of interstate movement of stolen automobiles. Shanahan and two other federal agents were waiting for him on Sunday, October 11, 1925, in a garage at 6243 Princeton Avenue on the South Side, intending to arrest him on warrants for possession of a car stolen in California and for shooting and wounding three policemen in December 1924. When Shanahan and the other agents approached Durkin as he was driving into the garage, Durkin opened fire without even leaving the car. Some of the five shots he fired hit Shanahan in the abdomen and near the heart. Shanahan died shortly after arrival at St. Bernard's Hospital. Durkin escaped and murdered police Sergeant Harry Gray and a civilian, Lloyd Austin, before leaving the area. Durkin was captured on a train in St. Louis on arrival from Texas on January 20, 1926. He was returned to Chicago and brought to trial. He maintained that he had fired on Shanahan in self-defense, believing that Shanahan and his men were approaching to rob him. Durkin was found guilty of the murder of Shanahan and sentenced to an Illinois penitentiary for thirty-five years (*Chicago Daily News*, July 10, 1926, p. 1). He was released in 1954 after serving for twenty-eight years. At the time of his incarceration in Illinois, he was said to be liable to fifteen additional years in federal prison for his violations of the Dyer Act.

THE REPORTERS: Come on, Hildy. Where is he! That's a hell of a trick, Hildy. I thought we were friends! *(Etc.)*

SHERIFF: *(Rushing back from the toilet.)* By God, I'll show you!

THE REPORTERS: Look here, Pete! What about Mr. Burns? Ask the Master Mind! Yeah. What's *he* doing over here? *(Etc.)*

SHERIFF: *(Grabbing WALTER's arm.)* Speak up, Burns! What do you know about this?

WALTER: *(Gently but firmly disengaging his arm.)* Listen Hartman . . .

MURPHY: The hell with that! Where is he?

WALTER: *(Continuing.)* The *Examiner* is not obstructing justice or aiding criminals. You ought to know that!

CARL: *(Pointing to the* Examiner *phone.)* Look! Somebody was talking on there! The receiver is off! *(McCUE jumps for the phone.)*

McCUE: I'll find out who it is . . .

SHERIFF: *(Also jumping.)* Leave that alone! *I'm* in charge here!

HILDY: Walter, listen! If I don't get out of here . . .

SHERIFF: Quiet, everybody! I'll handle this. It may be Earl Williams.

HILDY: Tell him to come on over.

SHERIFF: Sssh! *(Into phone, swallowing, then elaborately disguising his voice.)* Hello, Earl?

WALTER: *(Smiling.)* Scotland Yard.

SHERIFF: *(To McCUE, in a whisper.)* Trace this call—quick! *(McCUE jumps for another phone.)* Yes, this is Walter.

McCUE: *(Into another phone.)* Trace the call on twenty-one! In a hurry!

SHERIFF: *(Into* Examiner *phone.)* What? You gotta do what? Who is this?!!!

WALTER: You're talking to the *Examiner,* Hawkshaw![197] *(The SHERIFF wheels.)*

McCUE: That's right, Sheriff!

SHERIFF: Johnson, you're under arrest! You too, Burns!

WALTER: *(Calmly, without moving from his post at the desk.)* Who's under

---

[197]*Hawkshaw.* A detective, a character in Tom Taylor's play, *The Ticket of Leave Man* of 1863. At the time of the play, the character was well known from a comic strip, "Hawkshaw, the Detective," by Gus Mager, which ran in the Hearst papers regularly from 1913 to 1922, with occasional revivals thereafter. The strip was visually a parody of Sherlock Holmes; the use of an established literary character who had gone out of copyright was an effort to protect Mager from suit by representatives of Sir Arthur Conan Doyle.

arrest? . . . Listen, you pimple-headed German spy,[198] do you realize what you're doing?

SHERIFF: We'll see about this. Get the Mayor, Carl! Ask him to come over here! *(As CARL goes to the telephone the door opens and MRS. GRANT disheveled, with her hat over one ear, enters with two policemen.)*

FIRST POLICEMAN: *(Entering.)* . . . in here, Madam?

HILDY: *(Leaping forward, happily.)* Mother!

MRS. GRANT: *(To POLICEMAN.)* That man there! With the gray necktie! *(She points accusingly at Walter.)*

HILDY: *(Hugging her.)* Mother! Oh, my God, I'm glad to see you! Are you all right? Tell me! *(MRS. GRANT indignantly shakes HILDY off.)*

SHERIFF: What's the idea here?

POLICEMAN: This lady claims she was kidnapped!

SHERIFF: What?!!

MRS. GRANT: They dragged me all the way down the stairs—I tried to get help and they began to pinch me—I'm black and blue all over! Then they ran into another automobile and I was nearly killed! . . .

SHERIFF: Just a minute! What did this man have to do with it, lady? *(He points at WALTER.)*

MRS. GRANT: He was the one in charge of everything! He told them to kidnap me!

WALTER: *(Amazed.)* Are you referring to *me*, Madam!

MRS. GRANT: *(To WALTER.)* You know you did! You told them to take me out of here!

SHERIFF: What about this, Burns! Kidnapping, eh?

WALTER: *(Round-eyed.)* It's beyond *me*. Who is this woman?

MRS. GRANT: Oh! Oh, what a thing to say! I was standing right there . . . after the girl jumped out of that window!

SHERIFF: Did you get the Mayor? Was he in?

A DEPUTY: He's coming over.

WALTER: *(To MRS. GRANT.)* Now, Madam, be honest, if you were out joyriding—drunk! . . . and got in some scrape . . . why don't you *admit* it instead of accusing innocent people!

MRS. GRANT: *(Beginning to doubt her senses.)* You ruffian! You unprincipled man! How dare you say a thing like that!

---

[198]No doubt because "German spy" had more pejorative connotations by 1950 than it had in 1928, this passage is condensed into "you pimple head" in the acting edition.

HILDY: Please, Mother! He's just crazy! Don't! . . .

MRS. GRANT: I'll tell you something more, officer! I'll tell you why they did it!

WALTER: *(Fidgeting.)* Come on, Sheriff. We've got to get bail.

MRS. GRANT: *(Continuing crescendo.)* I was in here and they had some kind of a murderer—hiding him! *(This is a bombshell. The room is electrified by the old lady's announcement.)*

SHERIFF: Hiding him! Hiding him! In here!

MURPHY: Hiding him where!

HILDY: Mother!

THE REPORTERS: Where was he? Where did they have him? *(Etc.)*

WALTER: *(With superb indignation.)* Madam, you're a goddamn liar!¹⁹⁹ *(To emphasize his righteousness WALTER pounds on the desk three times—and then stands horrified. He remembers, too late, the signal.)*

REPORTERS: For God's sake, tell us where he was! Did they tell you where? Tell us! *(Etc.)*

SHERIFF: Shut up, everybody! Now! Where was he? Tell me, where he was!

MRS. GRANT: Well, I was sitting right in this chair. *(Three answering knocks come from WILLIAMS. The SHERIFF leaps as if the desk had bitten him.)*

SHERIFF: *(Whispering.)* What was that?

REPORTERS: My God, he's in the desk! For the love of Christ! Holy God, he's in there! *(Etc.)*

SHERIFF: Aha! *I thought so!* Stand back, everybody!

DEPUTY: Look out, Sheriff! He may shoot!

SHERIFF: Get your guns out! *(The police all take out guns.)*

HILDY: He's harmless, for God's sake!

SHERIFF: Don't take any chances! Shoot through the desk!

HILDY: He can't hurt anybody! You got his gun!

MRS. GRANT: *(Panic-stricken.)* Oh, dear! Oh, dear!

WALTER: *(To MRS. GRANT.)* You gray-haired old Judas!

---

¹⁹⁹*goddamn liar!* This was one of the uses of "God" proposed to be dropped by the People's Theatre, Newcastle, in its application for the Lord Chamberlain's license to produce the play in 1935. Whether anyone noticed or not, this would have eliminated one of the words necessary to bring forth Walter's three thumps on the desk. As stated in the introduction, the Newcastle production was not mounted, but the terms for granting the license it sought were applied to the production by the Manchester Repertory Theatre in January 1936. How that company dealt with this problem is unknown.

MRS. GRANT: Let me out! Let me out of here! *(Streaks for the door; exits. The reporters are going for the telephones.)*

MURPHY: *(Into phone.)* City desk! Quick!

SHERIFF: *(To policemen.)* Close the door. You stand there. You cover the windows. *(Indicates with his gun.)*

MURPHY: Look out where you're pointing that gun, Pinky!

McCUE: *(Into phone.)* Gimme Emil.

KRUGER: *(Into phone.)* Gimme the city desk.

MURPHY: Hold the wire! I've got a flash for you.

WALTER: *(To HILDY.)* Call Duffy.

SHERIFF: No, you don't!

WALTER: Do you want us to get scooped?

McCUE: *(Into phone.)* Emil? Hang on for a second.

SHERIFF: Now then! Everybody aim right at the center. And when I say three—

HILDY: Goddamn it! That's murder!

SHERIFF: Carl! Frank! One of you get on each side of the desk. Take hold of the cover. Now then! We got you covered, Williams—don't try to move. Now! Everybody quiet and ready for any emergency. I'm going to count three.

MURPHY: *(Phoning in the silence.)* I'll have it in a minute . . .

SHERIFF: One! . . .

KRUGER: Right away now!

SHERIFF: Two! . . . *(DIAMOND LOUIE enters, accompanied by three people he has picked up in the street. One is a boy in short pants, the second is a sailor, the third is a seedy old man of the Trader Horn type.[200])*

POLICEMAN: *(At the door, opposing them.)* What do you want? *(WALTER waves violently, LOUIE and his assistants disappear.)*

---

[200]*Trader Horn*. The reference is to the hero of a novel published in June 1927, initially entitled *The Ivory Coast in the Earlies*, but almost immediately renamed *Trader Horn* after its protagonist. The book purported to be the autobiographical account of the adventures in West Africa of a seventy-three-year-old man, Alfred Aloysius Horn, edited by Ethelreda Lewis (New York: Simon & Schuster, 1927). The book was an immediate success, to the extent that a reference to it in 1928 would be unambiguous. A motion picture based on the novel, starring Harry Carey as Horn, was released in 1931. It was one of the hits of the year, nominated for the Academy Award as best picture.

The reference to Trader Horn is dropped from the acting edition; rather, the stage directions state that Louie enters with a sailor and a colored boy in short pants.

SHERIFF: *(Wheeling.)* Who was that?

WALTER: *(White with rage.)* Double-crossing Sicilian!

SHERIFF: Shut up!

KRUGER: *(Into phone.)* Keep holding it!

SHERIFF: Now then! Keep everybody out of here! I want quiet! . . . There's a dozen guns on you, Williams! You can't escape! Do you surrender or not?

WALTER: *(Into phone.)* Duffy![201]

SHERIFF: Are you ready, boys!

CARL: Yah. . . .

SHERIFF: All right. Now everybody aim right at the center. *(Looking around.)* Are you all ready? *(To the men at the desk.)* You boys? *(From the deputies comes a whispered "Yes.")* Ready back there? *(This to the men at the door and windows; they give quick nods in reply.)* All right. Now then—up with it. *(CARL and FRANK raise the cover. The SHERIFF waits a discreet distance until he sees there is no danger. WILLIAMS is cowering in the desk, his hands over his face. The SHERIFF rushes on him, jabbing his gun into him.)*

WILLIAMS. *(A wail.)* Go on—shoot me!

SHERIFF: Got you, Williams!

THE POLICE AND DEPUTIES: Grab him, there! That's him! That's him! Don't let him shoot! Stick 'em up, you! Clout him! Give him the boots! Hold his arm! *(Through this the reporters are telephoning in. As they talk, the police drag the screaming little anarchist out. The SHERIFF follows them.)*

MURPHY: *(Into phone.)* Earl Williams was just captured in the pressroom o' the Criminal Court building hiding in a desk.

McCUE: *(Into phone.)* The Sheriff just caught Williams in a rolltop right here in the room.

KRUGER: *(Into phone.)* Just nabbed Williams hiding in a desk, criminal court pressroom.

McCUE: *(Into phone.)* Williams put up a desperate struggle but the police overpowered him.

MURPHY: *(Into phone.)* Williams tried to shoot it out with the cops but his gun wouldn't work.

KRUGER: *(Into phone.)* Williams was unconscious when they opened the desk . . .

WALTER: *(Into phone.)* Duffy! The *Examiner* just turned Earl Williams over to the Sheriff . . . *(The SHERIFF rushes back.)*

---

[201]In the acting edition this becomes the third explicit reference to "Duffy" Cornell.

SHERIFF: *(Indicating WALTER and HILDY.)* Just a minute! Put the cuffs on those two! *(The police obey.)* Harboring a fugitive from justice!

MURPHY: *(Into phone.)* A well-dressed society woman tipped off the cops. Call you back in a minute . . .

KRUGER: *(Into phone.)* An old sweetheart of Williams double-crossed him . . . Call you back . . .

McCUE: *(Into phone.)* More in a minute.

REPORTERS: Where's that old lady? Hey madam! . . . Wait a minute! . . . Where's the old dame? *(They exit in a hurry.)*

SHERIFF: *(Into phone.)* Hello, girlie! Gimme Jacobi! Quick! . . .

WALTER: Hartman . . . you're going to wish for the rest of your life you'd never been born! *(The MAYOR enters.)*

MAYOR: Fine work Pete! You certainly delivered the goods! I'm proud of you!

SHERIFF: *(Over his shoulder as he phones.)* Look kind of natural, don't they, Fred? *(Referring to the handcuffs.)*

MAYOR: *(Happily.)* A sight for sore eyes! Well, it looks like you boys stepped in something up to your neck!

HILDY: *(To His Honor.)* Go on! Laugh! You big tub of guts![202]

MAYOR: That's pretty, isn't it? Aiding an escaped criminal, huh?

SHERIFF: *(Rolling in catnip.)* And a little charge of kidnapping I'm looking into! *(Into phone.)* That's the jail! There must be *some* body over there!

MAYOR: Well! Looks like about ten years apiece for you birds.

WALTER: Does it? Well, whenever you think you've got the *Examiner* licked, that's a good time to get out of town.

HILDY: On a hand car.

MAYOR: Whistling in the dark, eh? Well, it isn't going to help you. You're through.

WALTER: Yeah? The last man that told me that was Barney Schmidt[203] . . . a week before he cut his throat.

MAYOR: Is that so?

WALTER: And remember George T. Yorke[204] blowing his head off with a shotgun? We've been in worse jams than this—haven't we, Hildy? But something seems to watch over the *Examiner. (He raises his eyebrows.)*

---

[202]This line is also dropped from the acting edition—the second excision of "tub of guts."

[203]*Barney Schmidt.* Barney J. Schmidt, a foreman at Swift & Company.

[204]*George T. Yorke.* George F. Yorke, a reporter who went to work for the City News Bureau on May 14, 1914. He may have dropped the *e* from his surname; a George F. York was a clerk at the First National Bank of Chicago in the 1920s.

HILDY: Yeah. When that minister sued us remember? False arrest?

WALTER: Oh, yes . . . *(Coolly to the MAYOR.)* The Reverend J. B. Godolphin[205] sued the *Examiner* once for . . . a hundred thousand dollars. It seems that we'd called him a fairy. Well, the day of trial came and the Reverend was on his way to court . . .

HILDY: With all his lawyers and medical witnesses.

WALTER: *(Orgiastic.)* Drowned by God! Drowned in the river! With their automobile, their affidavits, and their goddamn law books! And I got the same feeling right now that I had five minutes before that accident!

MAYOR: Your luck ain't with you now.

SHERIFF: *(Into telephone.)* Jacobi? . . . I caught him. Williams. Single-handed. . . . Yeah. They're bringing him right over. Notify everybody. We're going to proceed with the hanging per schedule. *(Wiggles telephone for another call.)*

WALTE: *(To the Mayor.)* You're going to be in office for exactly two days more and then we're pulling your big nose out of the feed bag and setting you out on your fat can![206]

SHERIFF: Give me the state's attorney's office.

---

[205]*Reverend J. B. Godolphin.* Reverend Francis Richard Godolphin, an Anglican clergyman. He was born in London on November 17, 1875, but spent his formative years in Canada. He was ordained in San Antonio, Texas, in 1903, and first served at St. James Church in Del Rio, Texas. After two posts at parishes in Michigan, in 1913 he became rector of Grace Church in Oak Park, Illinois, a position he held until 1930. Thus, he was a prominent Anglican clergyman in a major Chicago suburb throughout the time span to which the play can be assigned. He probably came to MacArthur's attention during MacArthur's initial employment in the Chicago area as reporter for *Oak Leaves*, the local newspaper of Oak Park. Rev. Godolphin's final appointment was as rector of St. Andrew's Episcopal Church on Staten Island.

Rev. Godolphin was a scholarly clergyman, a specialist in the Old Testament. Themes from the Old Testament abound in his sermons, and he was the author, with Ernest H. Salter, of *God and His People* (New York: Morehouse-Gorham Co., 1943), a manual for instruction in the Old Testament. Rev. Godolphin retired in 1944 and died at age eighty-nine on August 23, 1965, in Princeton, New Jersey, where his son, Francis Richard Bourroum Godolphin, was Professor of Classics. Rev. Godolphin had no known legal involvement with the *Herald and Examiner*, and the accident described is entirely fictional. When he resigned his post at Grace Church, Grand Rapids, the *Grand Rapids Press* specifically noted his masculine manner and described him as "a man's man." (Quoted in *Oak Leaves*, November 13, 1913, p. 4.) Accordingly, the implication of effeminacy in the passage, combined with

HILDY: And when you're walking up and down North Avenue with blue eye glasses selling lead pencils, we're not going to forget you, either!

SHERIFF: *(Merrily.)* We're going to be selling lead pencils, eh?

MAYOR: Don't even answer him.

SHERIFF: Well, I'll tell you what you'll be doing. Making brooms in the state penitentiary. . . . *(Into phone.)* Hello, Pyrstalski?[207] This is Hartman. Come right over to my office, will you? I've just arrested a couple of important birds. I want you to take their confessions. *(Hangs up.)*

WALTER: *(Seizing the* Examiner *phone.)* Duffy! Get Clarence Darrow[208]!!!!

MAYOR: Get anybody you want! All the Darrows in the world aren't going to help you!

WALTER: Schmidt, Yorke, Godolphin. . . . You're next, Fred.

MAYOR: The power of the press, huh? Well, it don't scare me! Not an iota!

SHERIFF: It's a big windbag! That's all it is! Take 'em along, Carl!

WALTER: Bigger men than you have found out what it is! Presidents! Yes . . . and kings! *(PINCUS, the governor's messenger, reels in, stewed.)*

PINCUS: *(Woozy.)* Here's your reprieve.

MAYOR: *(Seeing him, in panic.)* Get out of here!

---

drowning him the Chicago River, is an exercise in bad taste second only to the authors' treatment of Mrs. Petras. (Letter of Stephanie Walker, Assistant Archivist, the Archives of the Episcopal Church, Austin, Texas, to George W. Hilton, April 12, 1995. See also Rev. Godolphin's obituaries in the *New York Times*, August 24, 1965, p. 31 and the *Chicago Tribune*, August 24, 1965, sec. II, p. 6.)

[206]The acting edition drops "fat can," replacing it with a dash.

[207]*Pyrstalski.* John Prystalski, a leading prosecuting attorney and subsequently a prominent elective judge. Prystalski was born in Poland and brought to the United States at age seven about 1888. He worked in foundries of the Pullman Company in his youth but entered Kent College of Law and was admitted to the bar in 1906. He was in private practice until 1910, but then served for two years as city prosecuting attorney. As a prosecutor, he was reportedly distinguished in cross examination. He became assistant state's attorney in 1912, with an office in the Criminal Courts Building—the position consistent with the play. He held office until 1920, when he unsuccessfully sought election as municipal court judge, a position he had also sought without success in 1914. He was elected to the Cook County Superior Court in 1930 and to Circuit Court in 1933. He died in office at age sixty-nine on November 18, 1950. (Obituary in the *Chicago Tribune*, November 19, 1950, sec. I, p. 3.)

The misspelling of Prystalski's name may reflect something more basic than the usual concealment of identity to avoid suit. Hilding Johnson insisted that his rewrite men misspell "Prystalski" in retaliation for Prystalski's withholding information on an assault and murder investigation involving Mossy Enright. When Prystalski asked,

PINCUS: You can't bribe me!

SHERIFF: Get out of here, you!

PINCUS: I won't! Here's your reprieve!

HILDY: What's that?

PINCUS: I don't want to be city sealer or whatever it was.[209]

MAYOR: Who *is* this man?

SHERIFF: *(Frenzied.)* Throw him out, Frank!

HILDY: *(Seizing PINCUS with his free hand.)* Who was bribing you? *(WAL-TER also seizes PINCUS, already being pulled out of shape.)*

PINCUS: They wouldn't take it! . . .

MAYOR: You're insane!

WALTER: What did I tell you? An unseen power. What's your name?[210]

PINCUS: Irving Pincus!

MAYOR: You drunken idiot! Arrest him! The idea of coming in here with a cock and bull story like that!

SHERIFF: It's a frame-up! That's what it is! Some impostor!

HILDY: Wait a minute! *(To the deputies.)* Let go there!

WALTER: Murder, huh?

"Why can't you guys see that my name is spelled correctly?" Johnson replied that they would do so "when you level with us on the Enright case." (Harold Ricklefs, "How Hilding Handled 1920 News Barrier," *Press Vet* vol. XXI, no. 2 [August, 1967], p. 11.)

[208] *Clarence Darrow.* Chicago's most prominent defense attorney (1857–1938), at the peak of his reputation in the 1920s. As Walter was undoubtedly aware, Darrow's specialty was defense of unpopular clients. As noted in the introduction for the 1946 revival, MacArthur, who thought the reference to Darrow had lost currency, substituted "Harold Ickes." Although Ickes had been an attorney in Chicago, he was by 1946 mainly identified with his services to the administration of Franklin Delano Roosevelt. Darrow returns in the acting edition of 1950.

[209] The Covici-Friede edition drops "or whatever it was" from the quotation in *Theatre.* Note that although the Mayor offered Pincus only a position in the office of the city sealer, Pincus interpreted the offer as the position of city sealer itself. Apart from moral considerations, it would have been irrational for Pincus to take the job. For Samuel E. Pincus, a Democrat, taking a position of this secondary character in the cabinet of a Republican mayor who was held in fairly universal contempt would have ruined any prospects he had in Chicago politics, which, of course, were and still are almost monolithically Democratic. In addition, even if the position were the actual city sealer, this was no job for a successful lawyer. In 1923, when Pincus became city prosecutor of Chicago, his salary was $6,000 per year; the city sealer was paid only $3,600.

HILDY: Hanging an innocent man to win an election! All right, Mr. Mayor—
and Sheriff Hartman—you might as well take these cuffs off Johnson and
me. Your goose is cooked.[211]

SHERIFF: That's a lie!

MAYOR: I never saw him before in my life!

WALTER: *(To PINCUS.)* When did you deliver this first?

HILDY: Who did you talk to?

PINCUS: They started right in bribing me!

HILDY: Who's "they"?

PINCUS: *(Indicating the MAYOR and SHERIFF.)* Them!

MAYOR: That's absurd on the face of it, Mr. Burns! He's talking like a child!

WALTER: *(Really impressed.)* An unseen power.

MAYOR: Certainly! He's insane or drunk or something! Why, if this unfortunate man Williams has really been reprieved, I personally am tickled
to death! Aren't you, Pete?

HILDY: Go on, you'd kill your mother to get elected!

MAYOR: *(Shocked.)* That's a hell of a thing to say, Johnson, about anybody!
Now, look here, Walter, you're an intelligent man . . .

WALTER: *(Stopping the MAYOR.)* Just a minute. *(To PINCUS.)* All right, Mr.
Pincus. Let's have your story.

PINCUS: Well, I've been married for nineteen years . . .

WALTER: Skip all that.

MAYOR: *(Loudly.)* Take those handcuffs off the boys, Pete. That wasn't at all
necessary. . . .

SHERIFF: *(Springing to obey.)* I was just going to. . . .

MAYOR: I can't tell you how badly I feel about this, Walter. There was no
excuse for Hartman flying off the handle.

SHERIFF: *(Busy with the handcuffs.)* I was only doing my duty. There wasn't
anything personal intended.

HILDY: You guys had better quit politics and take in washing. *(They are set
free.)*

MAYOR: Sheriff. . . . *(He is looking over the reprieve.)* This document is authentic!

---

[210]This entire speech is deleted from the acting edition.

[211]The text in *Theatre* attributes this speech to Walter, consistently with the reference to Johnson in the second sentence. Only the first sentence appears in the
Covici-Friede edition, probably to get rid of the cliché in the third.

Earl Williams, thank God, has been reprieved, and the commonwealth of Chicago has been spared the painful necessity of shedding blood.

WALTER: Save that for the *Tribune*.

MAYOR: *(To PINCUS.)* What did you say your name was—Pincus?

PINCUS: That's right. *(Shows a locket.)* Here's a picture of the wife.

MAYOR: *(Trapped.)* A very fine-looking woman.

PINCUS: *(Mysteriously angered.)* She's good enough for me. *(PEGGY enters.)*

HILDY: I'll bet she is.

MAYOR: A real character.

PEGGY: Hildy, what's the matter? What are they going to do? Mother said—

HILDY: *(Seeing her.)* Peggy, don't bawl me out now.

WALTER: Nobody's going to do anything to anybody.

MAYOR: Of course not. My good friend Walter Burns and I understand each other perfectly, I trust.

SHERIFF: *(Eager.)* And so do I.

MAYOR: So do you *what,* you goddamn hoodoo! And now, Mr. Pincus, if you'll come with us we'll take you over to the Warden's office and deliver that reprieve.

PEGGY: But Hildy, mother said that they'd arrested you . . .

PINCUS: *(Being escorted out by the MAYOR.)* If I was to go home and tell my wife—

MAYOR: The hell with your wife!

PINCUS *(Drunkenly loyal to his mate.)* She *loves* me. *(Exit PINCUS and the MAYOR.)*

SHERIFF: *(Pauses. His eyes lower. He speaks winningly.)* By the way, Walter . . . We were going to have a little feed after the hanging . . . a sort of buffet breakfast. . . .[212]

MAYOR: *(Calling from the corridor.)* Hartman!

SHERIFF: *(Nervously.)* I'm coming, Fred. *(Coyly, as WALTER stares.)* What do you say we eat it now? . . . Hmm? *(Still the deadpan from WALTER.)* Delicious ham. . . and some of Mrs. Hartman's own preserves. . . .

MAYOR: *(Loudly from the hall.)* Hartman!!! *(The SHERIFF sighs. A plaintive shrug indicates that he has a great deal to contend with. He leaves.)*

---

[212]The entire colloquy on the proposed buffet breakfast is dropped from the acting edition. Its text resumes with Walter's line, "Wait till those two Greeks read the *Examiner* tomorrow."

WALTER: *(Dreamily.)* Wait till those two Greeks[213] read the *Examiner* to-morrow! *(Back to life.)* Hildy, I'll tell you what I want you to do.

HILDY: What?

WALTER: I want you to get this guy Pincus over to the office tomorrow—

HILDY: Nothing doing, Walter. I'm all washed up. I mean it this time, Walter.

PEGGY: Oh, Hildy, if I only thought you did.

HILDY: Listen, Peggy—if I'm not telling you the absolute truth may God strike me dead right now. I'm going to New York with you tonight if you give me this one last chance! I'll cut out drinking and swearing and every-thing connected with the goddamn newspaper business. I won't even *read* a newspaper.

WALTER: Listen, Hildy, I got an idea . . .[214]

HILDY: *(To WALTER.)* There's nothing you can say can make me change my mind. This time I'm through, and I *mean* it. I know I don't deserve you, Peggy. I've done everything in the world to prove that, I guess.

PEGGY: Hildy, please! Don't say things like that.

HILDY: I've gotta hell of a nerve to ask you to marry me. I'm a prize pack-age, all right. But if you'll take me, here I am. Thirty-four years old and look at me.[215]

PEGGY: Darling, don't talk that way. I want you just the way you are. *(Any-way PEGGY will always remember that she said this and always forget that she didn't mean it.)*

WALTER: God, Hildy, I didn't know it was anything like this. Why didn't you *say* something! I'd be the last person in the world to want to come between you and your happiness.

HILDY: *(Staggered.)* What!

WALTER: You ought to know that. . . . *(As HILDY continues to blink.)* I love you, you crazy Swede! *(To PEGGY.)* You're getting a great guy, Peggy.

HILDY: Never mind the Valentines. Good-bye, you lousy bohunk. *(They shake hands.)*

---

[213]*those two Greeks.* In a pejorative context such as this, "Greeks" probably means persons who engage in anal intercourse. See Spears, *Slang and Euphemism*, p. 173.

[214]*Listen, Hildy, I got an idea . . .* In the text in *Theatre*, this is immediately followed by "Get this fellow Pincus over to the office in the morning." This may have been replaced by an earlier line, or been discarded as redundant. What remains of the line was dropped in the acting edition.

[215]This sentence appears in the *Theatre* text, but is not present in the Covici-Friede edition. Thirty-four was the age of Hilding Johnson about 1923.

WALTER: You're a great newspaperman, Hildy. I'm sorry to see you go. Damn sorry.

HILDY: Well, if I ever come *back* to the business . . . *(To PEGGY.)* Which I won't . . . *(To WALTER, his arm around PEGGY.)* There's only one man I'd work for. You know that, don't you!

WALTER: I'd kill you if you ever worked for anybody else.

HILDY: Hear that, Peggy? That's my diploma. *(He hesitates.)* Well, Walter . . . I don't know what to say . . . except I'm going to miss you like hell.

WALTER: Same here, son.

HILDY: *(To PEGGY.)* Twelve years we've been knockin' around together . . . before you were born. . . . *(To WALTER his face lighting up.)* Remember the time we hid the missing heiress in the sauerkraut factory?[216]

WALTER: Do I! *(To PEGGY.)* Get him to tell you some time about how we stole Old Lady Haggerty's stomach . . . off the coroner's physician.[217] We *proved* she was poisoned. . . .

HILDY: *(Laughing.)* We had to hide for a week!

PEGGY: Darling . . .

HILDY: *(Back to life.)* What?

PEGGY: You don't want to go to New York . . . down deep.

HILDY: Aw . . . what do you mean? I was just talking. *(With a nervous laugh.)* I'd feel worse if I stayed, I guess. . . .

PEGGY: Hildy, if I thought you were going to be unhappy—I mean, if you really wanted to— *(Firmly.)* No. No. It's your chance to have a home and be a human being—and I'm going to make you take it.

WALTER: *(To PEGGY.)* Why, I wouldn't let him stay. . . . Go on, Hildy, before I make you city editor.

HILDY *(Starting.)* Hurry up, Peggy. He means it.

WALTER: *(As PEGGY follows.)* Any objection to my kissing the bride!

HILDY *(Stopping.)* It's O.K. with me. *(He looks at PEGGY. She smiles.)* Go ahead, Mrs. Johnson.

---

[216]In the acting edition the missing heiress becomes a bigamist.

[217]*Old Lady Haggerty.* Possibly the mother of Mike Haggerty, keeper of the No. 7 Saloon on Market Street just off Madison, apparently a speakeasy, according to Vern Whaley a principal haunt of Hearst reporters. Although "Haggerty" is obviously not a Polish name, this saloon may be the prototype for "Polack Mike's" prominent earlier in the play. Alternatively, this may be a use of the name of Christian Dane Hagerty of the Associated Press, who covered the Dayton flood simultaneously with Hecht. (See Hecht, *A Child of the Century*, p. 192.) In the acting edition, "off the coroner's physician" becomes "right out from under the coroner's nose."

WALTER: *(Removing his hat and kissing her chastely.)* Thank you. . . . What time does your train go?

PEGGY: There's another one at twelve-forty.[218] *(To HILDY.)* We came awfully near going without you.

WALTER: New York Central, eh? *(To HILDY.)* I wish there was time to get you a little wedding present . . . but it's awful short notice.

PEGGY: *(Straining to be gone.)* Thank you, Mr. Burns, but Hildy's all the wedding present I want. . . . *(Laughing a little.)* If I've really got him.

HILDY: Ah, forget it, Walter. *(He, too, is leaving.)* [219]

WALTER: Hold on! I want you to have something to remember me by. You can't just leave like this. . . . *(Thoughtfully reaching for his watch.)* And I know what it's going to be. . . . *(Produces the watch.)*

HILDY: *(Embarrassed.)* Aw, Jesus, no, Walter! You make me feel like a fairy or something!

WALTER: *(With affected brusqueness.)* Shut up! You're going to take it, I tell you! It was a present from the Big Chief himself![220] And if you'll look inside . . . *(Opening the watch.)* You'll find a little inscription: "To the Best Newspaperman I know". . .[221] When you get to New York, you can scratch out my name and put yours in its place, if you want to. . . .

HILDY: You know I wouldn't do that. . . .

WALTER: Here. . . . *(Giving him the watch.)*

---

[218]*There's another one at 12:40.* Unless Hildy planned for his party to spend the night at a Loop hotel, there was no train at 12:40. The Pennsylvania Railroad for its Broadway Limited and the New York Central for its Twentieth Century Limited established 12:40 P.M. as departure time effective November 24, 1912. Except for the World War I period, the two railroads observed this departure until the Pennsylvania gave it up on September 30, 1929; the New York Central followed suit on May 1, 1932. Accordingly, this was the departure time for both railroads' leading trains to New York at any time to which the play could reasonably be assigned. At no time was there a 12:40 A.M. departure.

[219]Harry C. Read, city editor of the *Chicago American,* in his article on the play noted a major flaw in the plot: Hildy leaves for New York without filing his story with the rewrite desk of the *Herald and Examiner.* Similarly, he makes no arrangement with Walter to file it for him. Given the importance Hildy and Walter have given the story, it is inconceivable that they would treat it in this slovenly fashion. (*Chicago American,* November 26, 1928, p. 22.)

[220]*The Big Chief.* William Randolph Hearst (1863–1951).

[221]When Charles MacArthur visited Walter Howey on his deathbed, MacArthur gave him a watch inscribed, "To the Best Newspaperman I know." (Hecht, *Charlie,* p. 54.)

HILDY: Aw, Walter! It's too good for me! I can't take it!

WALTER: You *got* to! *(To PEGGY.) Make* him!

PEGGY: Go on, Hildy . . . if Mr. Burns wants you to. You don't want to hurt, his feelings. . . . *(HILDY takes it. WALTER pats him on the shoulder, his face averted.)*

HILDY: *(A lump in his throat.)* Well, this is the first and last thing I ever got from a newspaper. . . .

PEGGY: Good-bye, Mr. Burns. . . . I always had a queer opinion of you, Mr. Burns. I *still* think you're a little peculiar, but you're all right . . . underneath. I mean I think you're a peach.

WALTER: *(Winningly.)* So are you! You look just like a little flower!

HILDY: *(Ushering PEGGY out.)* Good-bye, you big baboon. . . .

PEGGY: Good-bye. . . . *(They exit.)*

WALTER: *(Calling after, leaning against the door.)* Good-bye, Johnson! Be good to yourself . . . and the little girl. . . .

HILDY'S VOICE: The same to you and many of them!

(WALTER waits till HILDY and PEGGY are out of sight and earshot, then closes the door. He walks slowly to the telephone. The receiver is still off the hook, the obedient DUFFY still on the other end. WALTER hesitates sentimentally, the receiver in his hand. Then he heaves a huge sigh and speaks.)

WALTER: Duffy!. . . *(He sounds a bit tired.)* Listen. I want you to send a wire to the Chief of Police of La Porte, Indiana. . . . That's right. . . . Tell him to meet the twelve-forty out of Chicago . . . New York Central . . . and arrest Hildy Johnson and bring him back here. . . . Wire him a full description. . . . The son of a bitch stole my watch![222]

CURTAIN

---

[222]*The son of a bitch stole my watch!* The episode that closes the play actually occurred. Howey gave his watch to Charles MacArthur as MacArthur was preparing to leave for New York on the Pennsylvania Railroad with Carol Frink at some time known only to be after the close of the Republican convention of June 1920 and before their marriage by the groom's father, Rev. William MacArthur, at the Little Church around the Corner on August 29, 1920. When the train reached Gary, Indiana—which was not a scheduled stop—two detectives arrested MacArthur on Howey's complaint. When MacArthur asked the reason, one of the detectives responded that Howey had said, "The son of a bitch stole my watch!" If the detective was accurate, the famous curtain line is, in fact, Howey's own composition. MacArthur was taken back

to Chicago, but followed Frink to New York two days later. (See George Murray, *The Madhouse on Madison Street* [Chicago: Follette Publishing Co., 1965], pp. 279–82.) The excerpts from an earlier draft in *Theatre* read "son of a bum," but this is probably a bowdlerization by the magazine's editorial staff, rather than an actual quotation from the draft.

There is some evidence that when the play opened in New York, or alternatively, in earlier drafts, the text was true to the actual event. Percy Hammond in his review was explicit that the telegram requesting Johnson's arrest was sent to Gary. (*New York Herald-Tribune*, August 15, 1928, p. 14.) Hammond may have read an earlier draft of the play, in which the text may have read "Gary." The excerpts in *Theatre* show "La Porte," however. Because Hildy's new job in advertising had been placed in Philadelphia, "Gary" was necessarily used in the 1974 motion picture that starred Jack Lemmon, Walter Mathau, Carol Burnett, and Susan Sarandon.

This episode has long been treated as an innocuous practical joke, but it has a serious criminal element. Howey made a false complaint of a crime, incurring costs to the Gary police department and stopping and delaying a train in interstate commerce. At minimum he could be accused of the crimes of making a false police report and malicious mischief in Illinois and false arrest or wrongful detention in Indiana. The Indiana statutes on criminal libel specifically render it illegal to make false statements that would subject a person to criminal prosecution. (*Annotated Indiana Statutes*, Harrison Burns, ed., revised and annotated by Benjamin F. Watson [Indianapolis: Bobbs-Merrill Co., 1926], sec. 2438 [2258a], p. 1071.) Any such crimes committed in Illinois would have been misdemeanors, record of which would not have been preserved to the present. The microfiche record of felony prosecutions in the present Cook County Criminal Courts Building shows no indication of an action against Howey. Police complaints before 1980 have not been retained by the City of Gary, and neither the *Gary Post* nor the *Gary Tribune* reported the incident. Presumably the railroad company and the City of Gary could have taken civil action for recovery of costs.

One of the most unusual revivals of *The Front Page* was a benefit performance at Arena Stage in Washington, D.C., on January 29, 1996, in which an effort was made to cast the play with actual journalists and current politicians. Professional actors or actresses played Hildy, Walter, Mollie, and Mrs. Grant. In the first photograph actor Stacy Keach as Walter checks on Secretary of Labor Robert Reich as Earl Williams in the rolltop desk. In the second, the Republican Senator from Wyoming, Alan Simpson, right, miscast as the Democrat Pincus, confronts Representative Richard Armey, who played Sheriff Hartman. The third photograph shows Representative Barney Frank, at right, as Diamond Louie. At the table sits Jack Germond of the *Baltimore Sun* as Endicott. The final photograph shows television journalist Cokie Roberts at left as Peggy Grant. Actress Kitty Carlisle Hart, center, played Mrs. Grant. Casey Biggs, also an actor, was Hildy Johnson. The participants read their lines from typescripts, but the performance was very effective (Photographs by Lee Anderson).

EPILOGUE

This epilogue appears as a supplement, not paginated, to the Covici-Friede edition in its third printing, dated October 1928. It is not in the first printing, dated August 1928, on the basis of the copyright deposit copy in the Library of Congress. It is also not in the second printing, dated September 1928, held by the Enoch Pratt Free Library, Baltimore. It is in the copy of the third printing in Duke University Library. The fourth printing in the UCLA research library is unchanged. It appears in the copy of the fifth printing, dated March 1929, held by the University of North Carolina, and in the British edition, dated only 1929, in the British Library. The British edition differs only in the title page and on the basis of the typographical error of "Austen Avenue" on page 75, was printed from the American plates. On the basis of the use of German, the epilogue is by Hecht. On the addition of the epilogue, see Chicago Evening Post, December 1, 1928, page 7.

This epilogue is one of apology. When we applied ourselves to write a newspaper play we had in mind a piece of work which would reflect our intellectual disdain of and superiority to the Newspaper.

What we finally turned out, as the reader may verify if he will, is a romantic and rather doting tale of our old friends—the reporters of Chicago.

It developed in writing this play that our contempt for the institution of the Press was a bogus attitude; that we looked back on the Local Room where we had spent half our lives as a veritable fairyland—and that we were both full of a nostalgia for the bouncing days of our servitude.

The same uncontrollable sentimentality operated in our treatment of Chicago which, as much as any of our characters, is the hero of our play.

The iniquities, double dealings, chicaneries, and immoralities which as ex-Chicagoans we knew so well returned to us in a mist called the Good Old Days, and our delight in our memories would not be denied.

As a result The Front Page, despite its oaths and realisms is a Valentine thrown to the past, a ballad (to us) full of Heim Weh[1] and Love.

So it remains for more stern and uncompromising intellects than ours to write of the true Significance of the Press. Therefore our apology to such bombinators, radicals, Utopians and Schoengeisten[2] who might read this work expecting intellectual mayhem.

In writing it we found we were not so much dramatists or intellectuals as two reporters in exile.

—The Authors

NOTES

1. *Heim Weh.* Homesickness, or more literally home woe or home grief. Normal practice is to present it as one word.
2. *Schoengeisten.* Literally, people of beautiful spirit, or more idiomatically, esthetes.

Appendix A
THEATER AND FILM PRODUCTIONS

THEATRICAL PRODUCTIONS

The cast of characters in the Covici-Friede edition lists the policeman called Tony who enters to help drag off Mrs. Grant in Act II, but not Frank, the deputy, who takes the stage with Carl in Act III. Neither has any lines. I have endeavored to identify the actors who played both, where possible.

ATLANTIC CITY AND NEW YORK PRODUCTIONS

WILSON, *American*		Vincent York
ENDICOTT, *Post*		Allen Jenkins
MURPHY, *Journal*		Willard Robertson
McCUE, *City News Bureau*		William Foran
SCHWARTZ, *Daily News*		Tammany Young
KRUGER, *Journal of Commerce*		Joseph Spurin-Calleia
BENSINGER, Tribune		Walter Baldwin
MRS. SCHLOSSER		Violet Barney
WOODENSHOES EICHHORN		Jay Wilson
DIAMOND LOUIE		Eduardo Cianelli
HILDY JOHNSON, *Herald and Examiner*		Lee Tracy
JENNIE		Carrie Weller
MOLLIE MALLOY	Atlantic City:	Phyllis Povah
	New York:	Dorothy Stickney
SHERIFF HARTMAN		Claude Cooper
PEGGY GRANT		Frances Fuller
MRS. GRANT		Jessie Crommette
THE MAYOR		George Barbier
MR. PINCUS		Frank Conlan
EARL WILLIAMS		George Leach
WALTER BURNS		Osgood Perkins
TONY		George T. Fleming
CARL	Atlantic City:	Willard Mitchell
	New York:	Matthew Crowley
FRANK		Gene West
POLICEMEN, CITIZENS		—

WILSON, *American*	Jules Cern
ENDICOTT, *Post*	Willard Mitchell
MURPHY, *Journal*	Robert Pitkin
McCUE, *City News Bureau*	John Carmody
SCHWARTZ, *Daily News*	Jack Campbell
KRUGER, *Journal of Commerce*	Lloyd Nolan
BENSINGER, *Tribune*	John P. Lewis
MRS. SCHLOSSER	Olive Reeves-Smith
WOODENSHOES EICHHORN	James Kearney
DIAMOND LOUIE	Henry Sherwood
HILDY JOHNSON, *Herald and Examiner*	Roger Pryor
JENNIE	Zylla Inez Shannon
MOLLIE MALLOY	Antoinette Crawford
SHERIFF HARTMAN	Harlan Briggs
PEGGY GRANT	Wilva Davis
MRS. GRANT	Mabel Wright
THE MAYOR	Willard Dashiell
MR. PINCUS	Harold Grau
EARL WILLIAMS	Earl Ford
WALTER BURNS	Fuller Melish, Jr.
TONY	—
CARL	Jack A. Clifford
FRANK	Harry Light
POLICEMEN, CITIZENS	—

WILSON, *American*	F. Jac. Foss
ENDICOTT, *Post*	Bruce Gentle
MURPHY, *Journal*	Jack Carlyle
McCUE, *City News Bureau*	James Donlin
SCHWARTZ, *Daily News*	Clyde McCoy
KRUGER, *Journal of Commerce*	Kenneth Duncan
BENSINGER, *Tribune*	Franklin Parker
MRS. SCHLOSSER	Patricia Page
WOODENSHOES EICHHORN	Wilbur Higby
DIAMOND LOUIE	Eugene Borden
HILDY JOHNSON, *Herald and Examiner*	Roscoe Karns
JENNIE	Dorothea Wolbert
MOLLIE MALLOY	Doris Kemper
SHERIFF HARTMAN	Clarence H. Wilson
PEGGY GRANT	Marion Burns
MRS. GRANT	Lydia Knott
THE MAYOR	Tom McGuire
MR. PINCUS	Ethan Allen
EARL WILLIAMS	Buckley Starky
WALTER BURNS	Ralf Herolde
TONY	—
CARL	W. H. Cameron
FRANK	Francis Wilbur
POLICEMEN, CITIZENS	—

WILSON, *American*	Allan Mitchell
ENDICOTT, *Post*	John Shrapnel
MURPHY, *Journal*	James Hayes
McCUE, *City News Bureau*	Gawn Grainger
SCHWARTZ, *Daily News*	David Bradley
KRUGER, *Journal of Commerce*	David Ryall
BENSINGER, *Tribune*	Benjamin Whitrow
MRS. SCHLOSSER	Maggie Riley
WOODENSHOES EICHHORN	David Henry
DIAMOND LOUIE	Stephen Greif
HILDY JOHNSON, *Herald and Examiner*	Denis Quilley
JENNIE	Jeanne Watts
MOLLIE MALLOY	Maureen Lipman
SHERIFF HARTMAN	David Bauer
PEGGY GRANT	Anna Carteret
MRS. GRANT	Mary Griffiths
THE MAYOR	Paul Curran
MR. PINCUS	Harry Lomax
EARL WILLIAMS	Clive Merrison
WALTER BURNS	Alan MacNaughtan
TONY	Barry James
CARL	Kenneth Mackintosh
FRANK	Malcolm Reid
POLICEMEN, CITIZENS	Michael Essex, Paul Hetherington, David Kincaid, Roger Monk, Harry Waters, David Whitman

FILM ADAPTATIONS

1931 MOTION PICTURE

United Artists release. Howard Hughes production. Directed by Lewis Milestone. Adapted for screen by Bartlett Cormac. Running time 100 minutes.

WILSON, *American*	Phil Tead
ENDICOTT, *Post*	Eugene Strong
MURPHY, *Journal*	Walter Catlett
McCUE, *City News Bureau*	Frank McHugh
SCHWARTZ, *Daily News*	Fred Howard
KRUGER, *Journal of Commerce*	Matt Moore
BENSINGER, *Tribune*	Edward Everett Horton
MRS. SCHLOSSER	—
WOODENSHOES EICHHORN	Spencer Charters
DIAMOND LOUIE	Maurice Black
HILDY JOHNSON, *Herald and Examiner*	Pat O'Brien
JENNIE	—
MOLLIE MALLOY	Mae Clarke
SHERIFF HARTMAN	Clarence H. Wilson
PEGGY GRANT	Mary Brian
MRS. GRANT	Effie Ellsler
THE MAYOR	James Gordon
MR. PINCUS	Slim Summerville
EARL WILLIAMS	George E. Stone
WALTER BURNS	Adolphe Menjou
TONY	—
CARL	—
FRANK	—
JACOBI	Dick Alexander
POLICEMEN, CITIZENS	—

United Artists Release. Produced by Paul Monash. Executive Producer Jennings Lang. Directed by Billy Wilder. Screenplay by Billy Wilder and I. A. L. Diamond. Music Director Billy May. Running time 105 minutes.

WILSON, *American*	Noam Pitlik
ENDICOTT, *Post*	Lou Frizzell
MURPHY, *Journal*	Charles Durning
McCUE, *City News Bureau*	Dick O'Neill
SCHWARTZ, *Daily News*	Herbert Edelman
KRUGER, *Journal of Commerce*	Allen Garfield
BENSINGER, *Tribune*	David Wayne
MRS. SCHLOSSER	—
WOODENSHOES EICHHORN	—
DIAMOND LOUIE	—
HILDY JOHNSON, *Herald and Examiner*	Jack Lemmon
JENNIE	Doro Merande
MOLLIE MALLOY	Carol Burnett
SHERIFF HARTMAN	Vincent Gardenia
PEGGY GRANT	Susan Sarandon
MRS. GRANT	—
THE MAYOR	Harold Gould
PLUNKETT (PINCUS)	Paul Benedict
EARL WILLIAMS	Austin Pendleton
WALTER BURNS	Walter Matthau
TONY	—
CARL	—
FRANK	—
DR. EGELHOFER	Martin Gabel
JACOBI	Cliff Osmond
RUDY KEPPLER	John Korkos
DUFFY	John Furlong
POLICEMEN, CITIZENS	—

HIS GIRL FRIDAY

An adaptation of *The Front Page* by Louis Lederer, in which Hildy Johnson is made a woman, Walter's ex-wife, and the action is set in an unspecified city. A male character, Bruce Baldwin, played by Ralph Bellamy, was introduced as a substitute for Peggy Grant. Most of the secondary characters are used without change of names, except that Mr. Pincus is renamed Joe Pettibone. The film starred Cary Grant as Walter, Rosalind Russell as Hildy, and Helen Mack as Mollie. Columbia Pictures release, 1940. Produced and directed by Howard Hawkes. Running time 92 minutes.

SWITCHING CHANNELS

A very loose adaptation of *His Girl Friday*, set in television news reporting. None of the names of the characters from The Front Page are used. The film starred Burt Reynolds, Kathleen Turner, and Christopher Reeve. Tri-Star Pictures release, 1988. Martin Ransohoff production. Executive producer, John Carmody. Directed by Ted Kotcheff. Screenplay by Jonathan Reynolds. Running time 105 minutes.

Appendix B
Supporting Materials

William S. Conklin's review of The Front Page *in the* Asbury Park Evening Press *of August 7, 1928 (page 3) and Jimmy Murphy's letter to the* Chicago Journal, *November 27, 1928 (page 4) giving his views on the use of his name are both in sources not readily available. Both are reprinted here in full.*

MAYOR THOMPSON, ET AL.

"The Front Page," by Ben Hecht and Charles MacArthur, presented by Jed Harris at the Broadway theater, Long Branch, for the entire week, staged by George S. Kaufman.

There may be some persons in the audience at the Broadway theater last night who came with the belief that "The Front Page" is a play depicting the efforts of some person who would gain prominence by making "the front page" of the newspapers. If they had such an idea it was quickly dissipated after a few minutes of the first act. Instead, one found an interesting story of "hard-boiled" newspaper life.

It should be said at the beginning that "The Front Page" is not laid in the technics of newspaper life so that it loses interest to the average layman. Rather, we are inclined to believe, it is molded along a line which holds the interest of the average playgoer as keenly as a story may hold the attention of the average newspaper reader.

Again a leaf of the hectic history of Chicago of recent years is taken as the basis of the story. There is an interesting bit of love in a plot that moves quickly. An execution is scheduled and about the pressroom of the Criminal Courts building the "boys" are "covering" the story. A jail break and the efforts of the mayor and the sheriff to "pin something" on the managing editor and star of the anti-administration paper furnish the highlights.

Newspaper life has been exaggerated a bit in this play. Undoubtedly this has been done in an effort to make the piece more dramatic. It is excusable for in so doing the play has been strengthened. Then, we would have to meet the newspaperman who would fall into the "breaks" as occurs in this story.

Perhaps, also the fire regulations prohibited the use of cigarets for which newspaper offices have earned a reputation.

In presentation there are a few things which could have been bettered. The play appears to be in too fast a tempo with the result that reports from those who were fortunate enough to be seated midway in the house were to the effect that a great deal of the conversation of the characters is lost. The sitting of some of characters back to the audience may be responsible for this.

Lee Tracy, who appeared in "Broadway," is the star of the production. He handles the role of the star reporter to perfection and much good may be said for his acting. Osgood Perkins as the managing editor became a ready favorite with the audience and for the work of Dorothy Stickney and Frances Fuller there should be words of praise.

All in all, it maybe said that "The Front Page" is a good story. It is not intended as a propagandist vehicle for longer hours and less pay for newspapermen. It is not moralistic in tone, but only exposes that not infrequently a man's work becomes his first love, rather than the woman to whom he has pledged himself. And this is not alone akin to the newspaper business.

—William S. Conklin

P.S. We would advise those who have been annoyed by the language of truck drivers to remain away from this play. The employment of adjectives of this nature are quite frequent, almost too much so.

•   •   •

MR. MURPHY DEFENDS HIS GOOD NAME

Dear Art[1]

I saw "The Front Page" last night and, if you don't mind, I would like to defend my good name, which is given to one of the police reporters—a very tough egg—in the play. That "Jimmy Murphy of *The Journal*" is somebody else. The other lads covering police may talk like that, but not *The Journal's* boy. You ask Steve Trumbull or any of the other rewrite men if I ever say so much as a ----, or a ----, or even a ---- ---- ---- ---- ---- on the telephone. I do not.

Ben Hecht and Charlie MacArthur, the authors, are good guys, but they took my name in vain. What I mean is that they didn't manage to embarrass me by their Jimmy Murphy's profanity, because my wife knows I do not talk like a copper and she went with me to the play.

After the show was over, Ben invited us to join him in a little chat in the theater manager's office but, suspecting spiritus frumenti, I was compelled to decline the invitation. I had to do something to defend the reputation of Chicago's police reporters, which is so completely shattered in that swell show at the Erlanger. Tell Ben and Charlie that I'm not mad—just hurt. Because they made Hildy Johnson the hero and not me.

—Jimmy Murphy
Journal Police Reporter

NOTE

1. Arthur G. Sheekman, conductor of the column, "Little about Everything."

Because the play is most conspicuously concerned with the relations of the reporter, Hildy Johnson, with his editor, Walter Burns, casting of those two roles for the initial production was of prime importance. On the basis of reviews, the choice could hardly have been better. Lee Tracy (foreground) was cast as Hildy and Osgood Perkins (rear) as Walter. The photograph shows Hildy clutching his typewriter late in Act II (New York Public Library, Theater collection) .

For the role of Mollie Malloy, Phyllis Povah was chosen. Even by the standards of actresses, she was an exceptionally beautiful woman. Her discharge after extremely favorable reviews in the tryout performances remains a mystery (drawing from the *New York Times,* August 7, 1927).

The Criminal Court Building, in which the play is set, in a photograph of 1916. At right is the county jail from which Tommy O'Connor made his escape — one of the principal elements in the plot. The jail was razed in 1936, but the Court Building itself stands majestically among modern buildings after an impressive restoration as an office complex (Chicago Historical Society).

Fred A. Busse, mayor of Chicago, photographed in 1907. Behind him is his rolltop desk, around which much of the action of the play revolves (Chicago Historical Society).

Richard Sovey's set for the play as the curtain rises. Joseph Spurin-Calleia as Kruger strums "By the Light of the Silvery Moon" at far right (New York Public Library).

In one of the most inevitable pieces of casting in the history of the play, Edward Everett Horton took the role of Bensinger in the 1931 motion picture version. Behind him, left to right, are Eugene Strong as Endicott, Frank McHugh as McCue, Phil Tead as Wilson, and Fred Howard as Schwartz (UCLA Libraries).

The Governor. Lennington Small stands in an open car in a procession in 1921. Next to him in the rear seat sits William Hale Thompson (Chicago Historical Society).

"Diamond Louie" Alterie at left in this *Chicago Daily News* photograph, dating from 1932, four years after the play and three years before his assassination. He is talking with defense attorney William Scott Stewart (Chicago Historical Society).

Peter M. Hoffman, prototype for Sheriff Hartman, stands at center in 1915 during his tenure as coroner of Cook County. The tall man at right is Herman Scheuttler, chief of police during World War I, on whom the character Woodenshoes Eichhorn is based. Framed between them, wearing a flat-topped black hat and a flowing bow tie, is Dr. Joseph Springer of the coroner's staff, who is mentioned in the text (Chicago Historical Society).

The reporters man their phones to report the escape of Earl Williams, immediately before the end of Act I. Lee Tracy as Hildy waits, suitcase in hand, at the left of the door (New York Public Library).

George Barbier as the Mayor and Claude Cooper as Sheriff Hartman talk with Joseph Spurin-Calleia as Kruger. In the unlikely event that there were any doubt as to the Mayor's identity as William Hale Thompson, the broad soft hat in Barbier's hand would have clinched the point (New York Public Library).

Arnold Stang as Mr. Pincus in the 1969 revival of the play on Broadway reacts with horror to the Mayor's proposed bribe of a job in the office of the city sealer. John Mc-Giver is the Mayor, and Charles White, at left, is Sheriff Hartman (Photograph by Ted Yaple, from *Theatre World*, vol. 25 (1968–1969), p. 79. Used by permission of the publisher from UCLA Libraries).

George Leach as the condemned Earl Williams drops in on Hildy Johnson. Lee Tracy's expression demonstrates Hildy's recognition that the scoop of his life is at hand (New York Public Library) .

Hildy attempts to pacify his fiancée and alert his editor simultaneously. Lee Tracy demonstrates the conflict basic to the character (New York Public Library).

Dorothy Stickney as Mollie prepares to take her plunge from the newsroom window (New York Public Library).

Carl and Frank prepare to drag Hildy off to jail. Watching are Willard Robinson as Murphy and William Foran as McCue at left, along with Kruger and the Sheriff at right (New York Public Library).

"We're going to be selling lead pencils, eh?" The sheriff has a brief moment of exultation (New York Public Library).

The uncorruptable Mr. Pincus, played by Frank Conlan, delivers the reprieve for Earl Williams to the Mayor (New York Public Library).

The second London production of the play was at the Donmar Warehouse Theatre in 1997, directed by Sam Mendes. Griff Rhys Jones was a particularly harried Hildy. Here he assures Peggy, played by Rebecca Johnson, of his devotion and his reformation as the third act approaches its end (Mark Douet photograph, courtesy Donmar Warehouse Projects, Ltd).

Hildy and Peggy, played by Frances Fuller in the original production, bid farewell to Walter as they leave for the train to New York (New York Public Library) .

"The son of a bitch stole my watch!" Osgood Perkins delivers the curtain line (New York Public Library).

INDEX

Note: Page numbers referring to footnotes or endnotes on that page are followed by the letter *n*.

film adaptations, of *The Front Page*, 27n, 184n, 193–95, 201
Fitzgerald, Thomas Richard, 6, 152–53n
Fitzmorris, Charles C., 107n
Foote, Samuel, 8, 25n
Foran, William, 206
Fowler, Volney, 19
Frink, Carol, 2, 111–12n
Front Page, The
  acting edition of, 18, 37
  anachronisms in, 59n
  Atlantic City tryout of, 9, 36, 189
  British productions of, 1, 16–17, 20, 37, 45, 92n, 171n, 208
  characters, identifying in, vii–viii, 2, 3–4
  casting of, 9, 10
  censorship of, 9, 14–16, 17, 37, 122n, 164n, 171n
  Chicago production of, 7, 12, 21, 190
  Covici-Friede edition of, 8, 16, 36, 37, 86n, 104n, 109n, 123n, 177n, 178n
  critical success of, vii, 1, 9–10, 11, 12, 17, 20
  dating of, 6–7, 64n
  and depiction of newspaper life, 18–19, 31n
  epithets in, 13–14, 17
  as farce, 8–9, 10, 11, 12, 13, 1920, 25n, 29n
  film adaptations of, 27n, 184n, 193–95, 201
  Indianapolis tryout of, 19
  London production of, 1, 92n, 208
  Long Branch tryout of, 10, 11, 36
  Los Angeles production of, 191
  musical version of, 2, 5, 20, 65, 83
  naming of, 8, 24n
  Newark production of, 10
  New York City production of, 11, 189
  origins of, 2–3
  Philadelphia production of, 5, 27n
  problems with, 31n, 182n
  profanity in, 11, 13–15, 17, 37
  radio play of, 17
  reviews of, 1, 5, 10, 11, 14, 17, 18, 19, 20, 21, 25n, 31n, 92n, 143–44n, 150n, 184n, 196–97
  revivals of, vii, 4, 17, 185
  as satire, 3, 12
  structure of, 28n
  writing of, 2, 7–8
Fuller, Frances, 9, 26–27n, 208

Gaily, Gaily, 39
Gallagher, Nicholas, 163n
Garbo, Greta, 6, 127n
Gause, Noah C., 86
Gentlemen of the Press, 11, 28n
Gilbert, W. S., 18, 22, 29n
Gill, Richard S., 106n
Gilhooley, William, 109n
Gilpin, Charles, 35–36, 38n
God, use of word in *The Front Page*, 16, 171n
Godolphin, Rev. Francis Richard, 175–76n
Goldstein, Malcolm, 36
Gordon, C. L., 16
Grand Crossing, 62–63n
Grant, Peggy, 4, 5

Haggerty, Mike, 181n
Hammond, Percy, 14, 184n
Hamon, Clara Smith, 6, 113–14n
Hamon, Jacob L., 113–14n
Hand of the Potter, 153n
Harris, Jed, 8, 11, 20, 21, 24n, 35
Harrison Street Station, 65n

Hartman, Sheriff, 5, 6, 8. *See also* Hoffman, Peter M.

Hawkshaw, 169n

Hayes, Helen, 2, 11, 45, 103–4n, 111n, 112n, 114n

Hearst newspapers, 19, 46, 60n

Hecht, Ben, 2, 3, 8, 11, 12, 19, 36, 39, 40, 48–49, 153n

Helgesen, Terry, 127n

Hennessey, LeRoy "Spike," 39–40

Herald and Examiner. See Chicago Herald and Examiner

Hickman, Walter D., 19

His Girl Friday, 195

Hobson, Harold, 19–20

Hochstein, Harry, 125n

Hochstadter, Benjamin "Barney," 66n

Hoffman, Dennis E., 68n

Hoffman, Emma May, 99n

Hoffman, Peter M., 5, 6, 12, 94–95n, 151–52n, 154n, 203

Hollander, Theresa, 160n

Holmes, Sherlock, 4, 138–39n

Horner, Bartley T., 159n

Horner, Ella S., 159n

Horner, Rosalie, 20

Horton, Everett, 201

Hound of the Baskervilles, The, 4

Howey, Walter Crawford, 2, 3, 52, 114n, 154n, 158n, 182n, 183–84n

Hubka, Emil F., 61–62n

Illinois Staats-Zeitung, 43

Importance of Being Earnest, The, 1, 2, 28n

Indianapolis tryout, of *The Front Page*, 19

Jacoby, Edward L., 73n

Jennie. *See* Armbruster, Jennie

Johnson, Edwin C., 41

Johnson, Enoch M., 41

Johnson, John Hilding, 3, 5, 44–45, 86n

Johnson, Rebecca, 208

Jones, Griff Rhys, 208

Jonson, Ben, 8

Journal. See Chicago Journal of Commerce

Kaufman, George S., 8, 9, 10, 11, 24n, 35, 36

Kaufman, S. Jay, 11

Kenna, Michael, 96n

Keppler, Rudy, 84n

King's restaurant, 87

Koehler, Joseph, 24n

Kogan, Herman, 46

Krueger, Jesse, 42, 43

Kruger, Ernie, 6, 42–43

Kun, Henry, 109n

Lardner, Ring W., vii, viii

Lawson, Jack, 79

Leach, George, 205

League of Nations, 149n

Levin, Meyer, 44

Lewis, J. Hamilton, 118n

Lindberg, Richard C., 51, 116n

Lindsey, Benjamin Barr, 86n

Lingle, Alfred "Jake," 68n

Lipman, Maureen, 45–46

London production, of *The Front Page*, 1, 92n, 208

Long Branch (New Jersey) tryout, of *The Front Page*, 10, 11, 36

Loraine, Robert, 15, 16, 37

Lorimer, William, 12

Los Angeles production, of *The Front Page*, 191

Lovett, Robert Morss, 12

Lundin, Fred, 12

Lustgarten, Harry, 108n

Lustgarten, Paul A., 108n